Return to Babel

Return
to
Babel

Global
Perspectives
on the Bible

Edited by
Priscilla Pope-Levison
and
John R. Levison

 Westminster John Knox Press
Louisville, Kentucky

Book design by Sharon Adams
Cover design by Jennifer K. Cox

Detail from Brueghel, Pieter the Elder. *The Tower of Babel*, 1563.
Erich Lessing/Art Resource, NY.

First edition
Published by Westminster John Knox Press
Louisville, Kentucky

This book is printed on acid-free paper that meets the American National Standards Institute Z39.48 standard.

PRINTED IN THE UNITED STATES OF AMERICA

99 00 01 02 03 04 05 06 07 08—10 9 8 7 6 5 4 3 2 1

Library of Congress Cataloging–in–Publication Data

Return to Babel : global perspectives on the Bible / edited by
Priscilla Pope-Levison and John R. Levison. — 1st ed.
    p.   cm.
Includes bibliographical references and index.
ISBN 0-664-25823-9 (alk. paper)
    1. Bible—Criticism, interpretation, etc. 2. Christianity and
culture. I. Pope-Levison, Priscilla, 1958– II. Levison, John R.
BS531.R47 1999
220.6'09—DC21   98-49512
                                                        CIP

For Chloe and Jeremy
our children
our delight

Contents

Preface   ix
Contributors   xi
Introduction   1

Old Testament Texts

Genesis 11:1–9
A Latin American Perspective (José Míguez-Bonino)   13
An African Perspective (Solomon Avotri)   17
An Asian Perspective (Choan-Seng Song)   27

Exodus 20:1–17
A Latin American Perspective (Jorge Pixley)   37
An African Perspective (François Kabasele Lumbala)   43
An Asian Perspective (George M. Soares-Prabhu)   49

Psalm 23:1–6
A Latin American Perspective (J. Severino Croatto)   57
An African Perspective (Hannah W. Kinoti)   63
An Asian Perspective (Cyris Heesuk Moon)   69

Ecclesiastes 3:1–8
A Latin American Perspective (Elsa Tamez)   75
An African Perspective (François Kabasele Lumbala)   81
An Asian Perspective (Choan-Seng Song)   87

Isaiah 52:13–53:12
A Latin American Perspective (Jorge Pixley)   95
An African Perspective (François Kabasele Lumbala)   101
An Asian Perspective (Cyris Heesuk Moon)   107

New Testament Texts

Matthew 5:1–12
A Latin American Perspective (J. Severino Croatto)   117
An African Perspective (Hannah W. Kinoti)   125
An Asian Perspective (Helen R. Graham)   131

John 1:1–18
A Latin American Perspective (José Cárdenas Pallares)   139
An African Perspective (Hannah W. Kinoti)   145
An Asian Perspective (George M. Soares-Prabhu)   151

Acts 2:1–42
A Latin American Perspective (José Míguez-Bonino)   161
An African Perspective (Patrice M. Siyemeto)   167
An Asian Perspective (Helen R. Graham)   173

1 Corinthians 15:1–58
A Latin American Perspective (Elsa Tamez)   185
An African Perspective (François Kabasele Lumbala)   189
An Asian Perspective (Daniel C. Arichea)   193

Revelation 21:1–22:5
A Latin American Perspective (Jorge Pixley)   201
An African Perspective (Timothy G. Kiogora)   207
An Asian Perspective (Choan-Seng Song)   213

Select Annotated Bibliography   221
Index of Subjects   225
Index of Ancient References   229

Preface

This volume, as our former editor, Jon Berquist, quipped, will not soon be repeated. It contains thirty fresh essays—none previously published— from three continents, each following the same format. It has taken us as editors more than six years to bring this collection from inception to publication, with innumerable letters, faxes, and phone conversations. There were all sorts of glitches in communication: Patrice Siyemeto of Zambia had to turn off his phone to receive our fax at a prearranged time; George Soares-Prabhu bemoaned the frequent changes in phone numbers in India; letters were lost and delayed; numerous faxes could not be put through to what we believed to be legitimate numbers; and the differences in time zones wreaked their usual havoc in telephone conversations. Nonetheless, fifteen authors from the reaches of Latin America, Africa, and Asia overcame these obstacles and provided us with insightful and significant essays.

A volume such as this is typically the product of unseen hands. Wendy Kilworth-Mason, Paul Chilcote, and Jorge Pixley lent us the names of potential contributors, several of whom have written essays in this volume. Susan Perry, then of Orbis Books, provided lists of addresses that would otherwise have been extremely difficult to procure. Gail Chappell, Joan Lamorte, and Leslie Pardue of the Duke Divinity School administrative support staff, devoted their capable labors to typing forms and various essays. Leslie labored with us to proof this manuscript and to compile the Index of Ancient References. Westminster John Knox Press should also be credited with the advent of this volume; even before our first book with this publisher, *Jesus in Global Contexts,* was in print, Westminster John Knox Press provided a contract for this endeavor. We have had as well the fortunate opportunity to work alongside two very competent and careful editors, Jon Berquist, now of Chalice Press, and Cynthia Thompson, who first advocated the volume and has now managed the details of effectively bringing the project to fruition.

Although most of our own editorial work took place in the cracks and crevices of several academic years and summers, we were privileged to accomplish some of the initial communication and organizing of this volume during a pleasant sojourn in Tübingen, at the Evangelisch-theologisches Fakultät of the Eberhard-Karls-Universität Tübingen, where we were situated comfortably in the Institut für antikes Judentum und hellenistische Religionsgeschichte, directed by Professor Hermann Lichtenberger. Thanks to the initiative of Professor Martin Hengel, funding for that marvelous year was generously provided by the Alexander von Humboldt Foundation.

We have, finally, chosen to dedicate this book to our daughter, Chloe, and our son, Jeremy, who have filled our lives with a cacophony akin to Babel, who have built their own block towers on our kitchen floor, and who have, in eerie godlikeness, dispersed them with a kick into a houseful of rubble. We hope that, as they grow, Jeremy and Chloe will turn from these tiny Babels to set their hearts instead upon "the city that has foundations, whose architect and builder is God" (Hebrews 11:10).

Contributors

Latin America

JOSÉ MÍGUEZ-BONINO is Emeritus Professor of Systematic Theology and Ethics at ISEDET (Instituto Superior Evangélico de Estudios Teológicos), Buenos Aires. He is president of the Argentine Permanent Assembly for Human Rights, an elected member of the National Constitutional Assembly of Argentina, and is an ordained minister in the Iglesia Evangélica Metodista Argentina. He also served as a member of the Presidium of the World Council of Churches from 1975 until 1982. Míguez-Bonino has authored many books, including *Christians and Marxists: The Mutual Challenge to Revolution, Doing Theology in a Revolutionary Situation,* and *Toward a Christian Political Ethics.* He holds degrees from the Facultad Evangélica de Teología in Buenos Aires, Emory University in Atlanta, as well as a Ph.D. from Union Theological Seminary in New York City.

J. SEVERINO CROATTO is Professor of Old Testament, Hebrew Language, and Religious Studies at ISEDET (Instituto Superior Evangélico de Estudios Teológicos), Buenos Aires. A native Argentinian, and a former Vincentian Father, he is now a Roman Catholic layperson. He collaborates regularly in the Latin American Movement for the Popular Reading of the Bible through three channels: workshops, the Latin American "Curso Intensivo de Biblia," and writing for *RIBLA* (Revista de Interpretación Latinoamericana). Croatto was the first editor of the *Bibliografía Teológica Comentada,* issued by ISEDET, and is the author of fifteen books on topics such as biblical hermeneutics (*Biblical Hermeneutics: toward a theory of reading as the production of meaning*), Genesis 1—11, Exodus, and Isaiah. He studied at the Pontifical Biblical Institute in Rome and the Hebrew University of Jerusalem.

JOSÉ CÁRDENAS PALLARES is both a Roman Catholic priest in Salahua, Mexico, and a professor at the Universidad Pontifica in Thalpan and the Seminario de Colima in El Cóbano. He has served as a chaplain in various prisons and a hospital and now expounds on biblical themes in a weekly radio program. His many publications include five books on the Gospel of Mark, four on the Gospel of Luke, and others on the Gospel of John and the Song of Songs. He holds degrees from the Gregorian University and the Pontifical Biblical Institute in Rome.

JORGE PIXLEY is Professor of Bible at the Seminario Teológico Bautista in Managua, Nicaragua. Previously he taught at seminaries in Puerto Rico and in Mexico and is an American Baptist minister and missionary. Pixley has written several books, including *The Bible, the Church and the Poor* and *God's Kingdom: a guide for biblical studies.* He holds a degree from the Colegio Bautista in Managua, as well as a Ph.D. from the University of Chicago.

ELSA TAMEZ is rector of the Universidad Bíblica Latinoamericana in San Jose, Costa Rica. Originally from Mexico, she is now a member of the Methodist Church in Costa Rica. Tamez has authored many books, including *The Bible of the Oppressed, The Scandalous Message of James,* and *The Amnesty of Grace.* She holds a Ph.D. from the University of Lausanne in Switzerland.

Africa

SOLOMON AVOTRI is Associate Professor of Bible at Payne Theological Seminary in the USA. Originally from Ghana, he is now an ordained minister in the Presbyterian Church (USA). He holds degrees from the University of Ghana and United Theological Seminary (Dayton, Ohio), as well as a Ph.D. from the Iliff School of Theology in Denver.

HANNAH W. KINOTI is Associate Professor of Religious Studies at the University of Nairobi, Kenya. She is a Methodist lay preacher and a member of the Circle of Concerned African Women Theologians. Kinoti holds a degree from Makerere University in Uganda, as well as a Ph.D. from the University of Nairobi.

TIMOTHY G. KIOGORA is Associate Professor of Humanities at Eastern Kentucky University in Richmond, Kentucky. He is a Methodist from Kenya. Kiogora holds degrees from St. Paul's College in Kenya, Perkins School of Theology in Dallas, as well as a Ph.D. from the Iliff School of Theology in Denver.

FRANÇOIS KABASELE LUMBALA is Professor of Liturgy and Catechesis at the Catholic faculty in Kinshasa, Zaire, and Visiting Professor in the International Institute of Pastoral and Catechesis in Belgium. Kabasele Lumbala has edited *Faces of Jesus Christ in Africa* and *Celebrating Jesus Christ in Africa*. He holds a degree from the Strasbourg Human Sciences University and a Ph.D. from the Catholic Institute of Paris.

PATRICE M. SIYEMETO is Area Bishop in the Copperbelt Presbytery of the United Church of Zambia. He also lectures in Mission and Development Studies at the United Church of Zambia Theological College. Siyemeto holds degrees from Makerere University in Uganda and the University of Birmingham in England.

Asia

DANIEL C. ARICHEA is the resident bishop of the Baguio Episcopal Area of the United Methodist Church in the Philippines. Previously he worked with the United Bible Studies for twenty-six years, serving as translation consultant in the Philippines, Vietnam, Thailand, Singapore, Malaysia, and Indonesia, then as regional translation coordinator of Asia and the Pacific. Arichea holds a degree from Union Theological Seminary in the Philippines, as well as a Ph.D. from Duke University in Durham, North Carolina.

HELEN R. GRAHAM, a member of the Maryknoll Sisters, teaches at the Institute of Formation and Religious Studies, where she has taught since 1968, a year after she arrived in the Philippines, and also at the Maryhill School of Theology. She is also a member of the Association of Major Superiors in the Philippines Commission on Justice, Peace, and the Integrity of Creation and lends her support to various nongovernmental organizations that work for justice, peace, and women's issues. Graham holds an M.A. and a Ph.D. from Ateneo de Manila University in the Philippines and an S.T.M. from the Jesuit School of Theology in Berkeley, California.

CYRIS HEESUK MOON is Professor of Old Testament at San Francisco Theological Seminary. Previously he taught at the Presbyterian Theological Seminary in Seoul, Korea. An ordained Presbyterian minister, Moon is the author of *A Korean Minjung Theology: An Old Testament Perspective*. He holds a degree from Columbia Theological Seminary in Decatur, Georgia, and a Ph.D. from Emory University in Atlanta.

GEORGE M. SOARES-PRABHU, prior to his death, was a member of the Society of Jesus (Jesuits). He taught at DeNobili College in Pune, India. In 1995, he began United Cooperative Works, an organization to help poor people with limited educational skills receive training in carpentry, electronics, and vehicle repairs. Soares-Prabhu was the author of *The Formula Quotations in the Infancy Narrative of Matthew: an Enquiry into the Tradition History of Matthew 1—2* and editor of *Wir Werden Bei Ihm Wohnen: das Johannesevangelium in indischer Deutung.* It is our great regret that Rev. Soares-Prabhu's contributions are being published posthumously.

CHOAN-SENG SONG is Professor of Theology at the Pacific School of Theology and the Graduate Theological Union in Berkeley, California. He is a member of the Presbyterian Church in Taiwan and the Reformed Church in America. Song has authored many books, including *Third-Eye Theology, The Compassionate God,* and *Jesus, The Crucified People.* He holds degrees from National Taiwan University, the University of Edinburgh in Scotland, as well as a Ph.D. from Union Theological Seminary in New York.

Introduction

In the first lines of the first essay, José Míguez-Bonino has wonderfully encapsulated the impetus for this volume—though this was not his assigned task. Nevertheless, in his analysis of the Tower of Babel story (Genesis 11:1–9) from a Latin American perspective, a radical rethinking of the biblical story emerges to launch this collection, *Return to Babel*. His interpretation offers a paradigmatic glimpse of the kind of bold reopening of a text that occurs again and again from the insightful, challenging essays in this volume.

The thrust of his essay is an inversion of the usual interpretation of the Tower of Babel story, in which the "confusion of tongues" is a *fall* from "the one language," a divine *punishment* for the human act of arrogance. Míguez-Bonino chooses to explore this story out of the experience of his own people, with its collective memory of an era before there existed a single, European language.

> In 1552, the *conquistador* Pizarro disembarked in what is now Ecuador and began a *blitzkrieg* conquest of the whole Tahuantinsuyu (Inca) Empire. Thirty years later, the 7,000,000 inhabitants that he found had been reduced to 700,000. The weapons of destruction were wars, epidemics, forced labor, along with the total upheaval of the economic, political, and social structure. A new empire had reorganized life, redivided the land, reunified the former empire with a new center . . . *and a new language.*[1]

Following the thread of his experience through the Tower of Babel story, one can see the tower as the tangible manifestation of the workings of empire—Babylon—and as the visible symbol of the project of homogenization and unification that imperialism historically has pursued. By this line of thinking, the destruction of the tower and the resultant scattering and "confusion" of languages might arguably be seen not as the sign of God's punishment, but rather as the signal event in the restoration of a desirable diversity, of a positive return to indigenous tongues and thus to the multiplicity of nativist experiences that would otherwise be methodically suppressed and erased in the name of a false unity sanctioned and imposed by the conquering power.

The principal effect of God's intervention in this building project is, then, simultaneously to scatter the imperial builders and to create a cacophony of languages. In light of this interpretation, Míguez-Bonino contends that "God re-creates the diversity that some want to homogenize. . . . The question that remains for us is whether there *is a different kind of unity* . . . that does not rest in the elimination of all languages, the centralization of all locality, the submission to one city, or the worshiping of one tower."[2]

If we follow this thread further in its relation to biblical studies, we can see during the last decades a tendency toward a loosening of the hegemony of European and North American biblical interpretation. The original impulse for this loosening coincided in large measure with movements of independence in various regions of the Two Thirds World,[3] particularly in the 1960s. Pioneering authors began to raise the spectre of their own mode of biblical interpretation that took their own contexts seriously. J. S. Mbiti, author of *New Testament Eschatology in an African Background: a Study of the Encounter Between New Testament Theology and African Traditional Religion,*[4] in which he charted a course for subsequent African biblical interpretation, pressed European and North American theologians to share their domination by asking, "We have eaten theology with you; we have drunk theology with you; we have dreamed theology with you. We know you theologically. The question is, do you know us theologically? Would you like to know us theologically?"[5] A spate of compelling studies in which the Bible was interpreted from the perspective of concrete cultural contexts accompanied Mbiti's study. For example, L. Boff[6] and J. Sobrino,[7] in light of the class struggle that characterized their Latin American context, portrayed Jesus as a figure who sided with the poor and opposed the wealthy urban classes. In India, R. Panikkar[8] saw a point of resonance between Christianity and Hinduism at the deepest experience of mystery, while M. M. Thomas[9] observed that for centuries the Jesus of the Gospels—rather than the Christ of mystical experience—had produced a significant impact upon the public life of India.

Despite their diversity, these pioneering studies from the 1960s and 1970s declared in unison the conviction that the context of the interpreter has a decided and desirable impact upon the interpretation that eventuates from a reflection upon biblical texts. The cogency and clarity with which this challenge arose spawned a new generation of contextual theologians and biblical interpreters who believe that the Bible is relevant *for* their contexts and that the relevance of the Bible can best be grasped *from* the realities of their contexts—that differing vantage points in diverse contexts open fresh ways of reading the biblical text. Some of these studies are included in the Select Annotated Bibliography at the conclusion of *Return to Babel*. While the essays in this volume share the assumption of these studies,[10] what distinguishes this volume is how *coordinated* and *comprehensive* it is. *Return to Babel* is coordinated in that all thirty essays follow the identical format of context, text, and reflection. That is, each writer begins by foregrounding those aspects of his or her particular context that have the potential to provide a vantage point for fresh interpretations; each then engages those specific elements of the biblical text that most powerfully resonate with his or her context; finally, each creatively blends aspects of the biblical text with key elements of his or her respective Latin American, African, or Asian context.

Return to Babel is comprehensive in that the ten biblical texts range from the primeval history to the final vision of a new heaven and a new earth. In other words, the uniqueness of this volume is that it provides *common focuses for diversely situated interpreters from Latin America, Africa, and Asia* by selecting ten representative biblical texts, assigning the identical format for each essay, and gathering a diverse and distinguished collection of authors.

The ten biblical texts in *Return to Babel* are representative of the biblical canon.[11] Three interpreters—a Latin American, an African, and an Asian—have attended to each biblical text. These texts have been selected because they span the various divisions and genres that are found in the Jewish and Christian scriptures.

The five texts selected from the Old Testament encompass the three divisions into which Jews have traditionally apportioned their Bible: Torah, Prophets, and Writings.

Genesis 11:1–9

Exodus 20:1–17

Psalm 23:1–6

Ecclesiastes 3:1–8

Isaiah 52:13–53:12

Torah, or the Pentateuch, both of which are designations for the first five books of the Jewish Bible, from Genesis through Deuteronomy, is represented by two texts: Genesis 11:1–9, which is narrative in form, and Exodus 20:1–17, which, though set in the narrative context of the biblical book of Exodus, may loosely be identified as legal material.[12] The second division of the Jewish Bible, the Prophets, is represented by Isaiah 52:13–53:12. Psalm 23 and Ecclesiastes 3:1–8 belong to the third division, known as the Writings; the psalm represents Israel's hymnody and poetry, while Ecclesiastes belongs to Israel's wisdom tradition.

The five texts selected from the New Testament are:

Matthew 5:1–12

John 1:1–18

Acts 2:1–42

1 Corinthians 15:1–58

Revelation 21:1–22:5

These texts represent the various literary genres that are included in the New Testament. Matthew 5:1–12 is from one of the so-called Synoptic Gospels; the other Synoptic Gospels are Mark and Luke. John 1:1–18 comprises the Prologue to the fourth Gospel, which is significantly different in both form and content from the Synoptic Gospels. Acts 2 is a paradigmatic chapter in a volume on the early church that comprises a sequel to the Gospel of Luke. The letters of Paul are represented by 1 Corinthians 15, while the selection of Revelation 21:1–22:5 is a portion of a vision that is illustrative of a literary genre known as an apocalypse.[13]

The writers whose essays are gathered in this book represent a diverse range of experiences, as the brief biographies preceding this introduction suggest. The vocations of these writers range from lay preacher to pastor to priest to bishop to missionary to university rector to professor. Although all of these contributors possess the requisite academic training and publication records to qualify them as authors in their own right, they have also committed themselves to social change in their respective contexts. Essays in this volume are written, for example, by an elected member of the National Constitutional Assembly of Argentina who is also the president of the Argentine Permanent Assembly for Human Rights (Míguez-Bonino); by a member of the Association of Major Superiors in the Philippines

Commission on Justice, Peace, and the Integrity of Creation (Graham); by the founder of the United Cooperative Works, which provides mechanical training for the poor in India (Soares-Prabhu); and by a member of the Circle of Concerned African Women Theologians (Kinoti)—to mention a few more visible commitments.

The diversity of these authors is also apparent in their respective church affiliation. The five Roman Catholic contributors represent the Philippines, Zaire, Mexico, India, and Argentina. Methodists hail from Argentina, Costa Rica, the Philippines, and Kenya. The three Presbyterian writers were raised in Korea, Taiwan, and Ghana, while two other essays were written by a longtime American Baptist missionary in Nicaragua and a bishop in the United Church of Zambia.

The clearest signal of diversity in *Return to Babel* is apparent in what these contributors bring from their contexts to the interpretation of the Bible. The various geographical locales to which the reader is taken range from the tiny village of Cantomanyog on the southern part of the island of Negros in the Philippines to the large city of Nairobi, Kenya, from the city of Kwangju, South Korea, with its one million inhabitants, to the frontier city of Wiwili in the Northern mountains of Nicaragua. These essays reflect as well the enormous religious diversity of the contributors' contexts, which extend from Zambia, whose leaders declared it a Christian country, to India, whose religious pluralism is considered by George Soares-Prabhu to be India's "conspicuous feature."

The cacophany of cultures becomes louder with the introduction of various groups and tribes, such as the Nahua of Mexico, the Gikuyu of Central Kenya, and the Bantu of sub-Saharan Africa. A treasury of proverbs, songs, and tales from Latin America, Asia, and Africa are recounted in this book, including the African tale of the blue bird, the ancient Taiwanese story of the five brothers who were murdered by the Japanese, the East African Christian revival song, *Tukutendereza Yesu,* and Bantu maxims such as *kudia kua nsua mpa msua* ("Do not wait . . . one must eat in the ant's season"), to mention a few.

The writers bring, moreover, stories of individuals whose lives are paradigmatic of their cultures. There are individuals from every context who encounter daily suffering and oppression, such as Doña Catalina, a Nicaraguan mother of five children who could choose to send only two of her five children to school, and Yati, a twenty-three-year-old woman who works 130-hour weeks in the Reebok factory in Tangerang, Indonesia, although she clings tenuously to the dream of leaving the factory to become a secretary. There are as well individuals from every context who exhibit extraordinary courage in the face of adversity—Mrs. Mutahi, for example, who founded the Ngong Hills Children's Home not long after she began to feed a group of homeless boys and girls in Nairobi, Kenya, whom she found picking food from a common rubbish bin. There are those people from every context whose stories of martyrdom find testimony in this book: Maria Cristina Gomez, a Nicaraguan teacher dedicated to working with orphans and to organizing women who was taken from her classroom and shot to death; thirteen farmers who were murdered by the Philippine marines as they demonstrated to call attention to the plight of farmers; and Ciyamba, an innocent woman who, after having her legs and arms broken, was buried alive because she was chosen as the sacrificial victim to seal the alliance pact between the peoples from the Lubilanji basin in Africa.

Although diversity is the hallmark of *Return to Babel,* this diversity will not silence a profound unifying theme that emerges in the following thirty essays, namely, the juxtaposition of suffering and hope. As Cyris Moon explains, "Suffering and hope are, indeed, two simple words that cover the deepest and most complex realities of our existence as human beings."[14] Again and again in this volume, essays begin with tales of tribulation, stories of despair, accounts of political ordeals. Elsa Tamez, for instance, begins her essay on the resurrection of the body (1 Corinthians 15) with the harsh and pervasive reality of the abuse of women's bodies in Latin America. The poverty and social degradation of the *dalits* (ex-untouchables) in India is the touchstone for Soares-Prabhu's analysis of the Decalogue (Exodus 20). Prior to his discussion of the new community in Acts 2, Patrice Siyemeto of Zambia details the chaos of his country as it forges its own community in the midst of strikes, demonstrations, economic disorder, and political disquiet.

Nevertheless, although these writers begin with descriptions of misery and grief, they invariably proceed to wrest hope from the biblical text in their effort to withstand that suffering, to comprehend that chaos, to emerge undefeated from that distress. Tamez maintains that when one believes in the resurrection of the body—as Paul urges in 1 Corinthians 15— "then one's own body and others' bodies can be valued."[15] Similarly, in the Decalogue, "with its implicit proclamation of the equality of all human beings," Soares-Prabhu finds "the broad outlines of this liberative community toward which all dalits everywhere aspire."[16] There is hope, according to Siyemeto, in the church as an agent of the Holy Spirit to bring about reconciliation in Zambian society: "Therefore, commitment and openness to the leading and renewal of the Spirit are called for on the part of the church. It is this life once lived to its fullest by the church that will permeate our society."[17]

This uncanny and univocal ability to "hew a stone of hope out of a mountain of despair," as Martin Luther King, Jr., phrased it so aptly on the steps of the Lincoln Memorial in Washington, D.C., can be illustrated particularly well by the interpretations of Ecclesiastes 3—a biblical text that unreservedly acknowledges the hopelessness and futility of human existence—a text whose recurrent theme is that there is nothing new under the sun and that all of life is vanity, vanity of vanities, a text about whose author, C. S. Song, justifiably queries, "But who is this sage-teacher, who is preoccupied with the thought that the world is absurd and futile?"[18] Notwithstanding the despair evinced by Ecclesiastes, Kabasele Lumbala, Tamez, and Song invariably wrest hope from this text on behalf of the oppressed in their respective contexts. Tamez discovers hope "when the future cannot be known, the past has been forgotten, and the present is unbearable" because, although the chronological time of human drudgery grinds on, liberation can be grasped by the faith that "in God's timing . . . everything has its time and its hour."[19] Song robustly challenges the sage who authored Ecclesiastes and who neither expected nor offered hope; there is hope, according to Song, precisely in the unexpected. "But there is something he [the sage] has not expected: what he has said in total resignation can be taken up by the oppressed and victims of injustice as a challenge to change their fate. . . . Our sage-teacher is right: for everything there is a season. How true! It does not matter if he says it in despair. Nor does it matter if he means by it how futile things are. There is no question about the fact that 'for everything there is a season.' "[20] In the cadence of the phrase, "a time for," Kabasele Lumbala discerns the rhythm of life: "Where Qoheleth—the preacher, the philosopher—reads the incoherence of existence, which is shaken by contradictions, the Bantus perceive a chant in praise of life's multifaceted dynamism, and they bring a dance-step into the infinitely variable and unforeseeable rhythm of life."[21] The recurring contrasting pairs—be born and die, kill and heal, find and lose, fight and make peace—serve further to remind us "by their diversity, . . . how much God's behavior encompasses all of human activities, from the most banal to the most dramatic."[22]

In the first essay of this volume, Míguez-Bonino returned to Babel to alert us to the reality that the destruction of a dominant culture in the earliest chapters of the Bible is simultaneously a source of hope to cultures dominated by that imperium. In the final essay, Song returns to another city, the new Jerusalem (Revelation 21:1–22:5), to awaken us to another reality, that "from the old creation to a new creation is a long, long time."[23] Before John, exiled to the island of Patmos, was privileged to see the final, glorious vision of a new heaven and a new earth, he perceived destruction and annihilation everywhere and in all times. About this requisite and painful period of waiting, Song writes, "It takes all the tribulations, both personal and communal, for John the seer finally to envision that new heaven and earth."[24] Song can, from the delay of this vision, find hope for those who ache with suffering, heralding words that close his essay and express the hope of those who have brought their wisdom and faith to the task of biblical interpretation in this volume: "The road towards a new heaven on earth in Asia [in Africa and Latin America] is a long and hard one. . . . But the journey has already begun, and there is no turning away from it. This, after all, is the journey of none other than Jesus our Lord, who prayed that God's will be done on earth as in heaven."[25]

Notes

1. See page 13.
2. See page 16.
3. We shall usually refer collectively to the regions of Latin America, Africa, and Asia as the Two Thirds World.
4. Oxford: Oxford University, 1971.
5. "Theological Impotence and the Universality of the Church," in *Third World Theologies*. Edited by G. Anderson and T. Stransky (New York: Paulist, 1976) 16–17.
6. *Jesus Christ Liberator: A Critical Christology for Our Time* (Maryknoll, NY: Orbis, 1978).
7. *Christology at the Crossroads* (Maryknoll, NY: Orbis, 1978).
8. *The Unknown Christ of Hinduism* (London: Darton, Longman and Todd, 1964).
9. *The Acknowledged Christ of the Indian Renaissance* (London: SCM, 1969).
10. For concise analyses of the process of interpretation, see P. Pope-Levison and J. R. Levison, *Jesus in Global Contexts* (Louisville: Westminster/John Knox, 1992) 14–18; idem, "Global Perspectives on New Testament Interpretation," in *Reading the New Testament: Strategies for Interpretation*. Edited by J. B. Green (Grand Rapids: Eerdmans, 1995) 329–48; R. Grant and D. Tracy, *A Short History of the Interpretation of the Bible* (2nd ed.; Philadelphia: Fortress, 1984) 154–60, 181. Tracy here interprets H. G. Gadamer, *Truth and Method* (2nd ed.; New York: Crossroad, 1990). The relationship between text and context is understood as the fusion of two horizons by A. C. Thiselton, *The Two Horizons: New Testament Hermeneutics and Philosophical Description with Special Reference to Heidegger,*

Bultmann, Gadamer, and Wittgenstein (Grand Rapids: Eerdmans, 1980) 10–23. See also the paradigmatic essays of R. Bultmann, "The Problem of Hermeneutics," in idem, *Essays Philosophical and Theological* (London: SCM, 1955) 234–61; "Is Exegesis Without Presuppositions Possible?" in *Existence and Faith: Shorter Writings of Rudolf Bultmann*. Edited by S. Ogden (London: Hodder & Stoughton, 1961) 289–96.

11. We have adopted the Protestant canon for this project. The Roman Catholic canon would include additionally the Apocrypha, or Deutero-canonical literature, while the Jewish canon would include only what Christians have traditionally designated the Old Testament.

12. Scholars tend to divide the forms of legal material in the Hebrew Bible into so-called casuistic and apodictic law. Casuistic, or case, law usually has the form, "If/when someone [e.g., steals an ox]," or "Whoever . . ." followed by "then [the punishment is]. . . ." For example, Exodus 21:15 reads, "Whoever strikes father or mother shall be put to death." Or, "If someone's ox hurts the ox of another, so that it dies, then they shall sell the live ox and divide the price of it; and the dead animal they shall also divide" (Exodus 21:35). Apodictic law, on the other hand, of which the Decalogue is an example, consists of direct, second-person commands.

13. The title, Revelation, is simply a translation of the Greek word, *apokalypsis*.

14. See page 112.

15. See page 187.

16. See page 53.

17. See page 171.

18. See page 88.

19. See pages 77–78.

20. See page 89.

21. See page 85.

22. See page 84.

23. See page 216.

24. See page 217.

25. See page 219.

Genesis 11:1–9

Now the whole earth had one language and the same words. 2 And as they migrated from the east, they came upon a plain in the land of Shinar and settled there. 3 And they said to one another, "Come, let us make bricks, and burn them thoroughly." And they had brick for stone, and bitumen for mortar. 4 Then they said, "Come, let us build ourselves a city, and a tower with its top in the heavens, and let us make a name for ourselves; otherwise we shall be scattered abroad upon the face of the whole earth." 5 The L_{ORD} came down to see the city and the tower, which mortals had built. 6 And the L_{ORD} said, "Look, they are one people, and they have all one language; and this is only the beginning of what they will do; nothing that they propose to do will now be impossible for them. 7 Come, let us go down, and confuse their language there, so that they will not understand one another's speech." 8 So the L_{ORD} scattered them abroad from there over the face of all the earth, and they left off building the city. 9 Therefore it was called Babel, because there the L_{ORD} confused the language of all the earth; and from there the L_{ORD} scattered them abroad over the face of all the earth.

Genesis 11:1–9
A Latin American Perspective

José Míguez-Bonino

Context

In 1552, the *conquistador* Pizarro disembarked in what is now Ecuador and began a *blitzkrieg* conquest of the whole Tahuantinsuyu (Inca) Empire. Thirty years later, the 7,000,000 inhabitants that he found had been reduced to 700,000. The weapons of destruction were wars, epidemics, forced labor, along with the total upheaval of the economic, political, and social structure. A new empire had reorganized life, redivided the land, reunified the former empire with a new center . . . *and a new language.*

This was not an unknown experience for this people, for some 250 years earlier the Quechua dynasty had conquered and subjected the different tribes—"yuncas," "aimaraes," and others—and had built the most extended and powerful empire of the continent. *It had imposed its language* under the threat of severe punishment. Parents had to teach this language to their children. Nothing could be transacted outside of that language. Only the poets—the *amautas*—were able to sing with nostalgia about their old cultures.

This new language of the Spanish conquest was again a crucial issue. To accept the new language meant to deny everything that gave meaning to their lives—stories, traditions, the "naming of things," the music of words, the sounds of love. To keep to their own language, however, meant to be a stranger in their own land, to be "outside the law," to be unable to negotiate and to understand the language of power. The religious situation is a good example of the tensions surrounding a new language. Some missionaries wanted to keep the indigenous language in order to be able to communicate. However, the result of this was that the "Quechua-speaking converts" could not enter the ministry and in this way were effectively kept from being "agents" of their faith! Other missionaries wanted to use only the Spanish in order to integrate the people more fully into the "transplanted official Church." Who was favoring the aboriginal people?

The question of indigenous languages continues to be a dilemma. In the recent Constitutional Assembly in Argentina, sharp discussions took place around the "rights of the aboriginal people." Most agreed that they had the right to use their own languages—already a step forward! But not all of those who agreed were ready to pay the cost of a fully bilingual education. Even fewer were willing to include "the resources necessary" for these peoples to develop the material, economic, and judicial infrastructure that would make this "language" *work!* However, the pressure of the aboriginal people's own presence finally moved the right definitions through. Now, who will see these definitions to their enactment?

Text

The usual interpretation of this text is to view the "confusion of tongues," a fall from "the one language," as divine punishment for the human act of arrogance. I diverge from this interpretation, and I will call attention briefly to some aspects that lead me to another interpretation.[1]

The "project" of building begins in Genesis 11:2 with an undefined subject, "they," who "migrated . . . found a plain . . . and settled there." The only concrete reference is *Shinar,* possibly the name for Babylon in the Late Bronze Age. There they "settle" and carry out the "project" to which they had agreed (Genesis 11:2–3), which is characterized by three elements: (1) to build a "city"; (2) to build "a tower"; and (3) "to make a name for ourselves."[2] It is possible, by placing this story into its narrative context in Genesis, to gain a clearer sense of who "they"—the people who build the city in Shinar—are. This "project" should be related to what precedes it in Genesis 10:8–10, where the founder of Babel is mentioned and characterized: "Cush became the father of Nimrod; he was the first on earth to become a mighty warrior. 9 He was a mighty hunter before the LORD; therefore it is said, 'Like Nimrod a mighty hunter before the LORD.' 10 The beginning of his kingdom was Babel, Erech, and Accad, all of them in the land of Shinar." Here Nimrod, the founder of Babel, is identified as a "mighty warrior" and a "mighty hunter." The two epithets belong together, for the same Hebrew word, *gibbor,* is employed to describe Nimrod: he is a *gibbor* (a mighty warrior) and a *gibbor sayid* (a mighty warrior of beasts). Babel's founder was, then, a tyrant with respect to both humans and beasts, "a true prototype of the

Assyrian [i.e., Babylonian] monarchs."[3] The city, Babylon, the tower (perhaps a Babylonian ziggurat), and the "name" characterize the Assyrian-Babylonian empire. Are the storytellers a threatened people who look at the ruined and unfinished old Babylonian ziggurat and laugh at the arrogance of an empire whose dream was that it would never be "dispersed"?

The purpose of this passage, therefore, is *not* primarily the explanation of the origin of diverse languages, *but* the condemnation and defeat of the imperial arrogance and universal domination represented by the symbol of Babylon. God's action, then, is twofold: the thwarting of the project of the false unity of domination *and* the liberation of the nations that possess their own places, languages, and families. The punishment of imperial Babylon is simultaneously the liberation of diverse nations. Interestingly, the "going down" of God appears two times in the text, in 11:5, "to see" and in 11:7, "to act." Generally, this "going down" is thought to represent God's action only of judgment. What I am suggesting is that the act of defeating the "imperial project" is at the same time an act of deliverance: the peoples can return to their own nation, place, and language!

Reflection

Universality and diversity, universal time and diverse space, seem to be in conflict. We all live now in a "universal history" whose "times" affect everybody and every place. But babies are still born in a specific space, which means they stammer a certain language, are given certain names, and find certain people around them. We all belong simultaneously to one (universal) world and to one (particular) locality. Has our text anything to tell us about this conflict?

For one thing, Genesis 10–11 tells us that God wants to disturb the imperial attempt to unify all of humankind around one "emperor-warrior," one city, or one name. Does this mean that God is jealous of this empire they are building because God wants to make uniform everything and everybody in *God's own* one and only "empire"? Our author seems to imply this interpretation in 11:6–7: "And the LORD said, 'Look, they are one people, and they have all one language; and this is only the beginning of what they will do; nothing that they propose to do will now be impossible for them. 7 Come, let us go down, and confuse their language there, so that they will not understand one another's speech.'" But the author's own story of God's action as he tells it before and after this episode—in the narrative context in Genesis—suggests something different. *This context suggests that God's intention is a diverse humanity that can find its unity not in the domination of one city, one tower, or one language but in the "bless-ing for all the families of the earth"* (Genesis 12:3). This different kind of unity requires that the alleged unities of the Inca, the Spanish, the British, or the United States empires, all of which represent the "manifest des-tinies" of self-chosen "centers" in a declaration that the final and absolute city has been reached, be confused.

God re-creates the diversity that some want to homogenize. For this rea-son, God must constantly "scatter the proud in the imaginations of their hearts" (Luke 1:51), so that the humble may live in freedom. The question that remains for us is whether there *is a different kind of unity,* a different universality, that does not rest in the elimination of all languages, the cen-tralization of all locality, the submission to one city, or the worshiping of one tower.

Notes

1. While the Spaniards were landing in America, the Portuguese conquered the Western Coast of Africa. In 1778, by way of exchange, a part usually called West-ern Guinea came into Spanish hands, and in 1858 it was declared a colony. In 1988, J. M. Eko Eko Ada, a young student from Guinea who had suffered in his own childhood the physical and moral abuse of having to use the imposed lan-guage, came to Buenos Aires, Argentina, to do his graduate work at the Higher Evangelical Institute for Theological Studies. He was haunted by the question of language and the story of Babel. His master's thesis, "La Torre De Babel: Signo De Libertad" (Buenos Aires: ISEDET, 1991), has been a fruitful help in this ex-egetical section of this article.

2. There is perhaps a play on words between the Hebrew word *name* and the Hebrew word *sky,* which sound alike. Thus the name to be made is linked to the sky—the tower's destination. See J. P. Fokkelmann, *Narrative Art in Genesis: specimens of stylistic and structural analysis* (Assen: Van Gorcum, 1975) 16–18.

3. J. Skinner, *A Critical and Exegetical Commentary on Genesis* (Edinburgh: T. & T. Clark, 1930) 208.

Genesis 11:1–9
An African Perspective

Solomon Avotri

Context

One of the best-known myths found in many parts of the African continent is the African blue bird story, which tells of how God left the earth in order to separate Godself from human beings. E. W. Smith's reconstruction of the Akan version of the African myth is as follows:

> It is said that long ago men were happy, for *Nyame* (God) dwelt among them and talked with them face to face. These blissful days, however, did not last forever. One unlucky day it chanced that some women were pounding a mash with pestles in a mortar while God stood by looking on. For some reason they were annoyed by the presence of the Deity, and told him to be off; and as he did not take off fast enough to please them, they beat him with their pestles. Then God retired altogether from the world into the sky, and left it to the direction of the fetishes;[1] and still to this day people say: "Ah, if it had not been for that old woman, how happy we would be!"[2]

The Dinka people of the Sudan add that a rope hanging from the sky, now Nyame's abode, provided the means for people to get up and down from heaven, but God sent a blue bird to cut the rope so that people could no longer ascend to God so easily. According to the Nuer tradition, also of the Sudan, the reason people climbed the rope was to become young again. They had been in the presence of God, the source for the renewal of life, and they desired to return to earth to begin life all over again. Despite these variations, the whole story can be referred to as the African blue bird story.

Even though there is no mention of a city here, the myth is tied to a human community that becomes the meeting place of earth and Sky (Nyame). Nyame's dwelling among them and talking to them face to face may suggest some cultic (i.e., worship) connections. "It is hardly an exaggeration to say that every compound in Ashanti[3] contains an altar to the Sky God, in the shape of a forked branch cut from a certain tree which the Ashanti call *Nyame dua*, literally, *God's tree*. This forked branch holds a brass or earthenware pot containing ancient stones. People put daily offerings in these pots or on the roofs of their huts for the Great God of the Sky."[4] Many of these household forked branches have now disappeared, perhaps under the force of Christianity; nevertheless, this widespread African myth may have been associated at one time with memories of different cultic locations (cities) for the worship of the Sky God.

The addition from the Nuer tradition, which makes provision for the renewal of life in the presence of the divinity, can be understood as symbolic of the mere power to live. It is what V. Mulago refers to as a "vital union," "the bond joining together, vertically and horizontally, beings living and dead; it is the life-giving principle in all. It is the result of communion, a participation in the one reality, the one vital principle that unites various beings."[5] As E. Smith contends, what the African seeks is power, a vital union.

This craving for power is the driving force in the life of African religion. It has its origin in a feeling of incapacity and in an obstinate desire to overcome it; it is a search for help and comfort, a means of maintaining and strengthening life in the midst of a thousand dangers, and a way of conquering the fear which shoots its arrows from every hidden ambush. Man is weak, and what he needs is increased strength. The absorbing question for him is how to acquire some of this power[6] so that it may serve for his own salvation or that of the group for which he is responsible.[7]

The African myth attempts to explain why humanity does not have this power in the first place. Seemingly, Nyame has put a distinction between the divine and human worlds, thereby creating for humans the dilemma of alienation and divine inaccessibility. From an African perspective, the Tower of Babel story raises similar issues about the divine-human relationship.

Text

The Tower of Babel story not only forms the conclusion of the creation story in the first eleven chapters of Genesis, but it also tells a story concerning humanity in relation to God. Many commentators have viewed the

Tower of Babel story negatively as a story about sin and punishment in response to human pride and arrogance (e.g., Genesis 11:4a). In this interpretation, the human intention to build a tower with "its top in the heavens," and to make a name for themselves, is an expression of the human desire to become divine. E. van Wolde has compiled samples of these negative interpretations.[8] For example, one commentator writes, "The sin of those tower builders is undoubtedly the sin of pride and pretentious humanism." Similarly, another suggests that the action of the builders resembles the disobedience of Adam and Eve, who attempted to transcend their limits in order to become like God. I would suggest rather differently that Genesis 11:1–9, like the African blue bird story, presents the essential structure in which we can perceive divine reality, humanity, the depths and subtleties of human life, and the divine-human relationship. In this structure also is embedded humanity, set against the human experience of being alienated from God—an experience that has set humans on a path of constant quests for immortality.

Understood in this way, the Tower of Babel story follows integrally from the chapters that precede it. After Adam and Eve have eaten the forbidden fruit (Genesis 3:6), thereby offending God, the Yahwist[9] presents a progression of hostility between Yahweh (i.e., God) and humanity, as seen in Yahweh's attempt to distance himself from humans. Yahweh's response seems to stem from the fear that humanity might have full access to divine qualities. This fear is first expressed when Yahweh realizes that humanity has become like divine beings, knowing good and evil (Genesis 3:22a). Secondly, Yahweh is alarmed that humanity might attain immortality by eating from the tree of life (Genesis 3:22b). Thus, in spite of Yahweh's benevolence toward them demonstrated by clothing them (Genesis 3:21), Yahweh is still determined to take away from them the privilege of living in the garden; so Yahweh drives them out (Genesis 3:24a). In order to ensure that they never have any more access to the garden, Yahweh places cherubim with a flashing sword to guard the way to the tree of life (Genesis 3:24b). When the divine-human boundary is further broken by the mating of divine beings with human women, Yahweh's anger is vented on humanity. The divine reprisal is swift and severe; the human life span is limited to 120 years—an emphatic statement of the denial of immortality to humanity (Genesis 6:1–4).

In Genesis 6:5–7, Yahweh even regrets that he has made human beings in the first place and decides to blot them out by means of a flood (Genesis 7:1–24). Only Noah and his family are saved. Thus a relationship that began so propitiously has ended in disaster, so that as soon as humanity multiplies again, divine-human hostility resurfaces. With the Tower of Babel story, Yahweh is no longer accessible to humankind; Yahweh is even far away in the sky. For this reason, humanity strives to do for itself what it thinks necessary for its self-preservation (Genesis 11:4a). Reacting with fear similar to before (Genesis 3:22), Yahweh is threatened by human unity and its potential for greater achievements: "And Yahweh said, 'Look, they are one people, and they have all one language; and this is only the beginning of what they will do; nothing that they purpose to do will be impossible for them'" (Genesis 11:6).

Following his words with action, Yahweh destroys humanity's effort and its limitless possibilities of creativity in the unity of language (Genesis 11:7). As a result, the tower never reached heaven, and they never made a name for themselves. However, this divine act does not appear as a punishment for human arrogance or pride but as Yahweh's determination to keep himself transcendent and inaccessible to humankind.

When the Tower of Babel story is seen in the context of the progression of hostility between Yahweh and humanity, then the significance of the story is seen as evidence of the human dilemma about divine inaccessibility and the quest for immortality. In pursuit of linking the divine and human realms, humans design to do two things particularly for themselves:

11:4a: Let us build ourselves a city and a tower with its top in the heavens.

11:4b: Let us make a name for ourselves.

In Israel, there was awareness of the significance attached to a name and the power that resided in it. This significance of the name (Hebrew, *shem*) also finds expression in the idea that a man's name lives on in his descendants.[10] For example, Joseph prays in Genesis 48:16, "The angel who has redeemed me from all harm, bless the boys; and in them let my name be perpetuated, and the name of my ancestors Abraham and Isaac; and let them grow into a multitude on the earth." The Hebrew-translated "perpetuated" in this prayer is *qr'*, "to call, to give a name." Thus Joseph prayed that his name and those of Abraham and Isaac might be called, or might "live on," in his sons. The same idea is expressed to Abraham by God in Genesis 21:12: "For it is through Isaac that offspring shall be named [*yqr'*] for you." When Absalom, David's son, did not have any son to perpetuate his name, he said to himself: "I have no son to keep my name in remembrance." So he set up a pillar and called it by his own name: "Absalom's Monument" (2 Samuel 18:18). Thus the perpetuation of a name even after death suggests the idea of immortality. In other words, an aspect of the power that resides in a name is immortality. Similarly, with regard to the Babel tower, the builders will make a name for themselves by challenging the supremacy of Yahweh. Since the Hebrew word *shem*, meaning *name*, possesses connotations of fame, renown, and progeny, it seems clear that the city builders are engaged in an attempt to overcome the human fate of mortality.[11]

Reflection

Almost all African peoples associate God with the sky. A testimony of the Ewe people of West Africa, to which I belong, says, "There, where the sky is, God is too." This saying stems from the immensity of the sky, which invites one to gaze on it with his or her eyes and imagination. Similarly, God is thought of as dwelling far away in the sky, beyond the reach of human beings. The Basuto, for example, sing a wailing-song that speaks of the sky in this way:

We were left outside; we were left for trouble; we were left for tears;
Oh, if there were in heaven a place for me!
Why have I not wings to fly there!
If a strong cord hung down from the sky, I would climb it; I would go up;
I would go and dwell there.

This song can be interpreted as a lament over the transcendence of deity and the loss of physical accessibility to God—a loss of "vital union." It recalls the cord imagery in the blue bird story. In both cases, the cord exists no more, and thus the sky remains inaccessible either as a place where one escapes to from troubles or as a place to which one goes for life renewal before returning to earth.[12] But the dilemma of inaccessibility goes beyond spatial limits and translates into spiritual incomprehensibility. This is illustrated by the meanings of some African names for God, such as "the God of the unknown" (the *Lunda*), "the Unexplainable" (the *Ngombe*), "the Unknown" (the *Massai*).[13]

Still, the traditional African understanding of God's beyond-ness includes at the same time God's ongoing communion with humanity and the rest of creation in concrete terms. In the Akan version of God's departure from the earth, one interpreter states that "God has removed Himself too far away from men for direct approach; yet this is accompanied by the Ashanti belief that everyone has access to Him."[14] The point we are trying to make here can be summed up in what E. E. Evans-Prichard observed about the Nuer religion: "Nuer religious thought cannot be understood unless God's closeness to man is taken together with his separation from man, for its meaning lies precisely in this paradox."[15]

How, then, is this closeness of God experienced in African thought? An Akan proverb provides some insight—*wope asem aka akyere Nyame a, ka kyere mframa*—"If you want to say something to *Nyame* [God], say it to the wind." What this proverb indicates is that, even though God left the earth, God is not bound or limited to any particular region or space. God is like the wind. Therefore, in the midst of the ambiguities of daily living, the African, by this paradox, is able to fix at a safe distance a God who is sometimes unfair, capricious, and dangerous. At the same time, he or she is able to bring that same—but also dependable—God near enough to meet human needs.

A similar understanding of the concept of God is found in the stories of the African blue bird and the Tower of Babel. Both stories present God as the God of the sky, who, although much greater than humans, is nevertheless depicted in vivid anthropomorphic terms. For example, God exhibits anger and impatience. In both stories, God is presented less as the loving God than as the God who opposes human dreams and creates a harsh world for them. God's capriciousness and unfairness thwart human happiness. When the divine supremacy is threatened by the desire of human beings to obtain immortality from divine sources, God thwarts their efforts. In other words, God does not hesitate to inflict suffering in order to enhance God's own well-being. At the end of both stories, God is presented as preferring to live in isolation from human beings.

Another theme we encounter in the African blue bird story is the affirmation of life. The story ends with the words: "Ah, if it had not been for that old woman, how happy we would be!" These words express a yearning for relief and happiness in the midst of the harsh realities of African life. Like the story of the Tower of Babel, this African story presents the deity as one who has the power over life and death. Specific motifs, such as the tree of life (Genesis 3:22) and the renewal of life (the African story), emphasize life and God's identity with it. Life is the continuous flow of creative power and spiritual energy.[16] This is the essence of the divine reality, which, in biblical terms, is referred to as "the Spirit" or "the Breath of God" (Genesis 1:2).

Lastly, the idea of a great name also establishes a connection between the Tower of Babel story and the African blue bird story. J. S. Mbiti comments upon the blue bird story: "The original paradise was lost: men's direct link with God was severed or eclipsed, the closeness between the heavens and the earth was replaced by a vast gap without a bridge, the gifts of immortality and resurrection melted away, and death, disease and disharmony came and reigned ever since."

He continues, "Through marriage and childbearing, [people] are still able to achieve something of the original immortality." This "something of the original immortality" is recaptured in the notion of the survival of a person's name.[17]

The naming ceremony in Africa signifies how important names are among Africans. Prayers spoken during the ritual often invoke the ancestors and include an offering of food.

> *Your food is here,*
> *Let the children have good health,*
> *The women have childbirth,*
> *So that your* names may not be obliterated.[18]

The importance of names begins with the naming ceremony, which usually occurs on the eighth day of a child's life. Among the Ewes, the child is first taken out of the room at dawn. Water, dipped out with a fresh calabash, is thrown onto the thatch roof and allowed to drip on the child, who is then named by the family elders. A libation is made to the earth, and the child's feet are touched with oil. As G. Parrinder correctly observes, this ceremony explains the African understanding of the vital connection of the name with the very life itself.[19]

Along with the many similarities between the blue bird story and the Tower of Babel story, there is a significant difference between the two stories with respect to the names given to God. The name of God in the biblical text, Yahweh, has the particular association with being the God of Israel or the God of Israel's covenant. In this way, Yahweh is an ethnocentric God—the God of a particular people, Israel. Further, this ethnocentrism carries the implication of the Babel story into the stories of God's choice or election of Abraham and Sarah, which begin in Genesis 12. The God who *denies* the rest of humanity their effort to make a name for themselves now *confers* a name upon Abraham, Israel's ancestor. "I will make of you a great nation, and I will bless you, and make your name great, so that you will be a blessing" (Genesis 12:2). In contrast, Nyame, the God of the African story, is not related to any particular ethnic group by covenant or any other means. Other synonyms in the Akan language only conceive of Nyame in such universal terms as the Dependable One; Alone, the Great One; and the Powerful One. A well-known artistic symbol in Ghana, *Gye Nyame* ("Except God"), embodies many of these qualities of Nyame.

When the late Ghanaian artist, Kofi Antubam, was given the interpretation of the Gye Nyame symbol, it simply said, "This great panorama of creation originated from the unknown past: No one lives who saw its beginning. No one lives who will see its end, Except God."

Notes

1. For Smith's etymology and criticism of the use of the word *fetish,* see G. Parrinder, *West African Religion* (London: Epworth, 1961) 8.

2. E. W. Smith, *The Secret of the African* (London: Student Christian Movement, 1929) 126–27. For other versions of the myth, see G. Parrinder, *African Mythology* (New York: Peter Bedrick, 1986) 38–39. See also K. Gyekye, *An Essay on African Philosophical Thought.* The Akan Conceptual Scheme (rev. ed.; Philadelphia: Temple University, 1987) 196.

3. Ashanti are the dominant tribe of the Akan ethnic groups in West Africa. "God's tree" is widely recognized throughout Ghana for its medicinal powers.

4. R. S. Rattray, *Ashanti* (Kumasi: Basel Mission Book Depot, 1923) 142–43.

5. "Definition of Africa: Vital Union—The African Worldview," in *Homeward Journey: Readings in African Studies.* Edited by H. T. Neve (Trenton, NJ: Africa World Press, 1994) 9.

6. Parrinder (*West African Religion*, 16) suggests that the name *Nyam,* the shortest form of *Nyame,* may originally have been associated with a root, *nyam,* meaning power or supernatural force.

7. E. Smith, *The Golden Stool: Some Aspects of the Conflict of Cultures in Modern Africa* (London: Holborn, 1926) 29.

8. *Words Become Worlds: Semantic Studies of Genesis 1–11* (Leiden: Brill, 1994) 92.

9. Many scholars refer to the author of this story as the Yahwist. The author is not in fact known, but the alleged source of this and many other stories in the Torah is often designated the "Yahwistic source" because of its preference for the Hebrew name, Yahweh, to refer to God. By contrast, another alleged source of stories in Torah is the Elohist source, in which the preferred designation for God tends to be Elohim [editors].

10. H. Bietenhard, *onoma*, in *Theological Dictionary of the New Testament,* 10 vols. (Grand Rapids: Eerdmans, 1979) 5.252.

11. See J. S. Kselman, "Genesis," in *Harper's Bible Commentary.* Edited by J. L. Mays (San Francisco: Harper & Row, 1988) 93.

12. B. E. Idowu (*African Traditional Religion: A Definition* [London: SCM, 1973] 146) argues that the fact of a "hidden God . . . must be accepted as man's predicament, in his approach to the mystery of the sacred and the transcendent." He suggests (152) that God's transcendence emphasizes God's uniqueness and incompatibility, explaining that this uniqueness is "one reason why there are no images—graven or in drawing or in painting—of him in Africa." Accordingly, "The

African concept of God in this regard is an emphatic 'No one' and 'None' to the question 'To whom then will you liken God, or what likeness compare with him?'"

13. See J. S. Mbiti, *Concepts of God in Africa* (London: SPCK, 1970) 2.

14. K. A. Busia, "The African World View," in *African Heritage*. Edited by J. Drachler (New York: Crowell, Collier & Macmillan, 1963) 192–93.

15. *Nuer Religion* (Oxford: Clarendon, 1956) 9.

16. This idea is also expressed in John 1:4: "All that came to be was alive with his life, and that life was the light of men."

17. *Introduction to African Religion* (Portsmouth, NH: Heinemann Educational, 1989/91) 81.

18. Emphasis mine. The dominant idea in this prayer is that the birth of children ensures that the names of the ancestors are not forgotten. This remembrance is one understanding of immortality. For further insight on African prayers, see A. Shorter, *Prayer in the Religious Tradition of Africa* (Oxford: Oxford University, 1975) 52.

19. *African Traditional Religion* (London: Hutchinson's University Library, 1954) 57.

Genesis 11:1–9
An Asian Perspective

Choan-Seng Song

Context

Defeated by Japan in the Sino-Japanese War, China ceded Taiwan to Japan. The year was 1895. When the rumor of cession reached Taiwan, its inhabitants were first incredulous, then shocked. Soon panic spread. The Chinese governor and his cohort were secretly making plans to abandon the island and withdraw to China, which is separated from Taiwan by the waters of the Taiwan Strait 100 miles to the west. With their life and destiny in crisis, the island people rallied to take the matter into their own hands. They must be prepared for the imminent arrival of the Japanese occupation forces. Stories, written in tears and blood in the history of Taiwan, thus unfolded.

On May 29, 1895, the Japanese army, under the command of the newly appointed governor Kabayama, landed near a little fishing village on the northern tip of the island. In the midst of confusion, the simple and uninformed village folk decided to appease the invading army for peace. Five brothers of the leading family volunteered to repair to the Japanese army post and convey the goodwill of the villagers. But what to tell them? And *how* to tell them? At the village meeting hastily summoned, everyone was anxious and worried.

"This is what I am going to tell the Japanese," said the eldest brother. "We are only fishermen and farmers. We have neither soldiers nor guns. We will never resist you. Don't kill us. Just tell us what you need, food or money. We will give it to you. But please don't come and kill us."

"Easier said than done," responded the village elder. "All right, you may go and tell them that. But we speak Taiwanese; they speak Japanese. How are you going to talk with them?" The eldest brother, gentle and amicable, smiled. "I heard that the Japanese know Chinese characters," he informed them. "We bring a brush with us and make our wishes known to them by writing Chinese characters. Why do we have to talk?" "That's right," someone in the crowd shouted, very impressed. "Why did we not think of it sooner?"

Taking with them a brush, an ink stick, an ink slab, a small bottle of wa- ter, and some paper, the brothers set out to meet the Japanese troops. When they arrived, they were quickly surrounded by the armed soldiers. No sooner had the brothers raised the brush, ink stick, ink slab, paper, and the bottle of water above their heads as signs of surrender and walked towards the Japanese soldiers than the gunshots were heard. The next moment, the five brothers all lay dead on the beach . . .[1]

This was an ominous start of Japanese colonial rule in Taiwan that lasted fifty years. How much tragedy that rule was to bring to the people of Taiwan, tragedy to individuals, to families, and to the entire island community!

Text

This story from Taiwan brings us to the story of the Tower of Babel in Genesis 11. But are they not two different stories? One happened about 100 years ago. It can be dated. It is remembered. It is a part of the historical memory of the colonized people of Taiwan. As for the story of the Tower of Babel, it is not a history as one normally understands history to be. It cannot be dated in time. It cannot be located in a particular place. It is remembered, but it is not a *historical* memory. Is there, then, nothing in common between the two stories? Do they have nothing to do with one another? With questions such as these, let us look more closely at the story of the Tower of Babel.

"Come," said our ancient ancestors in the story, "let us build ourselves a city." In a few words, the storyteller tells us how human civilization started, and human beings have not ceased to be engaged in building ever since. Come, let us build ourselves a cave. Come, let us build ourselves a village. Come, let us build ourselves a town. And in modern times, human beings have been building metropolises and megacities. We have been building ourselves communities and habitats. We have also been building dwelling places for gods. From grand palaces to humble hamlets, from massive fortresses to thatched houses, from magnificent cathedrals and temples to simple churches and wayside shrines, human beings have transformed their religious devotion, their artistic imagination, their technological ingenuity, and their sheer energy and perseverance into villages, towns, cities, and places of worship. Human history is a history of building. Human beings are builders, among other things.

But the story of the Tower of Babel is not simply a story of how human beings become builders of cities. Our storyteller seems to have something else in mind. What would that be? It may be that the decision to build themselves a city was not made on the spur of the moment. It was not something out of the blue. Seated on the ground under the open sky, our ancient ancestors might have reached the decision to build a city after many hours of discussion.

What weighed heavily on their minds? What were the problems that concerned them? Why did they decide to build a city? It was, we are told, "to make a name for themselves" and for them "not to be scattered abroad upon the face of the earth" (Genesis 11:4b). United, we stand. Together we can accomplish something. This must be what they meant by "making a name for ourselves." Divided, we fall. Scattered, we become strangers to one another. We lose our kinship. We forget we are friends. We do not understand one another any more. And we easily turn into enemies of one another and resort to violence to overcome those who are different from us. We must build a city in which we can live together and prevent all this from happening.

Many conflicts must have existed in this ancient community of our ancestors. Each time, the conflict among themselves and with others brought destruction of property and loss of lives to the community. There was the tragic story of Cain murdering Abel, his own brother (Genesis 4:1–16). And was not there "a song of Lamech" telling us how our ancient ancestors committed revenge and bloodshed one against another (4:23–24)? "I have killed a man for wounding me," so sang Lamech to his wives, "a young man for striking me. If Cain is avenged sevenfold, truly Lamech seventy-sevenfold."

The conflict could begin with a disagreement over a little thing, acquiring a small plot of land, for example. At first it was not serious. They did not talk the matter over with one another. Perhaps they spoke different languages and could not make themselves understood to one another. It might also be that they meant different things even if they spoke the same language. The misunderstanding turned into a heated dispute, then became a shouting match, each saying something the other did not understand. What ensued was violence and bloodshed.

If we consider the fact that human history is a history of conflicts, what we have just said about the community of ancient builders may not be entirely far-fetched. From the beginning, we human beings have had to protect ourselves from nature, from wild beasts, and, above all, from one another. Our ancient ancestors in the story of the Tower of Babel were no exception. The mere fact that we speak different languages, more than 3,000 today, is truly daunting. How exasperating it must be to find oneself in a foreign country, neither able to speak the language nor able to understand when spoken to. If this is true with us today, it must have also been no less the case for our ancient ancestors.

Reflection

Are we fated to remain strangers to one another? Is there nothing we can do to change the situation? Summoned to a village meeting in the aftermath of the conflict that ended in tragedy, our ancestors in the story must have asked each other such questions. And as the story unfolds, God appears on the scene to give the story a strange theological twist. God now takes charge of the course of events, and things begin to take an unexpected turn.

The building of a city to ensure the unity of a people—a very basic condition of human survival in an inhospitable environment—is now said to be an audacious attempt on the part of human beings to storm heaven and challenge the supremacy of God. "Look," the storyteller has God say, "they are one people, and they have all one language." God is worried. "Nothing that they propose to do will now be impossible for them" (Genesis 11:6). God is scared. This is the human arrogance that stirs up concern and fear in the heavenly court. God wastes no time in doing what needs to be done.

The literary device of the storyteller here is ingenious. In parallel to the human beings who proposed and said: "Come, let us build ourselves a city, and a tower with its top in the heavens" (11:4), the storyteller now has God say: "Come, let us go down, and confuse their language there, so that they will not understand one another's speech" (11:7). This is the divine response, ingeniously crafted by the storyteller, to the human call to build a city and a tower that would reach the heavens.

That divine response was to result in tragic consequences: our ancient city builders found themselves unable to understand one another and became strangers to each other. Does this not remind us of those five Taiwanese brothers who set out to meet the Japanese invaders with brush and ink and met their death? Who is to blame for a tragedy such as this? God—who confused human language and made human beings not able to understand one another? God would also have to be responsible for most of the tragedies resulting from human incapacity to understand one another: it is God who is the very cause of it!

But is not here something that should puzzle us? Is this not theologically absurd and factually senseless? Why does God have to be afraid of human beings living in unity and harmony? Why does God feel threatened by human beings who speak one language and thus can understand one another? So many human tragedies could be avoided, so many misfortunes averted, only if human beings could communicate with one another without much difficulty! Is this not what God wanted? Should not God be overjoyed by it? Should not God be fully behind the human project to create a community of peace and harmony?

Most of the answers given to us have evaded the issues raised by these questions. God's intervention, which resulted in the confusion of language, is justified on the ground that "human beings, left to their own resources by the creator, are in the gravest danger because of their aspiration to burst their created limits, to acknowledge no longer that they stand before God, but to be like God or to reach to the heavens with their works."[2]

The implication here is clear. It takes us back to the garden of Eden, in which the seductive snake delivered those fatal words to the "unsuspecting" Eve: "You will not die; for God knows that when you eat of it [the fruit of the tree that is in the middle of the garden] your eyes will be opened, and you will be like God, knowing good and evil" (Genesis 3:4–5). Is this the sagacious snake making fun of God, making God appear to be afraid of human beings? Or is this that shrewd snake planting the seed of human revolt against God deep in Adam's and Eve's subconscious? In either case, most of us have been taught to believe that there existed from primordial times a conflict of power between God and humanity. What our Tower of Babel storyteller is showing us, then, is a small God, a fearful God, an insecure God, a God who regards human beings as potential rivals, a God created by human beings. Is *this how* we are also to understand our God who, according to the story of creation in the first chapter of Genesis, "created the heavens and the earth" (Genesis 1:1)?

Implied in the story of the Tower of Babel surely is not a conflict of power between God and human beings but *among* human beings—between parents and their children, between rulers and the ruled, between the haves and the have-nots, between men and women, between oppressors and the oppressed. The rich and powerful have been building "towers of babel" throughout human history. Dictators build them to decree what people must think and say. Religious authorities build them to control what believers must believe and how they worship. In this post-Cold War era of ours, it is the economically powerful who build economic towers of babel and perpetuate the unjust economic order of the world and control the destiny of humanity. It is this kind of "tower of babel" that has created untold miseries in human community from ancient times to the present day.

Those towers of babel are built and demolished. They are erected and torn down. People who have suffered oppression under a tower of babel rise up against it. Women and men who have endured hardship and misery under it are mobilized to work against it. And could the God who created the heavens and the earth and made human beings "to till and keep" the earth (Genesis 2:15) be totally unconcerned about people's struggle to do away with these towers of babel? Would that God be interested only in maintaining power over human beings, seeing to it that human beings are not going to be like God? This may be the God of the Christian church and the theology it has taught for centuries, but could it be the God who got involved in the demolition of the Tower of Babel in our story? Surely not.

That Tower of Babel must be the forerunner of those towers of babel erected and demolished in human history. If this is true, then God has to be at the very heart of it all. God is there, inspiring their struggle against those "towers of babel" and striving with men and women who engage themselves in the struggle. "Come, let us go down," says God in the story. God is not a mere onlooker. God stakes God's own self in human affairs. God is personally involved. This is the faith of many people, Christian or not, who engage themselves in the struggle for a society with more justice and freedom. And it is also their belief that God suffers with them and hopes with them, encouraging them when they get discouraged, empowering them when they feel powerless.

Is this perhaps another way of reading the story of the Tower of Babel, a reading inspired by what we know from history and prompted by what the majority of humanity is going through today in the world of "might makes right," the world in which "the weak falls victim to the strong" (*jwo iou chtiang she*), to use a Chinese expression?

The fact of the matter is that the world has always consisted of many languages and different words. This must be how God created it. Therefore, many languages and different words must be redeemed from the destructive power we human beings use against one another. Is it then not our task to strive toward that community in which "one language and the same words" can be heard in the world of "many languages and different words," a community in which the goodwill of the village people contained in the brush, ink stick, ink slab, paper, and a small bottle of water would not be met by the deadly force of the power to conquer, dominate, and dictate?

Notes

1. The story was abridged from T. F. Pai, *Waves and Sand: Stories of Three Families in the History of Taiwan during the Past Hundred Years,* 3 vols. (Los Angeles: Taiwan Publishing House, 1990) 1.33–38. Translation from the Chinese original by C. S. Song.

2. C. Westermann, *Genesis 1—11: A Commentary* (Minneapolis: Augsburg, 1984) 554.

Exodus 20:1–17

Then God spoke all these words: 2 I am the LORD your God, who brought you out of the land of Egypt, out of the house of slavery; 3 you shall have no other gods before me. 4 You shall not make for yourself an idol, whether in the form of anything that is in heaven above, or that is on the earth beneath, or that is in the water under the earth. 5 You shall not bow down to them or worship them; for I the LORD your God am a jealous God, punishing children for the iniquity of parents, to the third and the fourth generation of those who reject me, 6 but showing steadfast love to the thousandth generation of those who love me and keep my commandments. 7 You shall not make wrongful use of the name of the LORD your God, for the LORD will not acquit anyone who misuses his name. 8 Remember the sabbath day, and keep it holy. 9 Six days you shall labor and do all your work. 10 But the seventh day is a sabbath to the LORD your God; you shall not do any work—you, your son or your daughter, your male or female slave, your livestock, or the alien resident in your towns. 11 For in six days the LORD made heaven and earth, the sea, and all that is in them, but rested the seventh day; therefore the LORD blessed the sabbath day and consecrated it. 12 Honor your father and your mother, so that your days may be long in the land that the LORD your God is giving you. 13 You shall not murder. 14 You shall not commit adultery. 15 You shall not steal. 16 You shall not bear false witness against your neighbor. 17 You shall not covet your neighbor's house; you shall not covet your neighbor's wife, or male or female slave, or ox, or donkey, or anything that belongs to your neighbor.

Exodus 20:1–17

A Latin American Perspective

Jorge Pixley

Context

In Nicaragua, we are presently in a period that is, frankly, counterrevolutionary. National elections in 1990 put in place a government committed to returning the country to "normalcy" after more than ten years of national sovereignty and the implementation of military, economic, health, and educational policies geared to satisfy national needs. This previous policy meant prioritizing the basic needs of the majority in internal affairs—free education and health services and nationalized banks with generous terms of credit for small producers—and diversifying the dependence of this small country upon major external agents (the United States, Europe, the former Soviet Union, Arab countries, and the like).

The counterrevolution requires the acceptance of very specific dictates of the international financial agencies that control the organization of national life. The financial police are the International Monetary Fund (IMF), upon whose approval most foreign aid and loans depend in today's monopolar[1] world. The IMF requires policies of open markets and stable currency. In order to sustain the latter, the Nicaraguan government is forced to charge fees for public education and health services, to make loans in the banking system only at high interest rates and according to stringent terms, to strengthen the police force in order to break up labor actions, to pass and implement laws that will lead to a weakening of the labor movement, and to undertake similar antipopular measures. In order to open the Nicaraguan market (the first policy of the IMF), protective tariff measures must be eliminated, generous conditions must be created for foreign investment, and foreign access to natural resources (e.g., fishing, mining, and forestry) must be opened.

These measures are, of course, not unique to Nicaragua; these are the same conditions imposed on most countries in the Third World. In Nicaragua, they are seen for what they are: the imposition of counterrevolutionary policies by the global economic powers (corporations and governments) in order to eliminate workers' and peasants' alternatives to a capitalist society.

Text

These Ten Words[2] are presented in the Sinai narrative of the Book of Exodus (Exodus 19—24) as the "constitution" imposed on the newly constituted people of Israel by Yahweh, the God who freed them from slavery.[3] Exodus 20:2 sets the framework: "I am Yahweh thy God who brought thee out of the land of Egypt from the house of bondage."[4] Each Israelite is to stand before Yahweh as a freed man (women are not specifically included) who owes his freedom to this God. It is this debt that imposes the obligation to accept Yahweh's conditions.

The framing of these Ten Words is polemical in tone. It begins with the fundamental prohibition of recognizing "other" gods: "Thou shalt have no other gods before me" (Exodus 20:3). This is explained in Exodus 34:14 by reference to Yahweh as a "jealous God." As a slave nation that has been freed from Egyptian slavery without due legal process by the violent actions of its god, the new society into which the Israelite enters is threatened by other duly organized societies, their laws, and their gods.

The next two "words" further spell out the exclusive loyalty required by Yahweh. The Israelite is to make no image that might divide loyalties between various shrines and thus allow an unscrupulous king to control a cult at which worship is offered to Yahweh only in pretense. This is, of course, the interpretation given to Solomon's construction of Yahweh's temple in one strand of 1 Kings 5 and 12—the strand that speaks of the harsh yoke which Solomon imposed on Israel in order to build the temple.[5] The prohibition of speaking Yahweh's name in vain legislates above all the strict truth demanded in oaths which use that name; implied in this is that oaths in the name of other divinities need not be strictly truthful.

The next "two words" are more positive and less polemical. They are the transition to the prohibitions that protect other Israelite individuals who have also been freed from "thy" (singular) oppression. The Sabbath rest is modeled on Yahweh's creation rest and so signals one's loyalty to Yahweh; in this respect, it is a continuation of the first three words. Further, by forbidding overexploitation of the foreigner and the cattle on one's land,

GOD FELT THREATENED BY SOMEONE TRYING
TO-BE - GOD-LIKE

the Sabbath command prepares the way for the protective measures that follow. The command to "glorify thy father and thy mother" is tied as well to the gift of the land that Yahweh makes to the freed slave, and thus this command also serves as a transition to the protective laws concerning Israelite neighbors.

Little need be said about the other "words" that protect the Israelites from the aggressions of their fellows. All Israelites are put under the protection of Yahweh, the God who freed them from bondage in Egypt.

Reflection

Contemporary ideologues of market globalization justify their draconian measures by asserting that the market has its laws, which must be respected. In order to effect revival following a crisis, it is argued that the market demands sacrifices "if it is to generate wealth." On its own "economicist" terms, this is no doubt true, and it is attractive to that sector of the population which shares in the wealth generated by the market. For the rest, the vast majority, the market dictates misery, as it expels them from jobs in the name of efficiency, excludes them from schools and clinics because they are not paying clients, refuses them credit to plant their fields because they are not good risks, and creates laws that make it difficult for them to organize in defense of their salaries and jobs. In theological language, then, the market is a god who demands human sacrifice in order to produce wealth.

Like the Canaanite god, Baal, in biblical Israel, this god has his attraction. When the sacrificial measures are adopted, they do generate wealth — a wealth that is conspicuously displayed in advertising. Further, the presence of wealth set before the eyes of those who are incapable of satisfying their food and health needs makes people dream of sharing in that wealth.

It is equally clear, however, that the market is a false god because it is incapable of satisfying the life needs of the popular majority. The constitutional law of the Israelite tribes serves to unmask all false gods, that is, all gods who are incapable or unwilling to deliver slaves from bondage. The specific problem of kings who (like Solomon) impose forced labor on their populations and justify these measures by the requirements of their gods is, of course, not our specific problem. But the transfer of the polemical character of the Ten Words of Exodus 20 to our Southern context is not difficult. Like the elders of Israel who came before Samuel (1 Samuel 8:1–15) and insisted upon having a king, rather than Yahweh, in order to become like the nations surrounding them,[6] so are there many in the South, especially among the elite, who want "a market like all the nations of the earth" in this moment of transition after the collapse of the Soviet Union, when market ideologues feel emboldened to venture everywhere.

The Ten Words, in contrast to these false gods, remind us of the polemical requirements if we are to protect human life. Defending the life of the planet and the lives of the earth's millions of persons condemned to subhuman existence requires vigilance if the claims of false gods are to be detected. In Nicaragua and Latin America, the most dangerous false god in our time is the so-called free market. The struggles over labor conditions, represented in the Ten Words by the Sabbath command, are being aggravated by the devotees of the market. In Nicaragua, the government signed, in April 1994, a promise with the IMF to veto a new labor code under discussion if it did not create conditions for foreign investment. Specifically, this entailed severely controlling strikes by forbidding them in the public sector, limiting maternity leaves, facilitating dismissals by reducing required compensation, and expanding the length of the work week. Such an agreement amounted to a rollback of the labor rights that had been guaranteed in former labor codes. Such an agreement means sacrificing the workers in their health and living conditions to the demands of the false god, the market.

At this moment, fidelity to a God who defends life, and specifically the lives of the defenseless, the biblical "widow, orphan and sojourner," is unpopular. Such fidelity demands giving priority to a large sector of the world's population, which is seen by the promoters of so-called development as superfluous. Because of these conditions, the presence in the Bible of fundamental requirements to examine the gods who demand sacrifice in order to see if they are false, and to adhere only to "Yahweh, thy god who brought thee out of Egypt, out of the house of bondage," is a powerful incentive to renew our commitment to the defense of life and the conditions that sustain life.

Notes

1. That is, reflecting the post-Cold War dominance of the United States [editors].

2. Scholars tend to refer to Exodus 20:1–17 as the "Ten Words" or "the Decalogue" rather than as the "Ten Commandments" because the introduction to them in Exodus 20:1 refers not to commandments but to words: "Then God spoke all these words . . ." [editors]. Exodus 34:28 reads similarly, "He [Moses] was there with the Lord forty days and forty nights; he neither ate bread nor drank water. And he wrote on the tablets the words of the covenant, the ten commandments."

3. This narrative is viewed by some scholars as the compilation of two literary sources, designated the Jahwist source (J) and the Elohist source (E) [editors].

4. The archaic language is necessary in English to distinguish between second person singular and second person plural.

5. For example, 1 Kings 5:13 reads, "King Solomon conscripted forced labor out of all Israel; the levy numbered thirty thousand men."

6. For example, in 1 Samuel 8:4, the elders of Israel ask Samuel to "appoint for us, then, a king to govern us, like other nations" [editors].

Exodus 20:1–17
An African Perspective[1]

François Kabasele Lumbala

Context

Moral law and covenant play an important part in the life of the Bantu people of Africa. When a misfortune strikes someone, the first curses to come out of one's mouth are the following: "I have not stolen from anyone, I have seduced neither another's wife nor his daughter, I have not meddled in witchcraft . . . why then this misery?" Honest moral conduct is thus considered to be the source of happiness and the condition of a happy and peaceful life. When one lives in moral rectitude, one lives in harmony with the Creator and the order of the universe. The physical therapist nurse of a large hospital in the city of Mbuji-Mayi, for example, lectures newly arriving patients in these terms:

> You come here to be healed; your foot, your arm, your back . . . no longer obey you; we will do everything to ease your pain, with the Whites' techniques and with medicines; but realize that if you are not in harmony with the universe, with your family, with the Creator . . . all techniques and medicines will be of no use to you; for how will your arm obey you if you yourself do not obey your Creator; how can your foot be in harmony with you if you have severed this harmony with those who make up your very life blood? Above everything, always seek to re-establish harmony with God.

Any fetish, any traditional therapy always contains some moral prescriptions, or at least a particular practice. A Luba proverb says, "Follow the healer's prescriptions, so that you need not reproach him for his medicine's ineffectiveness."

HARMONIZE WITH ABOUT ALL – GOD. THEN YOUR BODY WILL "OBEY" YOU

Similarly, any introduction or access to a new social rank involves certain prohibitions. Those, in fact, who play a significant part in the life-growth of a society are the ones most bound by prohibitions, such as chiefs, healers, and women. Seeing, for example, the numerous nutritional or social prohibitions to which the female in Africa is submitted, one might too quickly presume that women are simply dominated by men. In reality, these prohibitions suggest primarily that the woman is considered to play a very important role in the birth and growth of life in society. For example, when a boy steals, his bad behavior will be reproached, but when a girl steals, she will be made to understand that her theft is a catastrophe for all society because woman represents the supernatural order, the order of life; she is the sacred being, *par excellence.*

Covenant is also a fundamental fact of our societies. Whether between members of a family or between neighboring peoples, the predominant mode of survival was covenant. For this reason, reconciliation rites were well developed and carefully prepared. Thus, for our African societies, love is the only sure way of self-defense against the invasion of the wicked and sorcerers. Wherever people are united and love one another, a sorcerer will have a hard time gaining admittance. The family is the first and ideal place of a covenant. A marriage is not understood principally as a contract between two people but as a covenant between two families. When a man comes to ask for a woman's hand in marriage, he addresses the woman's family, saying, "I would like to be born near you, I want to be your ally." In the church, to express the practice of Christ's salvation, the African Synod has chosen the term *Church-family,*[2] that is, a place of covenant between people based in relation to the covenant with God. Any serious and definite engagement in the church is expressed in our Bantu languages as a covenant *with God.*[3]

Text

The Decalogue is a very important text for the Jewish religion: it is considered to have come directly from God and was recited regularly and even daily during certain historical periods in the history of Judaism. In that text, God emerges as the guarantor and source of the law; God is guarantor of this law to the "thousandth generation of those who love me [God] and keep my commandments" (Exodus 20:6).

The objective of the Decalogue, moreover, is to maintain the freedom and life acquired and received from God. Thus, one basis offered for the sabbath is the need for freedom from work among all of God's created beings, from livestock to owner alike: "But the seventh day is a sabbath to the LORD your God; you shall not do any work—you, your son or your daughter, your male or female slave, your livestock, or the alien resident in your towns" (Exodus 20:10). Similarly, the motivation for obedience to the command to obey one's parents involves the extension of life: "Honor your father and your mother, so that your days may be long in the land that the LORD your God is giving you" (Exodus 20:12).

In addition to presenting God as guarantor and maintaining freedom and life, the essence of the Decalogue is the expression of the people's commitment in response to the benefits received from God. For this reason, faith and action are united in this text. That is to say, ethics are born from the gift of God; "the principal reason for which Israel must observe the commandments, is that Yahweh liberated her from Egypt."[4] The Decalogue begins, therefore, not with a prescription, but with God's action on Israel's behalf: "Then God spoke all these words: 2 I am the LORD your God, who brought you out of the land of Egypt, out of the house of slavery . . ." (Exodus 20:1–2). God's gift binds the beneficiary. That is the meaning of the relation of the Decalogue to the covenant.

The covenant is a fundamental notion in the Old Testament because it explains and orients the history of the Jewish people.[5] The unique force of the Decalogue, in relation to the covenant, is that God has already taken the initiative with Israel, so that the laws of the Decalogue are given by God, *not as the condition of God's love* toward the people of Israel, but as the people's response to God's love. In other words, God *already* loves Israel, has had compassion upon Israel, has heard Israel's groaning in slavery,[6] has led Israel to Mount Sinai; the Decalogue provides the people of Israel with a practicable mode of response to this love. The Decalogue is, then, the opposite of bilateral contracts which provide the conditions for covenants between people,[7] from start to finish.

Reflection

In small communities without priests, where the laity who are in charge of these assemblies preach, the weekly prayer ideally echoes this text. As in the Decalogue, certain key ideas, such as recourse to creation, to healing, to the vital communion expressed in a covenant pact, give strength to the law. God created us; God knows the secret of our makeup. Thus God is best situated to tell us how our "human machine" functions normally. The vital communion is true guarantor of the social ethic.

The following excerpts, which comment upon Exodus 20, come from observations made by community heads:

God = Tell us Human ma How we function normally

You know the healers. Each one of us has seen a doctor or a healer, either for oneself, or for a child, or one of his own people. We talk to the healer, and we very meticulously indicate where we hurt, which circumstances saw the pain which we feel come into view . . . And, after examinations, after investigations, the healer indicates to us a therapy. This can be for us a manner to behave with regard to nutrition. For example, for the stomach, for hypertension, manioc leaves, pepper, too much salt, etc . . . will be forbidden. Or else, we will be given pills or tablets to swallow over a certain number of days, such as for malaria (five days of quinine), ampicillins for urinary infections or tonsil inflammations . . . The same behavior is adopted by our traditional healers, when they give us plants or other ingredients to drink. Which one among us, if he wants to get well, can contest what the healer or doctor says? God, however, as creator and as author of our salvation, that is to say, our healer *par excellence,* gives us in his law the necessary therapy for our happiness. To go against this is to condemn oneself to death.

Another community head resorted instead to the meaning of creation:

Have you ever been to an electro-mechanic with a broken electrical plate which we use to cook foods? He opens it; he removes the wires; he cleans; he adds bits of metal or replaces resistors. Even more complex, it is a television which no longer gives images or sound . . . We are impressed by the quantity of wires rolled up against one another in there. The electro-mechanic manipulates them with ease because he knows the secrets of their manufacturing, the laws which govern the functioning of all these appliances. And so it is with God: more so than the electro-mechanic, he created us; he knows more than anyone how we function and what is needed for a harmonious and happy life. In this manner, he gave us his laws. If we do not choose them, we cannot be in harmony with ourselves or with nature as a whole which follows God's laws. If the present world is infested with wars and conflicts, it is because the people who govern and live in it do not follow God's laws.

In another context, but still on the subject of covenant, I lived through an interesting case of Bantu ethics, where the coercive capacity of a law was based on the covenant of life between members, on a sort of solidarity in life—what can be called a vital communion. In a conglomeration of villages surrounding a parish, nuns ran a secondary school and a boarding school for students. One night, during a school break, an unprecedented event took place: beds and mattresses and medical apparatus disappeared.

LAW OF NO COVENANT

In a country where the State is completely disorganized and where judicial services are practically nonexistent, there was no chance to find the culprits through the path of modern justice. The nuns appealed to the villages' chiefs, who in turn got together and decided on a covenant ritual.

With money pooled from all the nearby villages, they bought a sheep and a dog. On the appointed day, they summoned all the surrounding dignitaries and representatives. Dressed with their power insignias, they assembled themselves in the central market where the people of the area usually exchange their goods. They dug a hole like a tomb. The eldest of the chiefs then said:

> O God, master of the universe and source of life, we call upon you as witness. O you our ancestors, here we are, we, your descendants, in this meeting place which reinforces the life you have transmitted to us. The school which was founded on the soil of this region is for the growth of the life of your descendants; anyone who ate or drank in this region and who has betrayed the life of the region by striking out against the school of the Sisters is a false ally. The life covenant must pursue them. These same warnings apply to anyone who may have seen or may know the thieves and yet remain silent. We immolate this sheep and this dog by burying them alive; this is the blood we pour and the life we give as guarantors of this covenant and of the re-establishment of the severed balance in the region.

After having tied the two animals, they placed them in the hole. Then they dowsed them with white kaolin and filled the hole with earth. The people dispersed. Two days later, all the stolen goods were brought back in front of the nuns' courtyard. The coercive power of the covenant had brought back the social order.

Law based on covenant is the most powerful law among the Bantus because it receives its power, not from some judicial organization formed by people, but from life, from the vital communion between members of a society. And in the final analysis, the power of life is that which always triumphs. Thus God gave God's fundamental laws by finalizing a covenant, as did Jesus Christ, who gave his commandment by pouring out his blood to seal a new covenant.[8]

Notes

1. Translation by Laura Balladur.
2. M. Cheza (under the direction of), *Synode africain (Textes et interventions),* (Karthala, Paris, 1996.)

3. F. Kabasele Lumbala, *Covenants avec le Christ en Afrique* (2nd ed.; Karthala, Paris, 1994).

4. See F. Garcia Lopez's essay, "Décalogue," *Cahiers Evangiles,* 9n. 81.

5. Covenants were made according to the contractual schemata of the ancient Near Eastern peoples of that era, in this case perhaps, Hittite diplomatic treaties, by which victorious rulers bound vanquished peoples to them with: an account of what that ruler had done on behalf of those peoples; various prescriptions or laws to be obeyed; and curses awaiting those who violated the covenant or promises held out to those who adhered to the covenant. For examples, see J. B. Pritchard, editor, *Ancient Near Eastern Texts Relating to the Old Testament* (3rd ed. with a supplement; Princeton: Princeton University, 1969) 199–206; 529–41.

6. For example, Exodus 2:23–25 reads, "After a long time the king of Egypt died. The Israelites groaned under their slavery, and cried out. Out of the slavery their cry for help rose up to God. 24 God heard their groaning, and God remembered his covenant with Abraham, Isaac, and Jacob. 25 God looked upon the Israelites, and God took notice of them."

7. See P. Buis, *La notion d'covenant dans l'Ancien Testament* (Paris, 1976).

8. See, for example, Mark 14:22–25, which reads, "While they were eating, he took a loaf of bread, and after blessing it he broke it, gave it to them, and said, 'Take; this is my body.' 23 Then he took a cup, and after giving thanks he gave it to them, and all of them drank from it. 24 He said to them, 'This is my blood of the covenant, which is poured out for many. 25 Truly I tell you, I will never again drink of the fruit of the vine until that day when I drink it new in the kingdom of God.'"

Exodus 20:1–17
An Asian Perspective

George M. Soares-Prabhu

CASTE-SYSTEM

Context

About sixteen *16%* percent of India's 900 million people (nearly 145 million of them)[1] are (ex)untouchables, living on the margins of India's caste-structured society.[2] Because the Indian Constitution has outlawed untouchability and made its practice in any form a criminal offense,[3] these ex-untouchables are now described in official documents as members of the "scheduled castes." They belong, that is, to the castes mentioned in the official list or "schedule," which specifies the disadvantaged groups that are entitled to remedial privileges, like the reservation of jobs or of seats in the university. Mahatma Gandhi, in his unrealistic and unsuccessful attempt to rid Hinduism of untouchability without giving up caste, called them *harijans* or children of Hari (God). This is now seen as a condescending and perhaps even an unwittingly insulting designation (for in some parts of India, *harijan* is apparently a euphemism for an illegitimate child), which the ex-untouchables themselves rightly resent. A growing number of them, having reached political awareness, have begun to call themselves *dalits*, that is, people who are broken, crushed, oppressed. This is the acceptable name for the ex-untouchables in India today.

The name is eminently suitable. No segment of India's people, possibly no people anywhere in the world, are as shockingly oppressed as they are. Dalits occupy the very lowest strata in the caste system, which is an intricate, all pervasive and unbelievably tenacious structure of institutionalized inequality, unparalleled in the world for the damage it does to people.[4] Except for a tiny urban elite that is now emerging, partly as a result of remedial action by the state, the dalits are landless laborers, earning a precarious

livelihood in conditions marginally better than serfdom; or they are condemned to engage in religiously polluting and socially demeaning occu-
pations, like scavenging, handling the carcasses of dead animals, or
working in leather. They are the poorest of the poor.[5]

Their real problem, however, is not so much their extreme poverty as
the degrading social disabilities imposed on them by the so-called upper
castes. These treat them as ritually polluted, intrinsically inferior people
"with no rights [but] only the duty to submit to any order and any kind of
treatment by the members of the Hindu castes."[6] Despite the safeguards
against such treatment guaranteed them by the Indian Constitution, the dalits, in the rural villages where most of them live, continue to be "segregated." They remain confined to squalid and unhealthy sections of the
village and are denied access to public wells, schools, tea shops, temples,
and shrines. Attempts to assert their rights can provoke a violent backlash
from the upper castes, so that "atrocities" against the dalits are a regular
feature of rural India today.[7]

Such disabilities can remain even after their conversion to Christianity.
Dalit Christians, who make up about half of all the Christians in the country, continue in many parts of India to be treated by their fellow upper-caste
Christians as outcasts. They are forced to live in segregated colonies, even
in Christian villages. They are seated in separate, less conspicuous parts of
the church, are given no role in church services, and have no place in the
decision-making bodies of the community. They are treated with open contempt by their upper-caste fellow Christians, and often by their priests,
most of whom come from these "upper" castes. And, since caste proves
stronger than death, they may even be buried in separate cemeteries.[8] This
hurting discrimination, whose psychological damage is severe, has been
long tolerated by complacent church authorities who belong inevitably to
the upper castes. It is only recently that the emergence of a militant dalit
Christian movement claiming their rights has (hopefully) begun to make
the Christian churches conscious of their sin. Part of this movement is the
attempt to fashion a dalit theology that will read the Bible from a dalit point
of view. I attempt to do this here for the Decalogue in Exodus 20:1–17.

Text

The Decalogue of Exodus 20:1–17 is impressive. It surpasses all other
similar collections in the Bible (Exodus 34:14–26; Leviticus 18:6–18;
Deuteronomy 27:15–26) in its scope, its concision, and its authority. Its ten
commandments cover all the basic areas of human life—relationship to

God (Exodus 20:1–11), to human community (20:12–16), and to material possessions (20:17). In each of these areas, it touches on issues that are judged to be of singular importance. For though the Decalogue itself carries no sanctions, similar commands elsewhere in the Bible carry the penalty of death (Exodus 21:15–17; 31:15; Leviticus 20:10).

The Decalogue speaks on these issues with the utmost authority. This authority is grounded in its supposed origin. An introductory formula (Exodus 20:1), unique in the Bible, identifies its commandments as words spoken directly by God, "Then God spoke all these words" (20:1). The divine authority this implies finds an appropriate expression in the unusual form the Decalogue has assumed. Unlike other biblical collections of laws, where categorical commands ("you shall/shall not") alternate with case law ("if/when anyone does this . . . then"), the Decalogue is "consistently apodictical,"[9] that is, categorical. There may be parallels to its individual commandments elsewhere in the Hebrew Bible, but there is no formal parallel in the Bible (or in extrabiblical literature) to the collection as a whole.

The result of this universal authoritative formulation is that, unlike other series of biblical laws (e.g., the Covenant Code, in Exodus 20:22–23:19; the Holiness Code in Leviticus 17–26; or the Code of Deuteronomy in Deuteronomy 12–26), the Decalogue is not tied to any specific historical period or social situation in Israel's history.[10] It is wholly universal in its scope, valid always, everywhere, and for all.

Reflection

It is this universality that impresses the dalit who reads the Decalogue in Exodus 20, for the system that condemns her or him to dalithood is a system of innate inequality in which humankind is thought of as essentially hierarchical.[11] In such a system there can, of course, be no universal law valid for all, but only caste-regulations spelling out the duties incumbent on each caste. So the laws of Manu, the most significant codification of Hindu law, begin with the great sages requesting the lawgiver to tell them "the duties of all (four) castes, and also of the people who are born in between [that is, who are of mixed caste descent]" (1.1).[12] This, in fact, is what all Hindu law does. It spells out the *kula-jati dharma,* that is, the specific caste and family duties of a person. The Decalogue is quite unlike this.

What the dalit finds significant about the Decalogue, then, is not so much the content of its individual commandments as the thrust of its collective form. Taken individually, most of the commandments will seem banal. Two at least (the prohibition of images and the precept of Sabbath rest) will have little relevance outside Israel. But the significance of the commandments lies not so much in *what* they prescribe as in *how* they prescribe. Implied in their universal, categorical, and abstract formulation is the intiuition that everyone (priest, king, commoner, or slave) stands equally under the same basic God-given law.

There is no trace in the Decalogue, nor, strikingly, in the great codes of the Bible (Exodus 20:22–23:19; Leviticus 17—26; Deuteronomy 12—26), that applies the abstract norms enunciated in it to concrete situations, such as the kind of class differentiation that one finds in other Near Eastern codes, in Roman law, or, conspicuously, in the laws of Manu, where the penalty for the transgression of a law usually varies in inverse proportion to the social status of the transgressor. "A ruler who shouts abuse at a priest should be fined a hundred pennies," says Manu, "a commoner, a hundred and fifty or two hundred pennies; a servant should be given capital punishment. (8.267)." People, for Manu, are not equal before the law. In the Decalogue, they are. Only those who have lived in a caste system can appreciate the liberative significance of this.

All law serves both to legitimate the exercise of power in a social system and to erect defenses against its misuse. Law both empowers the strong and protects the weak. But where Manu tends to stress the first of these functions, the Decalogue favors the second. The Laws of Manu sustain a hierarchical order operating in favor of a privileged caste. Their bias in favor of the Brahman is plain.[13] The Decalogue shows no such bias towards any privileged group. Indeed, the great codes of the Bible (which in our present canonical text are to be read as applications of the Decalogue) actively favor the disadvantaged (Exodus 22:21–26; Leviticus 19:9–10; Deuteronomy 15:1–18) and seek to limit the power and wealth of the king (Deuteronomy 17:14–17). In contrast to the massive and sophisticated compendium of Hindu law, which sustains hierarchy, biblical legislation, inspired by a very different understanding of the human person, pursues the vision of an egalitarian society.

The ultimate basis of this vision is the creation story of Genesis, which, in the Bible as it now stands, offers a further horizon for the reading of the Decalogue. Humankind—all humankind—has been created in the image of God (Genesis 1:26–27). In whatever way this pregnant expression is to be understood, it certainly implies the sacredness of every human being. Everyone (man or woman, Jew or Gentile, clean caste or dalit) has therefore the right to the security of one's life and possessions, to the integrity of one's family, and to the safeguard of one's name.

This is what the Decalogue defends. For even though in its present set-

ting the Decalogue is presented as the core of *Israel's* law, given when the
covenant is sealed at Sinai (Exodus 34:28; Deuteronomy 4:13; 10:4), and
although it is understood as Israel's law in some other codes of the Bible
which ignore or sometimes explicitly exclude the Gentiles (Leviticus
25:39–46; Deuteronomy 15:1–3), the thrust of the text, when it is read in
the context of the biblical story, breaks through such ethnic boundaries.
The biblical story, which begins with the creation of the "heavens and the
earth" (Genesis 1:1) and ends with the breaking in of the "new heavens and
the new earth" (Revelation 21:1–4), is not just about Israel but about humankind. Israel is only a paradigmatic moment in this history. It has been
summoned (as the church is summoned) to be a contrast community that
will exemplify what the human community is meant to be. With its implicit
proclamation of the equality of all human beings, the Decalogue is one way
of drawing the broad outlines of this liberative community toward which
all dalits everywhere aspire.

Notes

1. The figures are based on the 1991 census of India, which gives the population of India as 846 million, of whom 15.8 percent belong to the scheduled castes;
and which projects a population growth of about 27 million a year. See *India 1993:
A Reference Annual* (New Delhi: Publications Division, Government of India,
1994) 7–19.

2. Indian society is made up of thousands of hierarchically arranged, heredi-
tary, endogamous groups, called *jatis* or castes, each of which is (1) associated
with some traditional occupation, though this may not be strictly followed today;
(2) part of a hierarchical system of social organization in which castes are ranked
according to the occupational and ritual status of the groups, determined by criteria which are by no means clear now; and (3) isolated from other groups, avoid-
ing contact, table fellowship, and above all intercaste marriages with them.
Theoretically the dalits fall outside the caste system. They are ritually polluted
"outcastes." In fact, they are a set of castes tagged on to the bottom of the caste hierarchy and regarded as ritually polluted and therefore "untouchable." A. Beteille,
"The Harijans of India," in *Castes: Old and New. Essays in Social Structure and
Social Stratification* (Bombay: Asia Publishing House, 1969) 90.

3. See the *Constitution of India,* article 17. Its provisions were given legal force
in the *Untouchability (Offences) Act* of 1955, amended into the *Protection of Civil
Rights Act* of 1976.

4. Some indication of what caste does to the lives of people can be construed
from the carefully documented, immensely moving life history of a 40-year-old
untouchable, Muli, reported in James M. Freeman, *Untouchable, An Indian Life
History* (New Delhi: Harper Collins, 1993).

5. See B. Das, "Untouchability, Scheduled Castes and Nation Building," in J. Kananaikal (ed.), *Scheduled Castes and their Struggle Against Inequality* (Delhi: Indian Social Institute, 1983) 11–39 [32–33]; J. P. Mencher, "The Caste-System Upside Down," in *Social Stratification* [Oxford in India Readings in Sociology and Social Anthropology]. Edited by D. Gupta (Delhi: Oxford University Press, 1992) 93–109.

6. S. Fuches, *At the Bottom of Indian Society: The Harijans and Other Low Castes* (Delhi: Manoharlal, 1981) 4.

7. J. Kananaikal, "The Scheduled Castes and their Status in India," in *Inequality, its Bases and Search for Solutions* [Dr. Alfred De Souza Memorial Essays]. Edited by W. Fernandes (New Delhi: Indian Social Institute, 1986) [89–92; 93–96]; Freeman (n. 4 above) 93.

8. See J. Kananaikal, *Christians of Scheduled Caste Origin* (Delhi: Indian Social Institute, 1983); A. Raj, "The Dalit Christian Reality in Tamil Nadul," *Jeevadhara* 22 (1992) 96–111.

9. B. S. Childs. *Exodus* (Old Testament Library; London: SCM, 1974) 395.

10. Childs, *Exodus,* 396.

11. See L. Dumont, *Homo Hierarchicus: The Caste System and its Implications* (Delhi: Oxford University, 1988) 2–4.

12. See *The Laws of Manu.* Translated by W. Doniger and B. K. Smith (New Delhi: Penguin, 1991) 3. I quote from this excellent translation, with occasional changes when greater literal fidelity to the original is needed.

13. But note that in 8.337, Manu surprisingly has: "For theft, the fine of the servant should be eight times (the value of the stolen object), of a commoner it is sixteen, and of a ruler thirty two; but of a priest it is sixty-four or a full hundred or even twice sixty four times, for he knows about virtues and vices." There is thus a counter tradition of *noblesse oblige* which emerges from time to time in the casuistic interpretation of this complex and sophisticated code. But this is rare. On the whole, the laws are shamelessly biased in favor of the Brahman.

Psalm 23:1–6

The LORD is my shepherd, I shall not want. 2 He makes me lie down in green pastures; he leads me beside still waters; 3 he restores my soul. He leads me in right paths for his name's sake. 4 Even though I walk through the darkest valley, I fear no evil; for you are with me; your rod and your staff—they comfort me. 5 You prepare a table before me in the presence of my enemies; you anoint my head with oil; my cup overflows. 6 Surely goodness and mercy shall follow me all the days of my life, and I shall dwell in the house of the LORD my whole life long.

Psalm 23:1–6
A Latin American Perspective[1]

J. Severino Croatto

Context

In the Latin American context, experiences of disorder such as the following are commonplace:

"Bad shepherds" abound, those who seek posts for their own gain rather than directing, orienting, or defending those whom they represent;

Disorientation about ideals, life projects, and the search for valid models to build a future;

Subsistence living in a world absorbed by capital and resulting inhuman conditions;

Emphasis upon personal self-realization goals that has prompted human beings to become simultaneously more selfish and more "lonely," less hospitable and more individualistic;

The absence of security, shelter, and protection in a world marked by violence.

How, in this situation which is reenacted on a daily basis, do we read and reappropriate the reservoir of meaning in this psalm, which begins by designating Yahweh, God, as "my shepherd," in relation to whom the psalmist affirms, "I shall not want"?

Text

This is the so-called "Psalm of the Good Shepherd," a designation that resonates with the well-known parable in John's Gospel in which Jesus proclaims, "I am the good shepherd"[2] (John 10:1–18). The difference is that in the Johannine parable, Jesus proclaims himself as the shepherd, while in Psalm 23, the speaker expresses *his own experience* of Yahweh as protector and giver of life. It is from such *personal* experiences that the image of shepherd originates.

The representation of Yahweh as a shepherd has a special resonance with a peasant cultural context. In Psalm 23:2, the psalmist describes in a few words the activity of a normal shepherd, who worries about the grass and the water available to his flock. It is basic sustenance; yet symbolically, the shepherd is the giver of it *all*. Another activity of the shepherd, which this psalm highlights, is his ability to *guide* the flock (23:3b)—"He leads me in right paths"—which at the same time evokes the motif of protection—"Even though I walk through the darkest valley, I fear no evil; for you are with me; your rod and your staff—they comfort me" (23:4).

These three qualities of Yahweh in Psalm 23:1–4—*sustenance, guidance,* and *protection*—provide the foundation for the psalmist's claim, "I shall not want." It is, further, the personal *experience* of the speaker, who talks in the first person and who, after describing God (vv.1–4a), suddenly, though not surprisingly in light of the affirmations of verses 1–4, addresses God directly in the second person in verses 4b-5: ". . . for *you* are with me; your rod and your staff—they comfort me. 5 *You* prepare a table before me in the presence of my enemies; *you* anoint my head with oil; my cup overflows."

Despite the prominence of the shepherd motif, the pastoral scene is only a background. When the psalmist affirms that Yahweh leads them "in paths of righteousness" (Psalm 23:3b), the image of the shepherd is in the background. At the primary level, it is Israel's saving history (e.g., the exodus) that is called to mind. For this reason, "paths of liberation" would be a better translation.

The formula, "I am with you," lying behind verse 4 is extremely common in the Bible; it appears more than 300 times and points to *Deus praesens* [God as present] in history. Startling, however, is that "I am with you" is not said here by Yahweh but by the psalmist, as an expression of supreme confidence in Yahweh: "you are with me." A still further significant nuance must not be circumvented: instead of "you are with me" (Hebrew, *'attâ 'immî*), the Hebrew text reads "you are next to me" (*'attâ 'immadî*), thus indicating not only the presence of Yahweh but also the *companionship* and protection of Yahweh[3]. The "name" mentioned in this verse refers to the tradition of the *magnalia Dei,* the mighty acts of God, that were associated with the name of Yahweh, such as the liberation from slavery in Egypt (Exodus 3:13–14[4]).

At the fifth verse, the scene changes. Now Yahweh is a host. From the sustenance of the sheep in the field (23:2), the psalm moves smoothly to a meal at a house: "You prepare a table before me in the presence of my enemies; you anoint my head with oil; my cup overflows" (23:5). The image of the overflowing cup reveals that the *hospitality* of Yahweh is exuberant. The gesture of anointing the guest's head suggests that this hospitality is also tender.

The sixth verse serves as a synthesis of the psalm as a whole. The occasion of the reception offered by Yahweh (23:5) produces great happiness and well being. The experience of liberation in two different contexts — in 23:3b (the scene of the flock) and 23:5a (the scene of the table) — evokes in the psalmist's prayer the presence of *hesed* ("grace" and "mercy"). This is a term with great theological density; it refers us to the concrete experience of Yahweh as saving actor throughout the history of Israel. In a form of fine irony, moreover, the Hebrew word *radaph,* which can be translated either as "follow" or "persecute," occurs in the expression "goodness and mercy shall *persecute* me." The irony occurs because this word recalls the frustrated enemies of verse 5: the psalmist is protected from those enemies, who wish to persecute him, and is persecuted instead by Yahweh, the shepherd who sustains, guides, protects, and acts as exuberant host. This shift in "persecutor" grants security and lasting peace to the psalmist. The final phrase, "all the days of my life," announces that this liberation is neither ephemeral nor incomplete. God's liberation, as it is evoked by the rich imagery of this psalm, is complete; dangers lurk no longer.[5]

Reflection

This analysis of Psalm 23 provides evidence that the psalmist speaks of his God (in the third person), or addresses God (in the second person), in periods of danger and persecution, and that he, moreover, finds in this Shepherd-God a generous host who offers security, liberation, happiness, and rest during such difficult periods. This psalm is, therefore, a "universal" psalm, for it fits any person who lives in a world like ours, which is full of dangers and needs.

But there are particular contemporary contexts in which the themes and motifs of the psalm become more relevant and generate a very deep identification with the speaker of the biblical text. For us in Latin America, this psalm affects us, not only in an individual way, but also in a collective, communal manner. We would like the speaker to be a "we" and not an "I" because we feel the needs, dangers, and persecutions to which the psalmist refs primarily in a communal manner, rather than in an individualistic manner. In our context, the social dimension lies always above the individual. In our context, therefore, the psalm stirs up feelings of solidarity with other people. Expressions from the psalm, such as "paths of liberation," "in the presence of my enemies," and "valley of the shadow of death," immediately bring up concrete referents to our collective experience.

However, we as hearers of this psalm must also heed a warning. Projecting onto Yahweh the security and satisfaction of needs does not eliminate the pressing need for human mediation and means. For instance, when Yahweh proclaims himself "shepherd" because the human shepherds have become corrupt (Ezekiel 34⁶), Yahweh is not replacing and denying those shepherds; rather Yahweh is criticizing and judging them *so that they will change in conformity with Yahweh's liberating, exuberantly hospitable shepherding*. Yahweh as shepherd thus becomes today, as in this psalm, a prototype of those who guide the community. Yahweh exemplifies how shepherds—leaders—in our world must provide security, sustenance, protection, and joy to those under their guidance.

Notes

1. Translation by Edgardo Colón-Emeric.
2. "'Very truly, I tell you, anyone who does not enter the sheepfold by the gate but climbs in by another way is a thief and a bandit. 2 The one who enters by the gate is the shepherd of the sheep. 3 The gatekeeper opens the gate for him, and the sheep hear his voice. He calls his own sheep by name and leads them out. 4 When he has brought out all his own, he goes ahead of them, and the sheep follow him because they know his voice. 5 They will not follow a stranger, but they will run from him because they do not know the voice of strangers.' 6 Jesus used this figure of speech with them, but they did not understand what he was saying to them. 7 So again Jesus said to them, 'Very truly, I tell you, I am the gate for the sheep. 8 All who came before me are thieves and bandits; but the sheep did not listen to them. 9 I am the gate. Whoever enters by me will be saved, and will come in and go out and find pasture. 10 The thief comes only to steal and kill and destroy. I came that they may have life, and have it abundantly. 11 I am the good shepherd. The good shepherd lays down his life for the sheep. 12 The hired hand, who is not the shepherd and does not own the sheep, sees the wolf coming and leaves the sheep and runs away—and the wolf snatches them and scatters them. 13 The hired hand runs away because a hired hand does not care for the sheep. 14 I am the good shepherd. I know my own and my own know me, 15 just as the Father knows me and I know the Father. And I lay down my life for the sheep. 16 I have other sheep that do not belong to this fold. I must bring them also, and they will listen to my voice. So there will be one flock, one shepherd. 17 For this reason the Father loves

me, because I lay down my life in order to take it up again. 18 No one takes it from me, but I lay it down of my own accord. I have power to lay it down, and I have power to take it up again. I have received this command from my Father.'"

3. This key verse, which is the center of the psalm's literary structure, must not be corrected. In other words, there is no need to suppress the "thou" at the beginning which is emphatic, or to modify the "they comfort me" into "they lead me" (*yanhunî* instead of *yenahamunî*).

4. Exodus 3:13 reads, "But Moses said to God, 'If I come to the Israelites and say to them, "The God of your ancestors has sent me to you," and they ask me, "What is his name?" what shall I say to them?' 14 God said to Moses, 'I AM WHO I AM.' He said further, 'Thus you shall say to the Israelites, "I AM has sent me to you." '" In this biblical tradition, the name of God means, "the one who is with," the one who accompanies, and not "the one who is" (a nuance in the Greek introduced by the translators of the Septuagint).

5. This conclusion (v.6b) has been understood in a variety of ways. The Masoretic Text reads, "I shall return (*shabtî*) to the house of the Lord," but the form preserved in Psalm 27:2b (*shibtî* "my residing"), with the same phrase as in our psalm, appears to conform better to the syntax of the psalm (see also the Septuagint translation of 23:6b: *to katoikein me*). This expression does not indicate a vow of dedication within cultic worship but a fervent desire to be near Yahweh. It is a way of speaking of the security and salvation found in Yahweh.

6. Ezekiel 34:1–16 reads, "The word of the Lord came to me: 2 Mortal, prophesy against the shepherds of Israel: prophesy, and say to them—to the shepherds: Thus says the Lord GOD: Ah, you shepherds of Israel who have been feeding yourselves! Should not shepherds feed the sheep? 3 You eat the fat, you clothe yourselves with the wool, you slaughter the fatlings; but you do not feed the sheep. 4 You have not strengthened the weak, you have not healed the sick, you have not bound up the injured, you have not brought back the strayed, you have not sought the lost, but with force and harshness you have ruled them. 5 So they were scattered, because there was no shepherd; and scattered, they became food for all the wild animals. 6 My sheep were scattered, they wandered over all the mountains and on every high hill; my sheep were scattered over all the face of the earth, with no one to search or seek for them. 7 Therefore, you shepherds, hear the word of the LORD: 8 As I live, says the Lord GOD, because my sheep have become a prey, and my sheep have become food for all the wild animals, since there was no shepherd; and because my shepherds have not searched for my sheep, but the shepherds have fed themselves, and have not fed my sheep; 9 therefore, you shepherds, hear the word of the LORD: 10 Thus says the Lord GOD, I am against the shepherds; and I will demand my sheep at their hand, and put a stop to their feeding the sheep; no longer shall the shepherds feed themselves. I will rescue my sheep from their mouths, so that they may not be food for them. 11 For thus says the Lord GOD: I myself will search for my sheep, and will seek them out. 12 As shepherds seek out their flocks when they are among their scattered sheep, so I will seek out my sheep.

I will rescue them from all the places to which they have been scattered on a day of clouds and thick darkness. 13 I will bring them out from the peoples and gather them from the countries, and will bring them into their own land; and I will feed them on the mountains of Israel, by the watercourses, and in all the inhabited parts of the land. 14 I will feed them with good pasture, and the mountain heights of Israel shall be their pasture; there they shall lie down in good grazing land, and they shall feed on rich pasture on the mountains of Israel. 15 I myself will be the shepherd of my sheep, and I will make them lie down, says the Lord GOD. 16 I will seek the lost, and I will bring back the strayed, and I will bind up the injured, and I will strengthen the weak, but the fat and the strong I will destroy. I will feed them with justice."

Psalm 23:1–6
An African Perspective

Hannah W. Kinoti

Context

In the rural areas of Africa, people take good care of their domestic animals at great expense to themselves. The pastoralists will move for miles with their animals in search of lush pasture, salt licks, and watering holes. These are the same items of survival sought after by the grazers among the wild animals such as zebras, buffaloes, and gazelles. Unfortunately, marauders and predators such as lions, leopards, and hyenas, out of necessity for food, do their hunting in the same localities. Often herdsmen and boys have a hard time keeping marauders from attacking them as well as their herds and flocks.

In places where inhabited areas border game reserves, real conflicts develop between humans and game reserve animals. The latter have government protection. The natural tendency is for people to track down the marauding animal that has snatched a sheep or goat and to kill it. In Kenya, the government often has to intervene because herdsmen will stop at nothing when their flocks and herds are in danger from wild animals.

Young Semoine was only twelve when he had to confront a lion. He was in the company of six boys who were grazing a herd of 300 cows in the Maasai Mara game reserve. The other boys scuttled away when the lion surprised them, but Semoine hesitated. The lion was about to strike Reoyi, the cow Semoine had milked that morning, and he was not going to see it die! He threw his spear and stabbed the lion in the chest. The wounded beast turned on the boy and struck his right leg, breaking it instantly before mauling his head. Then it limped away without touching the cattle. The boy might have died, but an emergency flying doctor's service airlifted him to a hospital in Nairobi, where he spent nearly two months receiving medical treatment. From his hospital bed, Semoine declared he would challenge lions again if they attacked his father's herd.

Even deep in the inhabited areas, hyenas, leopards, and pythons are known to take their loot from a herd or a flock. Recently an old man of eighty-three, Chege, fought a leopard that had menaced his herd of goats. He determined that before he died, that leopard must die. So he set up a trap that caught the leopard by a foreleg. Armed with a club, Chege moved too near and the leopard caught his leg below the knee. In spite of the searing pain, he concentrated on hitting the leopard's head until the animal died. Chege was later to declare, "I'm not proud of what I did. I just destroyed an enemy . . . The animal having wiped all my goats, I didn't care whether I lived or died in the process of fighting it."

Text

The psalmist in this psalm declares his confidence in God's protection even though he is surrounded by adversity (see also Psalms 11:1; 27:1–6; 62:1–8). Boldly he can testify that no good thing will be withheld from him (Psalm 23:6).

"Shepherd" is a very appealing metaphor, conveying God's devoted care for the well-being of the sheep (Psalm 23:1–3). The individual sheep in the flock is catered for personally with rich pasture and a place to rest before the journey through the dangerous pass ahead. God may ensure the national welfare of Israel, his flock (Psalms 79:13; 80:1; 95:7; Isaiah 49:10), but the individual can be confident of God's personal attention and concern, as illustrated by the Lord's parable of the lost sheep the shepherd searches for even though there are ninety-nine others in the fold. The shepherd is the guardian of the flock who recognizes each sheep individually (John 10:3–5, 14).

The shepherd ensures provision for material needs (pasture, water, rest, and shelter) so that the sheep is satisfied, refreshed, and revived. He also guides the sheep in paths that lead to life and well-being. With his staff, he keeps it from straying into wrong paths or into pathless bush—"And your ears shall hear a word behind you saying, 'This is the way, walk in it,' when you turn to the right or when you turn to the left" (Isaiah 30:21). The sheep follow the shepherd because they know his voice (John 10:4).

In this hazardous life's journey, even in the narrow pass where marauders may be lurking, the sheep need not fear because the shepherd's rod is a weapon of defense and offense, even as the staff is a tool of guidance.

These two symbols of combat power and gentle guidance through the right paths dispel all fear.

The Lord who leads and protects plays host at the journey's end (Psalm 23:5–6). Enemies may be threatening outside, but they are powerless as they watch the Lord provide hospitality complete with anointed head and overflowing cup. The enemy knows frustration because God's beloved is out of reach.

The trusting child of God has known nothing but God's goodness and mercy. There can be no doubt that these graces will continue in the life of the one who chooses to dwell in the presence of the Lord, both in this life and the next.

Reflection

Psalm 23 is popular in Africa. The metaphor of the shepherd is vivid and appealing to a people in close touch with their domestic animals—both traditional pastoralists and cultivators in rural communities. The metaphor of shepherd is a source of comfort in the face of current insecurity in Africa. Insecurity has many faces. There is food insecurity due to natural and sociopolitical factors. Individuals and communities are under constant threat of war due to political turmoil. The precarious national and regional situations that have created the refugee phenomenon have made individuals appreciate how very vulnerable everybody is. Individuals are displaced by the power of the gun from the only spot they could call home. The cry of many is, "Where are you, Lord?" Yet there is much evidence of people's trust in God. Every time a people emerges from a national crisis, they cannot but acknowledge that God has intervened on their behalf.

There is no doubt that prayer has assumed a new significance in Africa in these days of insecurity. And to see how often normal life is maintained in the midst of much calamity shows the confidence people have in a God who promises not a bed of roses but God's presence and protection from the ultimate defeat by evil. "Even though I walk through the valley of the shadow of death, I will fear no evil, for you are with me." Christ's presence with his suffering people is more reassuring and comforting than anything else. In his little book, *I Love Idi Amin*,[1] Festo J. Kivengere gives a moving account of the life of the church during Idi Amin's rule in Uganda. On one occasion, a busload of Christians were pounced upon by security forces just before they started their journey to Tanzania for a Christian revival convention. Some security advisor had intimated that the group's travelling to an "enemy" country, as Tanzania was then regarded, indicated that their mission was clandestine. The whole group was led to a prison yard where they could expect anything to happen in Amin's reign of terror. But they were each quietly praying and soon one of them started singing the familiar East African Revival song, *Tukutendereza Yesu,* in a subdued tone:

Tukutendereza Yesu	We praise you Jesus
Yesu Omwana gw'endiga	Jesus lamb of God
Omusaigwo gunaziza	Your blood cleanses me
Nkwebaza, Omulokozi	I praise you, Saviour

Within no time, the whole prison yard was alive with the resounding song. Prison wardens and soldiers came to watch in amazement as the prisoners sang joyfully and openly repented of the fear that had initially gripped them. Soldiers forgot their military etiquette, running to buy food and soft drinks for their prisoners.

Psalm 23 is pre-Christian and speaks of God, who at a later date in history was revealed in the person of Jesus Christ. Africans certainly knew of this faithful and caring God who protected and guided individuals and communities alike. My mother was an adult when she converted to the Christian faith, but her testimony of God's care for her stretches back to her early childhood. She was too young to rescue her mother, who had set their house on fire so they would both die, but something compelled her to jump out and spend the night in the bush. On another occasion, her young mind reasoned that the safest section of the river to draw water from was where the river was quiet and the water seemed calm. She was wrong, and a voice from the river called out to her to turn back! As a teenage orphan, she contemplated suicide and again a voice compelled her not to drown herself but to seek refuge among some distant relatives. She left the river that might have swallowed her, singing a happy song. My mother's favorite song since becoming a Christian has been Psalm 23. In my own childhood, Mother taught me, "take hold of God's hand and don't let it go"—an instruction she continued to give me every time I left home as a vulnerable teenager on long bus and train journeys to boarding schools in distant places.

Yes, one cannot reflect on this psalm without being personal, for the Lord is *my* shepherd. This is the shepherd that leaves the other ninety-nine sheep that are safe in the sheepfold and runs after the one lone, lost sheep, the shepherd who stretches out the staff and pulls out of the mire the one sheep that needs him most, the shepherd that lays down his life for the sheep.

God's word through the prophet Ezekiel, in which the leaders of Israel are depicted as wicked shepherds who defraud and destroy the sheep (Ezekiel 34),[2] is so graphically true of leadership in Africa today that the people have to say, "Yes, the Lord is my shepherd, nobody else." Entrusted to contemporary leadership that is political, civic, and ecclesiastical, to a large extent, the ordinary person is at the receiving end of a lot of injustices. As the mighty preoccupy themselves with feathering their nests at enormous costs to the citizenry, every overworked, overtaxed, abused common person would like to take Ezekiel's words to heart that, "He that keeps Israel will neither sleep nor slumber." That hope keeps alive in spite of the never-ending streams of refugees criss-crossing borders, traversing miles on foot, with no material possessions, food, or shelter. That hope keeps alive in spite of the many political assassinations, intimidations, and strong-arm styles of dealing with those who claim their rights as human beings. That hope persists in spite of the many evidences and demonstrations of a society of "man eat man." Many can say with the psalmist that the Lord is my shepherd because in the face of so many odds, in the presence of so many marauders, God has led, fed, given the peace that passes understanding, and given cause to laugh and be merry.

That God "fulfils himself as we need, not as we expect," every person in a dangerous and vulnerable situation can testify. By crying to God in desperation or by simply trusting God to find a way out of danger, God has proved himself to be faithful. God answers prayer. God has a way of spreading a table in the presence of one's enemies. When faith is tested in so many life and death instances, and the individual can see how God has dared the enemy to touch God's dear one, then one can boldly declare with the psalmist that, "Goodness and mercy shall follow me all the days of my life, and I shall dwell in the house of the Lord for ever." In God we put our trust as we push on our life's journey.

Notes

1. *I Love Idi Amin: The Story of Triumph Under Fire in the Midst of Suffering and Persecution in Uganda* (London: Marshall, Morgan and Scott, 1977).
2. "The word of the Lord came to me: 2 Mortal, prophesy against the shepherds of Israel: prophesy, and say to them—to the shepherds: Thus says the Lord GOD: Ah, you shepherds of Israel who have been feeding yourselves! Should not shepherds feed the sheep? 3 You eat the fat, you clothe yourselves with the wool, you slaughter the fatlings; but you do not feed the sheep. 4 You have not strengthened the weak, you have not healed the sick, you have not bound up the injured, you have not brought back the strayed, you have not sought the lost, but with force

and harshness you have ruled them. 5 So they were scattered, because there was no shepherd; and scattered, they became food for all the wild animals. 6 My sheep were scattered, they wandered over all the mountains and on every high hill; my sheep were scattered over all the face of the earth, with no one to search or seek for them. 7 Therefore, you shepherds, hear the word of the LORD: 8 As I live, says the Lord GOD, because my sheep have become a prey, and my sheep have become food for all the wild animals, since there was no shepherd; and because my shepherds have not searched for my sheep, but the shepherds have fed themselves, and have not fed my sheep; 9 therefore, you shepherds, hear the word of the Lord: 10 Thus says the Lord GOD, I am against the shepherds; and I will demand my sheep at their hand, and put a stop to their feeding the sheep; no longer shall the shepherds feed themselves. I will rescue my sheep from their mouths, so that they may not be food for them."

Psalm 23:1–6

An Asian Perspective

Cyris Heesuk Moon

Context

The year 1905 was a fateful year for the Korean people. That year, Korea lost its independence and sovereignty and became a protectorate of Japan. The Treaty of Protectorate robbed the kingdom of Korea of its diplomatic rights to deal with foreign powers. The Japanese established the office of governor general under the Korean king to control the Korean government. August 29, 1910, was a day of national humiliation for the Korean people. This was the day when Korea was formally annexed to Japan. The Korean people lost their country and became enslaved under Japanese military rule. The Korean *Yi* dynasty formally ended, and the right of government was transferred to the Japanese emperor.

The Korean people never accepted the legitimacy of Japanese authority. For Korean Christians, political neutrality was not possible. Living under the oppressive Japanese rule was inevitable suffering for a powerless *minjung*, those who were oppressed politically, exploited economically, alienated socially, religiously discriminated against, and kept uneducated in cultural and intellectual matters.[1]

The Japanese government strongly enforced the policy of Japanese ultranationalism in Korea. According to that policy, all values and institutions were under the control of the Imperial Authority of the Japanese Emperor. Hence, the government, the military, business, all truth, beauty, and morality belonged to the institution of the emperor. The infamous Education Rescript was an open declaration of the fact that the Japanese State, being a religious, spiritual, and moral entity, exercised the right to determine all values. This was the spirit of Japanese national policy, which was combined with the doctrine of the divinity of the emperor. This belief, championed by the Japanese military as the holy army of the emperor, launched the mission to bring the "light of the Emperor" to Korea. Japanese colonial rule lasted for more than thirty years until 1945.

Text

This is a psalm of trust or confidence that resulted from the life experience of Israel with their personal God, Yahweh. The people of Israel learned through their difficult and bitter historical circumstances how to put their trust in Yahweh, who always came to rescue them. By having trust in their Yahweh, they were able to find the strength not to be overwhelmed by their grief, suffering, and pain, for Yahweh was the shepherd. Furthermore, they were destined to be anointed, thus raising their status.

The Lord is my shepherd. The children of Israel were taught that Yahweh was their personal God who delivered their ancestors out of the bondage of Egypt into the Promised Land. Thus, in the event of suffering or pain, they learned to express their confidence in Yahweh not only as Just One (e.g., Psalm 11[2]) but also as their shepherd. It was common knowledge in ancient Israel that a god could be known as a shepherd.[3] The psalmist portrays Yahweh as his shepherd, expressing his confidence in Yahweh, not only because the psalmist needs nothing (Psalm 23:1b), but also because Yahweh makes him "lie down in green pastures," leads him "beside still waters," "restores his soul," and leads him "in paths of righteousness for God's sake" (23:2–3).

In this psalm, there is obviously a tension between the pleasant images of the shepherding of God and "the context of insecurity that forces open the question of needing to trust God."[4] That is to say, the psalmist has to realize that he must "walk through the valley of the shadow of death" (Psalm 23:4) in the presence of his "enemies" (23:5).

Thou anointest my head with oil. God is the anointer, and the psalmist is the one being anointed with oil. The psalmist is not thinking of being anointed with oil as a prophet or a priest, but is rather focusing on the anointing associated with becoming a king—not a king victorious at war, but a king who knows the harsh world of the lament psalms, a world of difficult and bitter historical circumstances. The presence of "the enemies" in the text indicates that the psalmist is being anointed with oil as a king, for the association of enemies and anointing is similar to the second psalm, which concerns the king of Israel: "Why do the nations conspire, and the peoples plot in vain? 2 The kings of the earth set themselves, and the rulers take counsel together, against the LORD and his anointed, saying . . ." (Psalm 2:1–2). Psalm 23, therefore, reflects the fear of death and the presence of Yahweh alongside the experience of the grim realities of life in battle. Within the context of the sociopolitical background of Israel, the threats of foreign powers, such as the Egyptians, Assyrians, Babylonians, and the Persians, can be envisaged here. The conclusion must be that the Israelites possessed their own status as kings with God.

Reflection

Given the extreme conditions of political oppression, economic exploitation, religious discrimination, and social alienation by a foreign regime, the Korean Christians had no positive outlet to express their feelings and aspirations other than biblical language. But those dreams were not empty dreams; they were powerful in their historical self-understanding. In their experience of oppression and alienation, Korean Christians found the God of the Old Testament, who was not only their shepherd (Psalm 23:1) but also their anointer in the presence of their enemies. (23:5)

There were also ways in which the pain and suffering they endured in silence was translated into faith trusting in God. The Korean *minjung* exposed the heart of a culture that is true and beautiful, revealing men and women and children in their poverty, oppression, exploitation, wretchedness, and helplessness trying to be human. By being human, they were able to recite their trust in God, saying, "since God is our shepherd, we do not need anything but God." This is reminiscent of Psalm 23:

> The Lord is my shepherd, I shall not want;
> God makes me lie down in green pastures.
> God leads me besides still waters,
> God restores my soul.
> God leads me in paths of righteousness for God's sake.
> (Psalm 23:1–3)

It is in this historical context that we must learn what God is doing with the *minjung* in Korea. The people of God as the community of believers have, in a special way, received the gift of the Spirit of God. They are called to confess anew their trust in God and witness the dynamic presence and activity of God as our shepherd in the whole world. They are called upon to make known their commitment to and trust in the presence of God as a distinct part of the realm of God.

In oppressive situations, the oppressed people in Korea had to learn to hide their feelings, even though they "walk[ed] through the shadow of darkness." Living under a repressive social, political, and religious system, they had to suppress their anger and sorrow. They had to swallow their tears. They did not put into sophisticated words the deep sense of injustice done to them. They did not use elaborate art forms to vent the anger gnawing their souls. But there were times when their long-suppressed anger and sorrow erupted from the abyss of their being in fury and frenzy like a volcano; then there would be protests, revolts, or revolutions. And all the while, Christians in Korea silently wished for their God to intervene and to make them the subjects of their own destiny, living in restored relationships with their enemies in the presence of their God. This restored relationship would no longer consist of fear of the enemies, for they would be the anointed ones, claiming their status as "kings." Their expression of faith went like this:

Even though I walk through the valley of the shadow of death [Japanese
     Imperial Government],
I fear no evil; for thou art with me;
thy rod and thy staff, they comfort me.
Thou preparest a table before me in the presence of my enemies [i.e.,
     Japan];
Thou anointest my head with oil, my cup overflows.
Surely good and mercy shall follow me all the days of my life;
And I shall dwell in the house of the Lord forever.

                                                             (Psalm 23:4–6)

Notes

1. *Minjung* is a Korean word composed of two Chinese characters that mean *people* and *the mass* (*jung*). Literally, then, this would be translated into English as "the mass of people." However, this simple translation does not fully reflect what is meant by the term, for *minjung* is not a concept or object that can be easily explained or defined. But as a starting point, I would like to posit the following general definition of *minjung:* "the *minjung* are those who are oppressed politically, exploited economically, alienated socially, religiously discriminated against, and kept uneducated in cultural and intellectual matters."

2. Psalm 11:4–7 reads, "The LORD is in his holy temple; the LORD'S throne is in heaven. His eyes behold, his gaze examines humankind. 5 The LORD tests the righteous and the wicked, and his soul hates the lover of violence. 6 On the wicked he will rain coals of fire and sulfur; a scorching wind shall be the portion of their cup. 7 For the LORD is righteous; he loves righteous deeds; the upright shall behold his face."

3. For example, Genesis 48:15; 49:24; Psalms 28:9; 74:1; 77:20; 78:52–53; 80:1; 95:7; 100:3; 121:3–8; Isaiah 40:11; 49:9–10; Jeremiah 23:1–4; 31:10; 49:19–20; 50:17–19; Ezekiel 34; Micah 4:6–8; 7:14 [editors].

4. J. D. Pleins, *The Psalms* (Maryknoll, N.Y.: Orbis, 1993) 51.

Ecclesiastes 3:1–8

For everything there is a season, and a time for every matter under heaven: 2 a time to be born, and a time to die; a time to plant, and a time to pluck up what is planted; 3 a time to kill, and a time to heal; a time to break down, and a time to build up; 4 a time to weep, and a time to laugh; a time to mourn, and a time to dance; 5 a time to throw away stones, and a time to gather stones together; a time to embrace, and a time to refrain from embracing; 6 a time to seek, and a time to lose; a time to keep, and a time to throw away; 7 a time to tear, and a time to sew; a time to keep silence, and a time to speak; 8 a time to love, and a time to hate; a time for war, and a time for peace.

Ecclesiastes 3:1–8
A Latin American Perspective[1]

Elsa Tamez

Context

Recently I met a Nicaraguan woman, Doña Catalina, who was distressed because she had to choose only two out of her five children to go to school. She chose Luis and Diego because she thought they were the most clever and could make the most of the opportunity to study. Lupita was more intelligent than Diego, but because she was a girl, her mother thought it would be more useful for Diego to go to school. Juan, who at fifteen was the oldest, had to work with his father in construction. Doña Catalina believed that she had made the right decision, but she was upset because she thought that all her children should be able to study. She had always believed that education would lift them out of poverty, and now she realized that an education was not within reach for all her children. I left her in distress but felt anguished because I did not have words of hope for her. She perceived that, and said to me with resolution, "Good times will come."

When a mother has to choose to send only two of her five children to school because she is unable to buy books and uniforms for all five, she feels desperate and enormously deceived. When a mother and a father have to work all day in order to survive and then are unable to enjoy either their work or a good salary for all their efforts, times are perverse. When a mother can see no real possibility for change anywhere under the leadership of some popular movement, and when, on the contrary, she hears constantly about the next Structural Adjustment Program,[2] the wells of messianic hope are drying up.

These extreme situations are now common in many of the countries of Latin America and the Caribbean. There is a desperate search for new messianic horizons. This occurs in the midst of the daily denial of real life and in the absence of a popular movement that might embrace the aspirations of the wretched sectors of the population. For this reason, when the indigenous movement of Chiapas, Mexico, rebelled with force, many looked toward Chiapas with a certain rejoicing astonishment.

Text

When Doña Catalina affirmed, "Good times will come," I thought of the beautiful poem in Ecclesiastes 3:1–8. In fact, this poem can be a key to inspiring faith in a situation of hopelessness in which the desired future is blocked. Qoheleth, through faith that everything has its time, offers a proposal that helps persons to resist the imposition of a dehumanizing present. Qoheleth affirms that there is nothing new under the sun; all is *hebel,*[3] an immense "emptiness"—translated often by the word "*vanity*" (1:2;[4] 12:8). Qoheleth's statement relativizes, in the face of daily experiences and contradictions, the common theology of traditional inherited wisdom as well as the messianic promises of the prophets. Their theoretical theological schemes do not respond to the historic challenges of the moment. There are no messianic solutions in sight, neither punishment for the wicked nor recompense for the just. All is *hebel.*

Nevertheless, the real world in which this text was written affirms the contrary. In the third century B.C.E., all was new. Scholars who analyze this Greco-Roman period offer evidence that astonishing, unprecedented structural changes occurred, especially during the time of the Ptolemies after the death of Alexander the Great.[5] In that context, the book of Qoheleth proves confrontational. It reveals the other face of the efficient Hellenistic technological system: the injustices (4:1),[6] the slavish toil without enjoyment of the fruits of labor (2:20–23),[7] the bureaucracy (5:8),[8] tyranny (8:3–4),[9] and the innocent suffering and the wicked prospering (8:14).[10] Ecclesiastes 3:1–8 must be read in the midst of this suffocating reality.

Nevertheless, Qoheleth affirms that everything has its propitious time ('*et* in Hebrew, *kairos* in Greek) and hour. To make this affirmation, however, one must struggle against the chronological, oppressive times that have conspired against human beings. Qoheleth does not find, either in the present, the future, or the past, the reins to grasp in order to develop a viable utopia in which he can deposit his faith. There is nothing new under the sun. The present is *hebel,* total frustration; the past has been forgotten, and in the future there is no glimpse of anything new.

A chronological understanding of time does not provide a structure of possibility; rather, the possibility comes through faith in the existence of mature, opportune time (*'et, kairos*). Qoheleth's confident affirmation that everything has its time and its hour is a utopian phrase that orders real life in the midst of slavish toil.[11] When the limits of the human condition are recognized, then hope can be reorganized. If there is a time to be born and a time to die, a time to embrace and a time to refrain from embracing, a time to love and a time to hate, there also has to be a time of *hebel* and a time of *no-hebel*. What is new here is that the narrator is announcing the time of *no-hebel*. When will this time come? No one knows. But one knows that it *will* come. Faith in the coming of the hoped-for time helps one to withstand and to resist with dignity the present time of death, destruction, weeping, nonembracing, hate, war . . .

Reflection

According to Franz Hinkelammert, the present hopelessness in the decade of the '90s has been the systematic work of capitalist ideology. A strategy has been established that intends to create "a culture of hopelessness," because to have hope for a different future threatens the stability of the present capitalist system, which believes it is on the road toward a perfect society.[12] The capitalist system claims to be everyone's hope. In this way, to create other hopes is to be against the only realizable hope. For this reason, one must not have expectations other than living in the expectation (with its respective adjustments) of the hope that has been promised. If this is true, then the task for our time, which cannot be postponed, is to reflect on a utopia for today. However, it is often the case that when the future becomes agonizingly impenetrable, utopias are hidden; they cannot take shape. As utopias become more impossible to create, humans are less able to act. And, as human action becomes more impossible, there is less possibility to develop a desired society.

In the case of Doña Catalina, the popular revolution of '79 in Nicaragua has been left behind. Hopes have vanished and the present denies the right for everyone to attend school, to enjoy a life with dignity, and to benefit from the fruits of labor. How can such impotence be overcome when the struggle for survival is endless, and there is no strong movement in sight that can carry forward the desire for a dignified life for the great majority of people?

Qoheleth, a book that many consider to be pessimistic, offers an interesting way to reflect on the reality of hopelessness when the future cannot be known, the past has been forgotten, and the present is unbearable.

Qoheleth's answer is to recognize this impotence and to hand it over to the divine, who knows the times. Although this answer is perhaps not the best way out, at least it permits breathing space and gives confidence that it is worthwhile to continue the struggle for life. Qoheleth's answer recognizes that everything has its time and its hour, and that something new can happen under the sun.

Qoheleth, as we have mentioned above, reorients the world toward *no-hebel* by assigning the propitious times to God. If the time of *hebel* neutralizes or paralyzes, then faith in God's timing—that everything has its time and its hour—liberates. This is the strength of the faith that God will act and judge with justice at the opportune time (3:17–18;[13] 8:12–13;[14] 12:14[15]). When one arrives at this point of faith, the affirmation of real life, an alternative explicit in Qoheleth, becomes possible in the joy of eating and drinking and loving your loved one (9:7–10[16]). This is neither irresponsibility nor indifference in the face of exploitation under the sun. It is a wager for life because it rests on the *no-hebel* of God.

Notes

1. Translation by Gloria Kinsler.

2. Structural Adjustment Programs are economic measures that governments must follow in accordance with the policies of the neo-liberal capitalist market, e.g., the World Bank, the International Monetary Fund, and the International Development Bank. These measures deal with issues, such as privatization, tariffs, cuts in spending for education and health, and the raising of prices for basic products.

3. The Hebrew term *hebel* has many meanings: empty, absurd, fleeting, useless, complete frustration, etc. (See E. Jenni and C. Westermann, *Theological Lexicon of the Old Testament*, 3 vols. (Peabody, MA: Hendrickson, 1997) 1.350–53 [editors].)

4. "Vanity of vanities, says the Teacher, vanity of vanities! All is vanity."

5. See M. Hengel, *Judaism and Hellenism* (Philadelphia: Fortress, 1974); M. Rostovtzeff, *Greece* (New York: Oxford University, 1963) 258–300; M. Ralf, *La epoca helenistica* (Buenos Aires, Paidos, 1963); H. Koester, *Introduccion al Nuevo Testamento, Historia, cultura y religion de la epoca helenistica e historia y literatura del cristianismo primitivo* (Salamanca: Sigueme, 1988) 73–345; S. de Jong, "Quitate de mi sol! Eclesiastes y la tecnocracia helenistica," *RIBLA* 11 (1992).

6. "Again I saw all the oppressions that are practiced under the sun. Look, the tears of the oppressed—with no one to comfort them! On the side of their oppressors there was power—with no one to comfort them."

7. "So I turned and gave my heart up to despair concerning all the toil of my

labors under the sun, 21 because sometimes one who has toiled with wisdom and knowledge and skill must leave all to be enjoyed by another who did not toil for it. This also is vanity and a great evil. 22 What do mortals get from all the toil and strain with which they toil under the sun? 23 For all their days are full of pain, and their work is a vexation; even at night their minds do not rest. This also is vanity."

8. "With many dreams come vanities and a multitude of words; but fear God."

9. "Do not be terrified; go from his presence, do not delay when the matter is unpleasant, for he does whatever he pleases. 4 For the word of the king is powerful, and who can say to him, 'What are you doing?'"

10. "There is a vanity that takes place on earth, that there are righteous people who are treated according to the conduct of the wicked, and there are wicked people who are treated according to the conduct of the righteous. I said that this also is vanity."

11. For a more complete analysis, see my article, "La razon utopica de Qohelet," *Pasos* 52 (1994).

12. See F. Hinkelammert, "La logica de la exclusion del mercado capitalista mundial y el proyecto de liberation," in *America Latina: resistir por la vida* (San Jose: DEI, 1994).

13. "I said in my heart, God will judge the righteous and the wicked, for he has appointed a time for every matter, and for every work. 18 I said in my heart with regard to human beings that God is testing them to show that they are but animals."

14. "Though sinners do evil a hundred times and prolong their lives, yet I know that it will be well with those who fear God, because they stand in fear before him, 13 but it will not be well with the wicked, neither will they prolong their days like a shadow, because they do not stand in fear before God."

15. "For God will bring every deed into judgment, including every secret thing, whether good or evil."

16. "Go, eat your bread with enjoyment, and drink your wine with a merry heart; for God has long ago approved what you do. 8 Let your garments always be white; do not let oil be lacking on your head. 9 Enjoy life with the wife whom you love, all the days of your vain life that are given you under the sun, because that is your portion in life and in your toil at which you toil under the sun. 10 Whatever your hand finds to do, do with your might; for there is no work or thought or knowledge or wisdom in Sheol, to which you are going."

Ecclesiastes 3:1–8
An African Perspective[1]

François Kabasele Lumbala

Context

The Bantu—a black people who populate l'Afrique du Cap at the equator—are considered to be "animists," people who believe that a mystery can be found in the most innocuous of things. The Bantu believe that behind a visible thing can lurk an invisible one, and that which is essential is invisible to the eyes. For the Bantu people, the world that we see is a mixture of what is beyond and what is here on earth. The world is populated by visible and invisible creatures who live in continual interaction and in a hierarchical interdependence. In this hierarchy, the invisible exists at the head of the hierarchy, while at the summit is God, the Supreme Being. The invisible is stronger; one must always follow it. Prayer, therapeutic cures, physical work to feed oneself or to acquire riches, the exercise of power—all of these lack substance if they are not based on the invisible, and if they do not occur in harmony with the invisible realities of God and the ancestors, as well as with the surrounding palpable and visible universe.

Happiness exists, therefore, only when there is harmony between this life, the life beyond, and the living cosmos. One finds oneself in this harmony when one lives at peace and communion with one's people, one's predecessors, and one's descendants; when one works and reaps the fruit of one's labor; and when one does not ruin the cosmos with all that would harm others' lives, such as hate, jealousy, witchcraft, curses, and theft.

The one who holds power among the Bantu people, moreover, must recognize that to be a leader means to be the ally and the defender of all in the name of the ancestors, those who have lived virtuously, died, and continue to exist in the invisible world. It also requires obedience to certain tenets, such as are illustrated by the following proverbs:

Only the father-in-law may lead the chief.

The rich must know that it is better to be surrounded by people than to be holed up with one's riches.

The sage should know that intelligence is like a small goat: it gets borrowed, sometimes from the oldest to the youngest, sometimes from the youngest to the oldest.

Humanity is designed to live on earth. Although we know that here on earth we are only transients, that according to a Bantu proverb our residence is in the ground, still the quest for a long and prosperous life is encouraged because in the hereafter we believe that we shall continue in accordance with what we had been on earth. This affirmation of life is apparent in yet more Bantu proverbs:

Kudia kua nsua mpa msua: Do not wait . . . one must eat in the ant's season;

Pa kudia mpaucidi wenda: It is while you are living that you can eat;

Kuleala nkuabanya meesu: To beget means to increase the number of your eyes.

The conception of time, further, is rather varied in Africa. We are familiar with several representations of time: linear time; cyclical time; mythical time, or the time of those in heaven which intervenes in all myths; and finally, human time. All of these times overlap, successively or in parallel, according to what life one is living or what story one is telling. Some believe in reincarnation, such as the Bambara, a people of West Africa. Others, such as the Bantu, believe in an uninterrupted progression during the course of which reincarnations can transpire. The most important thing about these times is not how long they last but what *happens* during their passage. Life expresses itself, grows, shrinks, and transforms, all behind the reality of time.

Text

Although the book of Ecclesiastes is a compilation of several authors, the central theme that runs through the book is the quest for human happiness. Therefore, whichever portion of the text one wishes to interpret, one must keep in mind the general theme of Ecclesiastes as it relates to this quest for happiness. Happiness does exist; it is not an illusion ("there is a time for everything . . ."). But in order to find happiness, it is necessary to reckon with God, to live within the range of God's will and during God's time. Human efforts to find happiness are in vain ("vanity of vanities . . .") if they remain merely human attempts.

Wisdom is, without a doubt, a powerful tool to possess on this search for happiness. Wisdom is a tool that draws upon the treasury of diverse human traditions, upon even such diverse philosophies as epicureanism (a philosophy of celebration), which barely hides behind the refrain of 5:18: "Behold, what I have seen to be good and to be fitting is to eat and drink and find enjoyment in all the toil with which one toils under the sun . . ." But epicureanism does not understand the celebration as a gift of God. The Jewish faith, the faith according to which God created the world and gave it to humanity to enjoy, manifestly comes to the rescue of the vanquished wise person through a God who is master of time and history and who accomplishes everything by his own glory. In this way, the faith of Ecclesiastes brings the sage even further towards union with, and conformity to, the will of God, who gives meaning both to pleasure and to the most bitter deception.

When the philosopher—an apt description of the authors of Ecclesiastes—observes this world, it seems to him that everything continues and that there is nothing new under the sun. Human activity for its own sake is nothing more than "striving after wind" (1:17). Vanity of vanities! But in keeping with God's will, this activity can become a lever to eternity, a meeting place with the divine. By doing God's will, humanity takes creation to its goal. Just as the abyss and the disappointing side of the world suggest to the wise person that there exists somewhere a summit, so also that which is humanly disappointing and troublesome comprises salvation when assessed from the perspective of faith.

Things are good when they are done in their proper season—which means in God's time:

> *to be born—to die*
> *to plant—to uproot*
> *to kill or harm—to heal*
> *to destroy—to build*
> *to groan—to dance*
> *to embrace—to abstain*
> *to find—to lose*
> *to keep quiet—to speak*
> *to fight—to make peace.*

These contradictory pairs, which all refer to the fundamental and most dramatic—"to be born—to die"—are multiplied just as much to shock the mind as to show, by their diversity, how much God's behavior encompasses all of human activities, from the most banal to the most dramatic.

Reflection

The first thing that a Bantu hears in Ecclesiastes 3, with its refrain, "a time to be born, a time to die, a time to laugh, a time to . . ." is the rhythm. The rhythm carries us to the heart of the universe's rhythm, which for us constitutes an essential element in the harmonization of existence. Indeed, we pay immense attention to rhythm because it is one of the essential components of our conception of the world and of life. We use dance as a fundamental element of every celebration because the most important thing is to harmonize everything with God's rhythm, which expresses itself in the rhythm of creation, the rhythm of life. And this rhythm reminds us of one of the facets of God's face, a disconcerting God, who creates life and death, who gives and who takes away:

> *Kambi kupa, kanza kaalua kanyi, kakuiminyi, muisu mualua mpoko:*
> If God gives, you will say that he's getting rid of things; but if God refuses, you will cry until the tears hollow out your cheeks.

The rhythm of the phrase "a time for . . . a time for" brings us also to appreciate the transformations and dynamism of life. It is not the moment but the *event* that counts; that which one does is more significant than how long the moment lasts. Therefore, let us grasp the time of living, for living is more important than all else. We dedicate *all* of time to everything that affects life. That is why we Bantu people have a reputation for long celebrations. This is good because for us, to celebrate is to live. We also have a reputation for the way we debate, a way that envelopes and hides the direct goal and does not go straight to the point of the discussion. For us who belong to the Bantu people, to circle around the point is to think about the words, giving them free run. The reason for this is that, in an oral civilization, the word is life, the word is personalized, and the word is often conjoined with the being itself because the word contains that being.

Therefore, the rhythmic pronunciations of Ecclesiastes would become for us a way to envisage the many sides of life, which at times begets, at times leaves the terrestrial, picks up here, but rejects there, at times embraces, at times remains impassive, here makes war, there makes peace, and so on. It is the multifaceted aspect of life and not merely of time that we perceive readily in this text. Where Qoheleth—the preacher, the philosopher—reads the incoherence of existence, which is shaken by contradictions, the Bantus perceive a chant in praise of life's multifaceted dynamism, and they bring a dance-step into the infinitely variable and unforeseeable rhythm of life.

The general observation of life in Ecclesiastes is contrary to our understanding as Bantus. Indeed, Ecclesiastes is pessimistic with regard to the general conception of the universe and events. For the Bantu, in contrast, life is *always* worth living. Whatever may be the difficulties of life or the bitterness of human existence, the Bantu opt for life, as still another proverb states:

> *cikole mmutu ku nshingu:* Provided that I am alive (or, more literally), provided that my head stays firmly on my neck.

Life is priceless, above all else. It is therefore, from the Bantu perspective, always worth living, whatever may be the conditions. This reality explains perhaps why there are very few suicides in this milieu and even fewer social revolts against conditions of life. The optimism of the Bantu people is radically opposed to the pessimism exhibited in Ecclesiastes.

Notes

1. Translation by Nancy Grey.

Ecclesiastes 3:1–8

An Asian Perspective

Choan-Seng Song

Context

Japan is admired for its beauty, elegance, and orderliness. The industriousness, ingenuity, and politeness of its people are proverbial. But little known to outsiders is the fact that there are more than two million people in Japan today called *burakumin,* literally, "hamlet people." Who are these *burakumin*? They are the outcasts in the society of Japan who are ostracized and discriminated against. They are Japanese in every sense of the word except for the respect and honor taken for granted by the majority of the Japanese. They are also called *hinin* (pariah or nonperson) and *senmin* (despicable people). Many of them make every effort to keep their identity a family secret, but once known, they are shunned by their colleagues and friends. They may even lose their jobs. Under strong family pressures, those engaged to be married to *burakumin* are often forced to renounce the prospective marriage.

Who are these *burakumin*? Why do they have to suffer such indignity and humiliation even today? They are descendants of those who labored and toiled as slaves and servants in the feudal society of Japan under the Tokugawa rulers (1603–1867). Their ancestors used to be treated with contempt by society and considered ritually unclean because of what they did for a living. After nearly 400 years, they still bear the stigma of that tradition and history. An entry in a young woman's diary speaks for itself:

> October 3, 1978, Tuesday. It is 3 a.m. Father, I heard and understood what you said to me. I cannot write it down in detail just now. . . . But I now know my history. Flowing in my veins is the blood of those

people who suffered discrimination. On this body of mine is engraved
the history that can no longer be hidden. Father, why did you not tell
me about it before? You must have suffered a lot. Your face, sometimes looking strong, sometimes lonely, and sometimes severe, used
to startle me. How often I felt hurt. I cried. Father, I did not know
what kind of pain you had to carry with you . . .[1]

What a heart-breaking story! One can see the pain in the young woman's
face and feel the agony in her heart.

Text

The Japanese woman who poured out her heart in her diary may find so-
lace in a strange book called Ecclesiastes (Qoheleth) in the Hebrew scriptures. That sage-teacher of Ecclesiastes seems to be giving advice to people
of his time to resign themselves to their lot in life when he says:

> *What has been is what will be,*
> *and what has been done is what will be done;*
> *there is nothing new under the sun.*
>   (Ecclesiastes 1:9)

Change is an illusion. Life is an endless repetition of the same thing.
History is what happens over and over. There is no use in fretting about
your fate.

If this is the case, then our sage-teacher is right. "Futility, utter futility,"
he intones, "everything is futile" (Ecclesiastes 1:2). This seems the end of
the matter. If "life is profitless, totally absurd," what are we to do? We are
told this is his answer: "Enjoy life if you can, for old age will soon overtake you. And even as you enjoy, know that the world is meaningless.
Virtue does not bring reward. The deity stands distant, abandoning humanity to chance and death."[2] This sounds like hedonism and moral anarchy. The sage-teacher lends himself to such a conclusion when he confides
to his readers: "This is what I have seen to be good: it is fitting to eat and
drink and find enjoyment in all the toil with which one toils under the sun
the few days of the life God gives us; for this is our lot" (5:18).

But who is this sage-teacher, who is preoccupied with the thought that
the world is absurd and futile? This is an important question if we are to
make sense of the musings and thoughts in his inner heart. Is he not one of
those who can afford to enjoy life with abandon? Does he not belong to the
class of men and women who can indulge in moral anarchy with impunity?
Is he not part of the rich and powerful, who are a law unto themselves?

Soaked in their riches and at the pinnacle of their power, they wake up one morning to realize that their riches and their power are their worst enemies. They have been deceived by their riches and betrayed by their power, and their life, the very thing their riches and power have enabled them to enjoy, is in decline. To their horror and sorrow, they are about to be overtaken by death. They have to concede that the life they have enjoyed with abandon is absurd, futile, and devoid of meaning!

But this is not all our sage-teacher is about; otherwise, he would not be a teacher, and on top of that, a sage. It does not quite do justice to him to say that his moral sensibility is in utter ruins, and his fear of God is entirely gone. Yes, he is at a loss and does not quite know what to make of life. He becomes morally impotent. But he does see "all the oppressions that are practiced under the sun" and "the tears of the oppressed—with no one to comfort them!" (Ecclesiastes 4:1). His mind condemns oppression and his heart goes out to the oppressed. One can even hear him sigh. But he seems to have neither the will nor the strength to do anything about it. All he can do is to envy the dead who are "more fortunate than the living" (4:2) and to lament that "better than both is the one who has not yet been, and has not seen the evil deeds that are done under the sun" (4:3).

This is all tinged with negativism and helplessness. He seems ready to let the matter stand there. But there is something he has not expected: what he has said in total resignation can be taken up by the oppressed and victims of injustice as a challenge to change their fate. And strangely, what he must have also said in utter helplessness can be heard as a call to action on the part of those who have suffered from a world that is hostile to them.

This brings us to his most familiar words in Ecclesiastes. "For everything there is a season," he says, "and a time for every matter under heaven":

> *a time to be born, and a time to die;*
> *a time to plant, and a time to pluck up*
> *what is planted;*
> *a time to kill, and a time to heal;*
> *a time to break down, and a time to build up;*
> *a time to weep, and a time to laugh;*
> *a time to mourn, and a time to dance; . . .*
> *a time to keep silence, and a time to speak . . .*
>   (Ecclesiastes 3:2–4, 7)

Our sage-teacher is right: for everything there is a season. How true! It does not matter if he says it in despair. Nor does it matter if he means by it how futile things are. There is no question about the fact that "for

everything there is a season." These words, though familiar, strike resonance deep in our hearts every time we read them. What would that resonance be? The story of *burakumin* helps us to hear it and grasp it.

Reflection

For 400 years, the lot of *burakumin* in Japan has been "to weep and mourn"
for the inhuman treatment inflicted on them. It is their duty "to keep silent"
about the extreme indignity they have endured. But now that time is over;
that season has ended. This is now the season "to speak, to dance, and to
laugh." In fact, more and more of them have decided not to accept the humiliation that society has imposed on them. They have taken actions to
break the shackles with which tradition has incarcerated them. They pour
out their pain and anger in words that have to make the entire nation
conscience-stricken, words such as these from a *burakumin* poet:

> *Please listen to us who live as* burakumin,
> *please understand the suffering of us* burakumin.
> *You who have heart to feel, please search our history.*
> *Despicable people—*
> *uneducated and poor—*
> *This is why*
> *we are despised.*
> *But what is the cause of it all?*
>
> *What and who made us so and when?*
> *It is the tradition-bound society*
> *that made us so.*
> *We are merely its victims.*
> *How can we restrain our tears?*
> *How can we not cry our hearts out?*[3]

Used and exploited, suffering in silence as the dregs of society for 400
years, *burakumin* have finally spoken out. They now struggle to be heard
and recognized as human beings. They have begun to mobilize themselves
to challenge the conscience of the nation and to shatter the chains of fate.

If our sage-teacher of Ecclesiastes were to hear this cry from the heart
of *burakumin,* he would perhaps first be puzzled. True, he would say, I
have said that for everything there is a time and a season, a time to be born
and a time to die, and so forth. But what I wanted to point out is the negative side of it: a time to die, a time to kill, a time to weep, a time to mourn.
This is what my faith and my life have taught me. That is why I did not ne-

glect to say these words: "That which is, already has been; that which is to be, already is; and God seeks out what has gone by" (Ecclesiastes 3:15).

If our sage-teacher had his way, he would have the *burakumin,* and for that matter, the outcasts in India and those women, men, and children who are humiliated and dehumanized in other societies on account of their race, sex, class, or creed, to continue to mourn, weep, and keep silent. It is not that he did not see them suffer. He did see it. "I saw under the sun . . . ." He did share his concern when he said, "that in the place of justice, wickedness was there, and in the place of righteousness, wickedness was there as well" (3:16). But he thought it better to leave it to God, for "God will judge the righteous and the wicked, for he has appointed a time for every matter, and for every work" (3:17). Yes, God will take care of everything, including what you *burakumin* have been through these four centuries. It is not for you *burakumin* to decide when to speak out, when to laugh, and when to dance; it is for God to decide.

That is why our sage-teacher would be puzzled by *burakumin*'s decision to break their silence. He would then be taken aback when *burakumin* decided to defy their fate and break it. He would not be quite prepared for them to take to heart what he also said about time and season and put it into practice, although he did say there is also a time to be born, a time to plant, a time to heal, a time to build up, a time to laugh, and a time to dance. *Burakumin* have gotten themselves mobilized to break down the shackles of history and the fetters of tradition. They have proceeded to remove that stigma of inhumanity branded on their person for centuries. For them, the season has arrived after four centuries. For them, the time has come after years of enduring their lot in silence. They are not going to resort to violence and killing, but they are determined that whatever wrongs done to them must be righted and whatever wounds inflicted on them must be healed. It is now the time of tearing down in order to build up, and it must begin with the *burakumin.* As early as 1922, they made known what they were determined to do:

> I am *eta* [dirty fellow]! I am proud to shout and call myself *eta*. I don't want to be renamed as "new commoner," or "special people." These new names will do nothing to help us. I am *eta*. This is enough. I am proud of being *eta*. Wait and see. Time will come when the whole society will respect the name *eta*. I believe that time must come. All of us in the same category of people, should we not be proud to be called *eta* and to call ourselves *eta*? When that time arrives, who will despise those of us who have struggled to change our lot?[4]

This is a powerful manifesto! It must have roused the community of *burakumin* from their silence. And it must have pricked the conscience of the nation.

Note the emphasis on time in this manifesto. The time to change things, the season to right wrongs, has come. *Kairos* has broken out of the historical time of Japan. The moral discernment for the time of action and for the season of change—the discernment not even entirely alluded to by our sage-teacher, enfeebled by the riches and the power he enjoyed—is transformed into the power to build a society of justice and love. Things are going to be different for *burakumin*. And things have to be different too for the people of Japan as a whole.

Just as the untouchables in India refuse to be called *harijans*, children of God, a euphemism that disguises their plight rather than redressing it, so *burakumin* of Japan refuse to be renamed and kept in the same fate that has lasted four centuries. Inadvertently, the wisdom of resignation enunciated by the ancient sage-teacher in our Bible proves that things can change, that if there is a time to hate, there must be a time to love; that if there is a time for war, there must be also a time for peace (3:8). To discern that time and to seize that season, the oppressed and the disinherited in the world today have stood up.

What would our sage-teacher say to all this? He would perhaps say, in his seasoned wisdom and faith, "God has done this, so that all should stand in awe before him" (3:14).

Notes

1. From *Yibara no Kanmuri, The Crown of Thorns* (Tokyo: Shinkyo Publishing Company, 1983). Quoted by K. Teruo in his *Keikan no Shingaku, Theology of the Crown of Thorns* (Tokyo: Shinkyo Publishing Company, 1991) 110. The English translation, based upon the Japanese original, is by C. S. Song.

2. J. L. Crenshaw, *Ecclesiastes, a Commentary* (Philadelphia: Westminster, 1987) 23.

3. This poem, "I Ask that You Know," by N. Tamiye, is quoted by K. Teruo in *Keikan no Shingaku,* 151. The English translation, based upon the Japanese original, is by C. S. Song.

4. Quoted by K. Teruo in *Keikan no Shingaku,* 154. Translation from the Japanese by C. S. Song.

Isaiah 52:13–53:12

See, my servant shall prosper; he shall be exalted and lifted up, and shall be very high. 14 Just as there were many who were astonished at him—so marred was his appearance, beyond human semblance, and his form beyond that of mortals—15 so he shall startle many nations; kings shall shut their mouths because of him; for that which had not been told them they shall see, and that which they had not heard they shall contemplate. 53:1 Who has believed what we have heard? And to whom has the arm of the LORD been revealed? 2 For he grew up before him like a young plant, and like a root out of dry ground; he had no form or majesty that we should look at him, nothing in his appearance that we should desire him. 3 He was despised and rejected by others; a man of suffering and acquainted with infirmity; and as one from whom others hide their faces he was despised, and we held him of no account. 4 Surely he has borne our infirmities and carried our diseases; yet we accounted him stricken, struck down by God, and afflicted. 5 But he was wounded for our transgressions, crushed for our iniquities; upon him was the punishment that made us whole, and by his bruises we are healed. 6 All we like sheep have gone astray; we have all turned to our own way, and the LORD has laid on him the iniquity of us all. 7 He was oppressed, and he was afflicted, yet he did not open his mouth; like a lamb that is led to the slaughter, and like a sheep that before its shearers is silent, so he did not open his mouth. 8 By a perversion of justice he was taken away. Who could have imagined his future? For he was cut off from the land of the living, stricken for the transgression of my people. 9 They made his grave with the wicked and his tomb with the rich, although he had done no violence, and there was no deceit in his mouth. 10 Yet it was the will of the LORD to crush him with pain. When you make his life an offering for sin, he shall see his offspring, and shall prolong his days; through him the will of the LORD shall prosper. 11 Out of his anguish he shall see light; he shall find satisfaction through his knowledge. The righteous one, my servant, shall make many righteous, and he shall bear their iniquities. 12 Therefore I will allot him a portion with the great, and he shall divide the spoil with the strong; because he poured out himself to death, and was numbered with the transgressors; yet he bore the sin of many, and made intercession for the transgressors.

Isaiah 52:13–53:12
A Latin American Perspective

Jorge Pixley

Context

In July 1978, I spent a week in San Salvador teaching a course to laypersons of the Immanuel Baptist Church. I lodged in the home of an accountant and his wife and four children. Immanuel is a local congregation with a great outreach, including courses in sewing for poor women and an orphanage for war orphans and others in their war-ravaged nation. As the years went by, I occasionally saw some of the children during trips they made to Mexico, where I taught up until 1985 at the Baptist Seminary. They were already young people involved in social work, and I heard that their mother, Maria Cristina Gomez, had become a leader in the work with orphans and in the organization of women, both within the Baptist Association and in the public arena. Maria Cristina had gone back to teaching at the Baptist School after her children no longer demanded her full-time attention. Then, on April 5, 1990, armed men came into her classroom and took her away. Her body was discovered an hour later in a nearby cemetery. She had been shot to death. Maria was not yet fifty years old.

Javier Barahona was the son in a Baptist family that had a tradition of leadership in public affairs in the Northern mountains of Nicaragua in the Department of Nueva Segovia. His father fought with Sandino in the 1920s. Javier himself was active in the Sandinista revolution in the 1970s and 1980s, and, after the electoral defeat of the Sandinistas in 1990, he settled down to a quiet life of service as Vice-Mayor of the frontier city of Wiwili. On March 21, 1994, he took the bus from Wiwili to La Maranosa. The bus was intercepted by an armed band on the highway, and he was taken off. That evening, his mutilated body was discovered beside a stream nearby. Javier was sixty-eight years old.

These are two of the lesser-known martyrs of the twentieth century, which has also produced famous martyrs like Martin Luther King, Jr. (United States), Malcom X (United States), Steve Biko (South Africa), Oscar Arnulfo Romero (El Salvador), and Ignacio Ellacuria (El Salvador). The number of martyrs has again made martyrdom a social issue, as it was during the first three centuries of the Christian Era.

Text

This text has a long and disputed history of interpretation. For our purposes, we can highlight only a few significant points. First, this text is the last in a series of four "Servant Songs" in which the Servant of Yahweh carries out a mission to the nations (Isaiah 42:1–4) and to "Jacob," the people of Israel (Isaiah 49:1–6). Second, within the context of Second Isaiah, this Servant-Minister must be presumed to be the nation Israel—not an individual (Isaiah 41:8; 44:1; 45:4; etc.). The Servant's mission is to make known the justice of Yahweh and Yahweh's saving power (Isaiah 42:1–4).

This mission of Israel, a nation presently in exile but soon to be returned to Jerusalem (Isaiah 40:1–11), is closely tied to the world-conquering mission of Cyrus, the ruler of Persia, who will subdue all the kingdoms of the earth (Isaiah 41:1–5; 45:1–7).[1] The prophet of the exile speaks enthusiastically about Cyrus (45:1–3): "Thus says the LORD to his anointed, to Cyrus, whose right hand I have grasped to subdue nations before him and strip kings of their robes, to open doors before him—and the gates shall not be closed: 2 I will go before you and level the mountains, I will break in pieces the doors of bronze and cut through the bars of iron, 3 I will give you the treasures of darkness and riches hidden in secret places, so that you may know that it is I, the LORD, the God of Israel, who call you by your name." While Cyrus conquers the world, then, Israel, by peacefully teaching justice (Isaiah 42:2–4; 50:4), interprets his successes as the saving actions of Yahweh.

This mission of the Servant provokes violence against him: "I gave my back to those who struck me, and my cheeks to those who pulled out the beard; I did not hide my face from insult and spitting" (Isaiah 50:6); "He was despised and rejected by others; a man of suffering and acquainted with infirmity; and as one from whom others hide their faces he was despised, and we held him of no account" (Isaiah 53:3). The reason for this violence can be explained by the historical context of Isaiah 40—55. In the context of the Babylonian exile, a pro-Babylonian party within the exilic community would have drawn the attention of the Babylonian authorities to the Persian sympathies of the "Servant-party," which preaches a new world system led by Cyrus of Persia (Isaiah 45:1–7). The violence suffered by the Servant would have been a natural result of the historic mission of the Servant and, hence, historical in character.

But the Servant expresses the assurance that he will be vindicated by Yahweh (Isaiah 50:7–8): "The Lord GOD helps me; therefore I have not been disgraced; therefore I have set my face like flint, and I know that I shall not be put to shame; 8 he who vindicates me is near. Who will contend with me? Let us stand up together. Who are my adversaries? Let them confront me."

Then, in the Fourth Song, the poet puts in Yahweh's mouth the assurance of that vindication, even to the point of being able to divide the spoils with the strong (Isaiah 53:12). This vindication, however, is a vindication after the Servant's death, which is announced in Isaiah 53:8–9. In other words, it is a form of resurrection, along the lines of the vision of dry bones in Ezekiel 37.[2] The nation that is dead will be raised to new life, but this new life will find its meaning in the mission-provoked innocent death it has experienced.

The Servant's historic *raison d'etre* is the mission that led to his historically meaningful death at the hands of those whose (pro-Babylonian) projects were threatened by the (pro-Persian) project promoted by the "Servant." The Servant Songs as a whole, and the Fourth Song in particular, reflect in quite a strict sense upon resurrection, not as personal life after death, but as national life that derives its power from "death with a mission." All of this reflection occurs, of course, in the concrete context of the exilic community in Babylon, which is disunified in its political understanding (for example, with respect to pro- and anti-Babylonian sympathies) and has been compelled to submit to the pressures of the Babylonian authorities.

Reflection

The impetus for this reflection is the correlation of the vision of a mission for Israel, which includes its persecution and "death" at the hands of the nations, with the twentieth-century social reality of martyrdom. Is violent death as the culmination of divine calling really being exalted in Isaiah 40—55? We know from experience that a calling to social transformation brings opposition and makes an early and violent death likely; should martyrdom, then, be included in a modern vision of Christian spirituality?

It would seem that the answer to both of these questions is yes. In a social situation where the fullness of human life is denied by dominant structures, the love for life leads to a view of divine calling that includes the preparation for violent death in the call of duty. Martyrdom, then, is not a value in itself, but rather a life-affirming value when it is assumed to be an element in the struggle for life in its fullness. Again, there seems to be a valid correlation between the twentieth century, the sixth century B.C.E. (exile), and the third century C.E., with its many Christian martyrdoms.

The Servant of Yahweh in Second Isaiah, however, is first a collective figure and only secondarily an individual prophet. What then are the difficult issues related to collective national death and resurrection? In Nicaragua, this experience of national death and resurrection is a vivid reality related to the Sandinista revolution, which encompasses past, present, and—hopefully—future.

The overthrow of General Anastasio Somoza Debayle in 1978–79 was experienced by Nicaraguans as the coming to awareness of themselves as a people with the potential for doing what seemed impossible, that is, to defeat a powerful army, the National Guard. Under the leadership of the Sandinista Front during the next eleven years, all sorts of amazing things were done. One, in particular, was the literacy campaign. Not only did this campaign lower illiteracy dramatically, but it also brought the country together, as young people in the cities devoted one school year to travel to remote regions and live with isolated peasants in order to teach them to read and write.

The revolution also became a powerful military apparatus that not only organized the defense of the nation during years of war, which was promoted and directed by the United States, but also spawned a military apparatus that imposed itself on the population of Nicaragua. A revolution that had begun from below (the people) became a revolution imposed from above (the government). Then, in 1990, this revolution was defeated at the electoral polls. Even though the elections were heavily influenced by funds and political and media support from the United States, as much as fifty-five percent of the Nicaraguan people themselves voted to end the Sandinista government. Does Isaiah's proclamation of the Servant of Yahweh provide an image for assimilating this defeat?

Perhaps we are to understand that the mission of realizing justice among a people denied life for centuries must pass through defeat on the way to becoming part of the national life. Nation-building that includes the poor—women, indigenous peoples, peasants, the elderly—is not a project that can be done for these people by a triumphant benefactor class. It must become a people's project, and defeat is one step on that pathway. This is the same message that Jesus' disciples had to learn after the defeat of Calvary. Resurrection does not cancel death but draws it into an ongoing victorious struggle for life.

The kings will shut their mouths (Isaiah 52:15) when they come to perceive that "he was wounded for our transgressions" (Isaiah 53:5). The prophet sees the defeat of Israel as a conversion experience for the kings of the nations. The Sandinista revolution evoked great hopes among the peoples of the world that an alternative way of nation-building which included all the small people of the world was possible. The defeat of that experience may be the path to building slowly from below what in Nicaragua was attempted from above. If so, martyrdom again will prove a powerful life-giving force, not only in the lives of churches, but also in those of nations.

Notes

1. Many scholars consider Isaiah 40—55 to be the product of a prophet who lived during the final years of Israel's exile in Babylon during the sixth century B.C.E. Cyrus, a Persian emperor, decreed that Israel, and other conquered nations that had been deported from their homelands under Babylonian rule, should return to their homelands. This decree, issued in 539 B.C.E., officially marked the end of the enforced Babylonian exile of Israel: "Thus says King Cyrus of Persia: The LORD, the God of heaven, has given me all the kingdoms of the earth, and he has charged me to build him a house at Jerusalem in Judah. 3 Any of those among you who are of his people—may their God be with them!—are now permitted to go up to Jerusalem in Judah, and rebuild the house of the LORD, the God of Israel—he is the God who is in Jerusalem; 4 and let all survivors, in whatever place they reside, be assisted by the people of their place with silver and gold, with goods and with animals, besides freewill offerings for the house of God in Jerusalem" (Ezra 1:2–4; see 6:3–5) [editors].

2. Ezekiel 37:1–13: "The hand of the LORD came upon me, and he brought me out by the spirit of the Lord and set me down in the middle of a valley; it was full of bones. 2 He led me all around them; there were very many lying in the valley, and they were very dry. 3 He said to me, 'Mortal, can these bones live?' I answered, 'O Lord GOD, you know.' 4 Then he said to me, 'Prophesy to these bones, and say to them: O dry bones, hear the word of the LORD. 5 Thus says the Lord GOD to these bones: I will cause breath to enter you, and you shall live. 6 I will lay sinews on you, and will cause flesh to come upon you, and cover you with skin, and put breath in you, and you shall live; and you shall know that I am the LORD.' 7 So I prophesied as I had been commanded; and as I prophesied, suddenly there was a noise, a rattling, and the bones came together, bone to its bone. 8 I looked, and there were sinews on them, and flesh had come upon them, and skin had covered them; but there was no breath in them. 9 Then he said to me, 'Prophesy to the breath, prophesy, mortal, and say to the breath: Thus says the Lord GOD: Come

from the four winds, O breath, and breathe upon these slain, that they may live.'
10 I prophesied as he commanded me, and the breath came into them, and they
lived, and stood on their feet, a vast multitude. 11 Then he said to me, 'Mortal,
these bones are the whole house of Israel. They say, 'Our bones are dried up, and
our hope is lost; we are cut off completely.' 12 Therefore prophesy, and say to
them, Thus says the Lord GOD: I am going to open your graves, and bring you up
from your graves, O my people; and I will bring you back to the land of Israel.
13 And you shall know that I am the LORD, when I open your graves, and bring
you up from your graves, O my people. 14 I will put my spirit within you, and you
shall live, and I will place you on your own soil; then you shall know that I, the
LORD, have spoken and will act, says the LORD.'"

Isaiah 52:13–53:12

An African Perspective[1]

François Kabasele Lumbala

Context

The Bantu people have an intimate knowledge of suffering and difficult lives. These are a part of our daily life:

> The rector of the Grand Seminary hired a cook, Maman Victorine, a 50-year-old widow and mother of eight children, of whom one was epileptic and another mentally retarded. One day we were eating lunch when our cook suddenly entered in tears; she had just been told that her oldest daughter had been arrested for allegedly insulting their local leader. The leader's court mandated a heavy fine. But everyone knew that this poor widow was unable to pay it. To prevent the abuse of her daughter in the corrupt surroundings of prison, she presented herself in place of her daughter. She had no choice but to leave the two sick children at home with the five other young children. In this neighborhood prison, there was no plumbing, food, or visitation. When she emerged three days later, Maman Victorine told us that what tortured her the most was not being hungry, nor was it the stench of excreta on the very floor where they all slept. What tortured her most was, rather, knowing that there was no one in her house to wipe the saliva from her epileptic child during her seizures, and no one to prevent her mentally retarded child from throwing herself into the fire.

Witchcraft consists of wishing harm on others by jealousy, hate, or nastiness. It is the principal evil against which a people mobilizes itself. But it is possible to wrongly accuse someone of being a witch, and it can lead to the death of the person who is despised, especially if it is an older person, for they are considered irretrievable. One day, in the middle of the day, two young people are seen dragging an old woman and throwing her into a hut, after dowsing her with gas. She cries from inside, "Mercy, I did nothing; I am not guilty of the death of your children." These cries fall on deaf ears, and no one dares to intervene, for the two young executioners are this woman's grand-children, and they accuse their grandmother of the successive deaths of their infants—through witchcraft. Little by little, slowly but surely, as the hut burns, the cries die out.

Some, like Ciyamba, suffer because they have been sacrificed so that their blood may be used to sign a pact. Ciyamba was an innocent woman who was violently killed in order to establish an alliance be-tween the peoples from the Lubilanji basin. When these people were reconciled, and the internal wars were at an end, they chose a victim whose name was Ciyamba. Her legs and arms were broken, and then she was buried alive next to the road. Any who would destroy this al-liance by any kind of treason would be followed by Ciyamba, who had just been sacrificed.

The Suffering Servant, one who sacrifices oneself or who is sacrificed for the good of humanity, is a figure found in the Bantu culture and history. As the case of Ciyamba illustrates, such people appear throughout the his-tory of alliances between peoples among whom certain pacts necessitated the sacrifice of a victim for the common cause. To understand these meet-ings and ruptures, it is necessary to consider the ideological springboards from which operate both the biblical figure of the Suffering Servant, in Isa-iah 52—53, and the victims of Bantu alliance pacts.

Text

Two issues underlie the biblical figure of the Suffering Servant in Isaiah 40—55: (1) the suffering of the righteous and of the innocent; and (2) the bearing of others' sins. The second will provide our focus, for it is the one that Second Isaiah[2] addresses during exile when he says, "Surely he has borne our infirmities and carried our diseases; yet we accounted him stricken, struck down by God, and afflicted" (Isaiah 53:4). The earlier chapters of the book of Isaiah present a figure who was constantly en-meshed in advising the king about political events and dangerous alliances during the eighth century; Isaiah of Jerusalem had advised the kings of Judah about their relationships to nations as far away as Assyria and Egypt or as close as the Northern Kingdom of Israel and Syria. His successor, Second Isaiah, who prophesied centuries later during the period of Babylonian exile, worked tirelessly to prevent his exiled people from sinking into despair. The chapters that include the Suffering Servant's Fourth Song (Isaiah 52:13–53:12) announce in particular the imminence of deliverance and the time of messianic blessing which this Servant will realize:

> How beautiful upon the mountains are the feet of the messenger who announces peace, who brings good news, who announces salvation, who says to Zion, "Your God reigns." 8 Listen! Your sentinels lift up their voices, together they sing for joy; for in plain sight they see the return of the LORD to Zion. 9 Break forth together into singing, you ruins of Jerusalem; for the LORD has comforted his people, he has redeemed Jerusalem. 10 The LORD has bared his holy arm before the eyes of all the nations; and all the ends of the earth shall see the salvation of our God (Isaiah 52:7–10).

> . . . so he shall startle many nations; kings shall shut their mouths because of him; for that which had not been told them they shall see, and that which they had not heard they shall contemplate (52:15).

This realization will reestablish Israel as the light of all nations, but at the enormous cost of the Servant's suffering to the point of an indescribably painful and disfiguring death. What is the nature of this suffering? This suffering is:

> first, the result of an unjust curse: he does not deserve death, he is unjustly condemned;

> second, the product of being misunderstood by those for whom he wishes to do good;

> third, the suffering of violence itself, when one undergoes the punishments of torture, disfigurement, and ignominious burial among criminals.

During the entirety of this test, however, the Servant is aware of carrying out a mission on God's behalf. He is conscious of being the intermediary between God and God's people. He is supported by God, who sent him, and that is why the Servant will persevere to the very end despite this torture and testing.

Reflection

This biblical text resonates with the daily experiences of our Bantu peoples, who are the victims of so much suffering. The *hope* that the Servant's chant releases is for us good news which proclaims that there is something *beyond* suffering: "Out of his anguish he shall see light; he shall find satisfaction through his knowledge. The righteous one, my servant, shall make many righteous, and he shall bear their iniquities. 12 Therefore I will allot him a portion with the great, and he shall divide the spoil with the strong; because he poured out himself to death, and was numbered with the transgressors; yet he bore the sin of many, and made intercession for the transgressors" (Isaiah 53:11–12). The Servant's *commitment* to the people's cause, and especially his *indestructible attachment* to God, speaks to us even more: "He was oppressed, and he was afflicted, yet he did not open his mouth; like a lamb that is led to the slaughter, and like a sheep that before its shearers is silent, so he did not open his mouth. 8 By a perversion of justice he was taken away. Who could have imagined his future? For he was cut off from the land of the living, stricken for the transgression of my people. 9 They made his grave with the wicked and his tomb with the rich, although he had done no violence, and there was no deceit in his mouth" (Isaiah 53:7–9).

It is not adequate to apply the characteristics of the Servant to Jesus in order to grasp the entire meaning of the text, or to create a resonance between him and us. Rather, even without interposing the figure of Jesus, this text raises questions for and about our context: What hopes can this text arouse in our suffering people? What commitments can it bring to a life of suffering, so that the people remain loyal to God? Does this suffering people have a mission for the church, for the world, through its suffering? In a word, can the meaning that Isaiah gives to the suffering of the righteous in this song shed light on the daily suffering in our present-day Bantu societies? Do we suffer so terribly in present-day Africa because we atone for the sins of humanity, because we atone for our own faults and imprudence, because we are called to a mission for humanity?

Isaiah remains hopeful because he knows that his "savior" is alive, that he is loved by God. For our people who suffer atrociously and who stagnate in misery, faith is a powerful, living force. It allows my people to feel that God is there, next to them, and that is enough. Sometimes it is laughingly said, "Africans believe a lot because they are poor and they do not take care of themselves." Or, sometimes, seeing the growing number of priestly and religious vocations, it is said, "It is because life becomes unbearable that the youth rush into the convents." This is a simplistic view, inspired by human reason, totally void of faith, for no one can live happily in a convent just because there is food available. Rather, God can use every circumstance to call someone to a given mission. For instance, Moses was approached to see the vision of a bush that burned without being consumed.[3] Thanks to his curiosity, he heard God's call. If the churches are filled in Africa, it is because they allow the suffering man or woman to feel the presence of the one who loves them. A Luba proverb states, "The sweet word from a friend's mouth is priceless, even if the friend does not bring us a present."

But what commitments should one make in these situations, not only to remain loyal to God but also to escape from their suffering? Suffering is not the goal of our existence. If the Suffering Servant endures suffering, it is for the happiness of his people, even for all people. One must persevere in justice, in good, and in the struggle against evil. To stimulate this perseverance, this refusal to yield to evil, this commitment to the triumph of good, Africans have composed religious songs. One example of this is a "credo" sung every Sunday by the Tshikapa Kele parish, a Christian community from Kasayi:

Everybody sing your Savior
Sing and glorify his name
Sing and glorify his name among the peoples
The Zaire nation and all the black nations, all of Africa,
sing the God of your ancestors, sing . . .
Sing the water, origin of salt, sing . . .
Sing the hero who never flees in the face of the enemy, sing . . .
Sing the wind which can never be trapped, sing . . .

1.

Sing "Mawefa" who sees all, who gives without counting
"Mikombo son of Kalewo," who alone created,
The water, origin of salt, the master of all

2.

Sing Jesus, the hero of innumerable arrows,
the shield on which heroes are smashed,
the rainbow which stops the rains,
Jesus the son of the leader,
who dies for us,
conquered death and gave us life;
everlasting life.

3.

Sing God the wind which fills the universe,
if it follows you are unhappy, even your clothes abandon you;
but when he makes you his ally,
he sends you to proclaim the good news to the poor,
to the prisoners, the Savior's deliverance,
to the blind, that they will soon see,
take to the frightened comfort and courage.

4.

I bless you the Master of Heaven and of earth,
for those things that you had hidden from the wise and powerful men,
but that you deigned to reveal to the poor and small.
Yes, you the small,
you who are oppressed and humiliated by the powerful of the earth,
here the hour has come to take back your rights,
the time to affirm yourself and to liberally praise your God.

The echo of the Suffering Servant resounds in this chant, especially in the hope that is integrally tied to his mission and his commitment to remain God's ally.

Notes

1. Translation by Nancy Grey.

2. Many scholars consider chapters 40—55 to have been written by a prophet or group of prophets other than the author of Isaiah 1—39, who is usually referred to as Isaiah of Jerusalem and who prophesied during the later eighth century and earlier seventh century B.C.E. The appellation, Second Isaiah, in contrast, refers to the author who wrote toward the end of the exile, as the great figure of Cyrus loomed on the horizon (Isaiah 45:1), sometime before 539 B.C.E. These prophecies, which are collected in Isaiah 40—55, contain the references to the so-called Suffering Servant, who is the focal point of Isaiah 52:13–53:12 [editors].

3. Exodus 3:1–6: "Moses was keeping the flock of his father-in-law Jethro, the priest of Midian; he led his flock beyond the wilderness, and came to Horeb, the mountain of God. 2 There the angel of the LORD appeared to him in a flame of fire out of a bush; he looked, and the bush was blazing, yet it was not consumed. 3 Then Moses said, 'I must turn aside and look at this great sight, and see why the bush is not burned up.' 4 When the LORD saw that he had turned aside to see, God called to him out of the bush, 'Moses, Moses!' And he said, 'Here I am.' 5 Then he said, 'Come no closer! Remove the sandals from your feet, for the place on which you are standing is holy ground.' 6 He said further, 'I am the God of your father, the God of Abraham, the God of Isaac, and the God of Jacob.' And Moses hid his face, for he was afraid to look at God."

Isaiah 52:13–53:12

An Asian Perspective

Cyris Heesuk Moon

Context

> The minjung[1] of Kwangju was wounded for our transgressions . . .
> was bruised for our iniquities . . .

It was open insurrection—the worst outbreak of violence that Korea had experienced since the Korean War. It occurred in Kwangju, a city of one million inhabitants, the capital of the South Cholla province. According to a report issued by the Martial Law Command, the Kwangju Uprising was triggered on the morning of May 18, 1980, when some 200 Chosun University students began an antigovernment demonstration on campus. By 2:00 p.m., the demonstration had expanded to include some 5,000 people. The Martial Law Command dispatched special paratrooper forces to deal with the protestors. As the students and "hot-blooded young soldiers" confronted each other, the Kwangju citizens began to join in, emotionally driven by reports that at least one young woman had been stripped to her underwear and dragged about by a soldier. The confrontation intensified and the paratroopers began responding with indiscriminate brutality. The violence then exploded:

> . . . Junior high school girls were stripped in a public square and had their breasts cut off before being killed. A pregnant woman had her fetus ripped out by a bayonet. Paratroopers searched and destroyed homes and other buildings in search of anyone resembling students. A group of taxi drivers were brutally slaughtered when they were caught helping demonstrators escape. Dead bodies were loaded onto military trucks and taken away to mass graves.[2]

By May 19, the number of demonstrators had climbed to 20,000; by the next day, to 200,000. At this stage, after machine-gun fire, 290,000 rounds of ammunition, 600 boxes of dynamite, 552 grenades, and 318 military vehicles had gunned down several hundred people, the demonstrators began to do open battle with the paratroopers. On May 21, the military retreated to the outskirts of the city, and Kwangju belonged to the demonstrators. During the next five days, they conducted peaceful rallies in downtown Kwangju, calling for an end to martial law and the release of the dissident leader, Kim Dae Jung. Meanwhile, the military paratroopers surrounded the city. Twenty-four hours later, on the morning of May 27, they quickly attacked and, within three hours, reclaimed Kwangju. Most of the leaders of the uprising were killed; thousands more were arrested. The final death toll from the uprising was estimated at more than 2,000.

Was this uprising an isolated, random event, in which "mob psychology" had taken hold of citizens, inflamed by "false rumors evidently spread by impure elements"?[3] It should now be evident that it was not an isolated incident (especially after the arrest of nine people, including Chu Doo Hwan and Roh Tae Woo, who were involved in manipulating the incident); rather, Kwangju was the climax of a cycle of confrontation between state and *minjung* forces that had been building up for some time. Moreover, Kwangju was an appropriate stage for this climax for several reasons. First of all, it clearly symbolized the economic and political marginalization that formed the foundation of the antigovernment movement. The Cholla province, of which Kwangju was the capital, was the poorest region of the country and had been consistently and deliberately neglected by Park during his rule. While the rest of the country had enjoyed the benefits of dramatic industrial growth, no industries had received government encouragement to locate in Cholla. Politically, Chung Hee Park's government had also overtly excluded Cholla residents. Park, a native of Cholla's bitter rival, the Kyungsang province, had openly favored Kyungsang residents to the extent that Kyungsang natives had dominated the upper ranks of the government, military, and business establishments. Furthermore, the discrimination that Cholla natives had felt during the Park era was exacerbated by the fact that dissident leader Kim Dae Jung was a native of the South Cholla province. In contrast, Chun Doo Hwan, the man who had taken control of the country after Park's death, was from the Kyungsang province.

Kwangju was an appropriate stage for the uprising for another reason. Cholla had a centuries-old tradition of striking back at national rulers, a tradition that had been born during the time of Christ (by Western measurement of time), when the area had fought against the dominant *Silla* dynasty.

Again, in the eighteeenth century, it had become a center of the rebellion against the *Chosen* dynasty. Finally, during the Japanese occupation, it had been the center of student opposition to foreign rule. Because of this history, the fact that the 1980 uprising occurred in Kwangju served as a metaphor for the historical continuity of the anti-establishment movement itself and a symbol of being wounded for the transgressions of the Korean people, especially the political leaders.

Text

This biblical text is usually known as the song of the Suffering Servant. The identification of the Suffering Servant has been problematic. Scholars have disagreed about the identification of this figure. Some prefer to interpret the Suffering Servant as an individual during the exile or anticipated as a deliverer from the exile, while other scholars interpret the Suffering Servant corporately as Israel or as a righteous group within Israel. This distinction between the individual and corporate realities, however, was far less apparent to ancient Israelites than to contemporary readers. Individuals such as Abraham and Sarah could be understood primarily in corporate solidarity with others, as in Isaiah 51:1–2, with its reference to one human in relation to many: "Listen to me, you that pursue righteousness, you that seek the Lord. Look to the rock from which you were hewn, and to the quarry from which you were dug. 2 Look to Abraham your father and to Sarah who bore you; for he was but one when I called him, but I blessed him and made him many." Further, Israel was often viewed less as a collection of individuals than as a corporate personality that could be addressed singularly. For example, in another song of the Servant, God addresses the people of Israel as this Servant: "And he [God] said to me, 'You are my servant, Israel, in whom I will be glorified'" (Isaiah 49:3).[4] The Suffering Servant, therefore, has a distinctively corporate dimension, and it is this dimension that resonates particularly with the *minjung* of Korea.

During the exilic period, the people of Israel experienced much suffering because of their sociopolitical situation of being exiled in Babylon, where they were not even allowed to remember Zion. This point is vividly evident in Psalm 137:1–3: "By the rivers of Babylon—there we sat down and there we wept when we remembered Zion. 2 On the willows there we hung up our harps. 3 For there our captors asked us for songs, and our tormentors asked for mirth, saying, 'Sing us one of the songs of Zion!'" The historical experience of suffering accentuated two Israelite commitments, both of which are vividly seen in the text of Isaiah 52:13–53:12: a corporate solidarity and suffering with hope.

The LORD will go before you (Isaiah 52:12). God is compassionate and deeply involved in human suffering. This idea of involvement in human suffering is manifest in the concept of the Suffering Servant in Isaiah 52 — 53, where God refers more than once to the Servant as *my* servant (52:13; 53:11). In order to liberate the people of Israel from exile and other nations, God is willing to be identified with the Suffering Servant. This divine commitment represents Yahweh's desire to have solidarity with the suffering people of the world, with those whose existence is marred by pain beyond recognition. In fact, God takes the initiative in this situation and "goes before" those who suffer. This aspect of the song of the Suffering Servant, then, gives insight even into the incarnation of God in the person of Jesus the Christ. The incarnation was not something passive but profoundly active: God went before suffering people in the person of Jesus the Christ.[5]

He was wounded for our transgressions (Isaiah 53:5). Throughout this text occur many words to describe suffering: sorrow (53:3, 4), grief (53:3, 4), afflicted (53:4, 7), bruised (53:5, 10), stricken (53:4, 8), despised (53:3), wounded (53:5), chastisement (53:5), stripes (53:5), marred appearance (52:14), cut off (53:8), and death (53:12). The suffering that the prophet was describing was not a mere vision; it was real and vivid. During the exile, when this song of suffering may have been written, Israel interpreted suffering as God's punishment for sin. For instance, the editors of 2 Kings attributed the ability of Babylon to conquer Jerusalem a few decades earlier to Israel's sin: "In his days King Nebuchadnezzar of Babylon came up; Jehoiakim became his servant for three years; then he turned and rebelled against him. 2 The LORD sent against him bands of the Chaldeans, bands of the Arameans, bands of the Moabites, and bands of the Ammonites; he sent them against Judah to destroy it, according to the word of the LORD that he spoke by his servants the prophets. 3 Surely this came upon Judah at the command of the LORD, to remove them out of his sight, for the sins of Manasseh, for all that he had committed, 4 and also for the innocent blood that he had shed; for he filled Jerusalem with innocent blood, and the Lord was not willing to pardon" (2 Kings 24:1–4). But the prophet known as Second Isaiah, who was responsible for Isaiah 40—55, was telling the Israelites something new as he prepared them for their mission: "See, my servant shall prosper; he shall be exalted and lifted up, and shall be very high. . . . so he [the Servant] shall startle many nations; kings shall shut their mouths because of him; for that which had not been told them they shall see, and that which they had not heard they shall contemplate"

(Isaiah 52:13, 15). The pains, afflictions, and grief that they, the Suffering Servant, would experience were part of God's plan to liberate others, both nations and individuals. For the new nations, the new revelation—that God suffers along with those who suffer—would create a way out of the dead-end suffering caused by war, destruction, brokenness, and a refugee experience in exile, and lead into wholeness (*shalom*), healing, and hope.

Reflection

The Kwangju incident was a crucial moment, the foundations for which had been laid by a particular fusion of past and present, a fusion that had allowed present struggle to become transformed into an ongoing, mythological narrative. This had resulted in the buildup, among sectors that were marginalized under the dominant regime, of intellectual and symbolic momentum. This resentment, in turn, had enabled economic and political powerlessness to be replaced by feelings of empowerment, leading to a cycle of confrontation between state and antistate forces. The government's violent response to such confrontations then created a cycle of violence which, given its symbolic dimensions, was ultimately transformed into a moral discourse. The culmination of all this moral discourse created the momentum that empowered the oppressed and suffering *minjung* of Kwangju to stand against the ruling military elite for the benefit of bringing liberation to their lives and the lives of others.

The Suffering Servant in Isaiah 52:13–53:12 can be related to the *minjung* in Kwangju when we recognize how deeply embedded the notion of corporate personality is in the Old Testament. The Suffering Servant is people joined together in such a way that they can be understood and addressed as one body, one personality. From this perspective, the Servant's suffering represents the suffering of all the *minjung*. Further, the suffering of both the Servant and of the *minjung* is in fact a contradiction—for this suffering and weakness and loss of life is a testament to the strength and fullness of their humanity as the people of God, as a people dedicated to a life of peace, harmony, justice, and love, and to the realization of God's will "on earth as in heaven."

The *minjung* in Kwangju challenged the individuals and social structures that maintain and sustain sin and evil governments. The *minjung* in Kwangju had to suffer on behalf of the people of Korea; *they were wounded for the transgressions of others*. The *minjung* of Kwangju, blemished or unblemished, suffered as the Servant did, for they were bound to a world of power structures that commit evil and sin against them. Of both the *minjung* and the Suffering Servant, it could be said, "By a perversion of justice he was taken away. Who could have imagined his future? For he was cut off from the land of the living, stricken for the transgression of my people" (Isaiah 53:8). In the hope for deliverance lies the knowledge that the *minjung* live on. Here lies the liberating and hopeful message of the Suffering Servant for the *minjung* of Korea.

Many aspects of suffering were accentuated in Kwangju, since many people were economically exploited, as well as oppressed politically and religiously. The people in the Kwangju area lacked the capacity to cope with the crises of daily suffering and had no resources to offer hope to the masses. For thousands of the people in Kwangju, the simple battle for survival was the only focus for their lives. But this realization is not the totality of their suffering. One can believe that God is present and active in human history, that the struggle of the *minjung* attests to this. It is a fact and not an illusion. Whenever and wherever *minjung* struggle for their human rights and dignity, there is God, who wishes to bring justice and freedom. We do not see God as someone somewhere beyond the blue sky; rather, we see God as living among the *minjung,* in solidarity with human struggle, pain, agony, and despair. In the words of Isaiah 52:12, "The LORD will go before you." Thus, we have hope in the midst of suffering.

Suffering and hope are, indeed, two simple words that cover the deepest and most complex realities of our existence as human beings. They have been the theme of every great religious teacher and prophet. Philosophers of every age have debated their meaning. In Korea, we have been taught that even Buddha began his ministry with a sermon at Benares on the topic of suffering. The Chinese sages ask how the righteous person can find hope in the world. Likewise, the figure of Job in the Old Testament wrestles with human misery and suffering, and Jesus not only accepts but also lives in solidarity with the suffering of the world in order to give hope to all people. The dual themes of suffering and hope hold special relevance for the people of Kwangju. The *minjung*'s suffering and hope are more widespread and pressing than at any previous time in history. In terms of numbers alone, the massive population in many cities and countries makes the magnitude of the problem much greater.

Do we then hope in the midst of such suffering, or do we go on hoping despite the suffering? When we confront the scavenger looking in the rubbish heap for food, what hope do we offer? When we speak through the bars to an activist imprisoned without charge for many months, what does hope mean? Do only those who share the suffering know the hope? Christians have often seen in the Suffering Servant a prefiguration of Jesus the

Christ. This identification raises above all the basic theological question, "Where is Jesus the Christ in the people's suffering and hope?" Although there are no immediate answers to the above questions, we do need to raise such questions constantly in order to create a new community. We who are the embodiment of Jesus the Christ need to move from isolation to solidarity to create a corporate solidarity in the world.

Notes

1. *Minjung* is a Korean word composed of two Chinese characters meaning *people,* and *jung,* which translates as *the mass.* Literally, then, this would be translated into English as "the mass of people." However, this simple translation does not fully reflect what is meant by the term, for *minjung* is not a concept or object that can be easily explained or defined. But as a starting point, I would like to posit the following general definition of *minjung:* "the *minjung* are those who are oppressed politically, exploited economically, alienated socially, religiously discriminated against, and kept uneducated in cultural and intellectual matters."

2. Korean Support Committee, *Korea: The Forgotten Struggle* (Oakland, CA: Korean Support Committee, 1984) 8.

3. Young-Hak Hyun, "Rumors and Minjung" (unpublished manuscript).

4. For a clear discussion of these interpretations, see B. W. Anderson, *Understanding the Old Testament,* 4th ed. (Englewood Cliffs, NJ: Prentice Hall, 1986) 488–95.

5. L. Boff, *Passion of Christ, Passion of the World* (Maryknoll, NY: Orbis Press, 1988) 11.

Matthew 5:1–12

When Jesus saw the crowds, he went up the mountain; and after he sat down, his disciples came to him. 2 Then he began to speak, and taught them, saying: 3 "Blessed are the poor in spirit, for theirs is the kingdom of heaven. 4 "Blessed are those who mourn, for they will be comforted. 5 "Blessed are the meek, for they will inherit the earth. 6 "Blessed are those who hunger and thirst for righteousness, for they will be filled. 7 "Blessed are the merciful, for they will receive mercy. 8 "Blessed are the pure in heart, for they will see God. 9 "Blessed are the peacemakers, for they will be called children of God. 10 "Blessed are those who are persecuted for righteousness' sake, for theirs is the kingdom of heaven. 11 "Blessed are you when people revile you and persecute you and utter all kinds of evil against you falsely on my account. 12 Rejoice and be glad, for your reward is great in heaven, for in the same way they persecuted the prophets who were before you."

Matthew 5:1–12
A Latin American Perspective[1]

J. Severino Croatto

Context

The historical reality of Latin America, in which I am immersed, is characterized by all forms of deficiencies: the suffering and the anguish of so many people who do not have what is indispensable for living, who are not happy, or who are persecuted for their ideas and convictions. There are those who are excluded from the system, ignored as almost nonexistent or marginalized from all possibility of realization. Those who search for justice do not find it in the places where it is proclaimed because corruption invades all social strata, especially the political and administrative arenas of society. Public honesty is becoming rarer all the time, or at least is unable to manifest itself, and the result is an atmosphere of oppression that is spreading everywhere.

Alongside this, violence abounds. In television broadcasting, in the cinema, in video games, in sports itself, expressions of violence become more prominent all the time. Even entertainment is violent! The Rambo and Schwarzenegger of the theater have become in reality implanted in the hearts of very many people. The "violent art" generates real violence in society and, vice versa, reclaims those visual expressions. Abetting unbelief is the acceptance of violence in society as "normal" in the visual media of communication. Such acted violence is the same that appears later—"acted" in newscasts.

The Latin American context is characterized by a supreme lack of justice and excessive violence. In this context, how do we read the Beatitudes of Matthew 5:1–12?

Text

The Beatitudes constitute the overture to the Sermon on the Mount. The designation, sermon, distorts in part the sense of the discourse of Matthew 5:3–7:27, which is neither a sermon nor a series of exhortations.

Attention must be paid to the immediate context, given in verse 1: "When Jesus saw the crowds, he went up the mountain . . ." As in this, the *beginning* of the teachings of the earthly Jesus to the "disciples," so also in his last instruction in Matthew 28:16–20, where the resurrected One speaks to the eleven "disciples," Matthew indicates carefully that Jesus speaks on a *mountain*. So we have two parallel discourses on a mountain: the first an indication of the Christian *ethos or ethic* (Matthew 5—7), the second of the *missionary task* of the community (Matthew 28). It is evident, in the whole context of Matthew's work, that the mountain on which Jesus speaks is the equivalent of the one at Sinai, from which Yahweh spoke, first to the community of Israel, to grant it the Decalogue,[2] and later to Moses, to give the laws.[3]

If we press this parallelism, we see that the programmatic discourse of Matthew 5—7 is the counterpart to the laws given at Sinai, and the Beatitudes in particular are analogous to the Decalogue, which is a global and "cosmo-visional" program that is later particularized by more concrete norms. From this perspective, Jesus is understood to be the "new Moses" who must be followed in this new divine order, and the gospel of Matthew, with its five "discourses" (chapters 5—7; 10; 13; 18; and 23—25) is the Christian "Pentateuch"—mirroring the five books of the biblical Pentateuch: Genesis, Exodus, Leviticus, Numbers, and Deuteronomy.

What then are the essential themes addressed in the Beatitudes? It is generally accepted that the themes of economic necessity and of suffering for the faith, highlighted in the Beatitudes of Luke 6:20–23, are completed and transposed in Matthew's gospel by the addition of words such as "in spirit" ("Blessed are you who are poor" in Luke, but "Blessed are the poor *in spirit*" in Matthew) and "justice" ("Blessed are you who are hungry now" in Luke, but "Blessed are those who hunger and thirst for justice" in Matthew). The inclusion of Beatitudes found as well in Luke, with these additions, allows them to complement the four that are original to Matthew (Blessed are . . . the meek, the merciful, the pure in heart, the peacemakers). In this way, the Beatitudes of Matthew do not touch the economic necessities but suggest an *interior* ethic that separates it completely from the so-called pharisaic ethic.[4]

In no way, however, does this imply that Matthew "spiritualizes" and "de-socializes" the message of Jesus. He may change the plane—the economic—but the Beatitudes remain in the plane of social praxis. In which way? we may ask.

1. The poor in spirit (Matthew 5:3) are neither those who have the soul of a poor person, so to speak, nor rich people who help or provide work. Rather they are—in light of the same expression used in the Dead Sea Scrolls[5]—the humble who trust in God (as opposed to the self-sufficient). Another possibility is that they are the ones of low intelligence who do not know or practice the law and are thus marginalized from the world of the "just." According to either interpretation, the "kingdom of heaven" is synonymous with the "kingdom of God," and this will take place in this *earth,* in a concrete history. It is future because it denies the present system, which generates poor people; it is utopian, and for this reason generates hope.

2. The meek (Matthew 5:5) may be those who are nonviolent; the description associates them with the "poor in spirit" of the first beatitude. The basis for this association of verses 3 and 5, of the "poor in spirit" and the "meek," is the direct dependence of Matthew 5:5 upon Psalm 37:11, by way of the Septuagint. The Hebrew reads, "The *poor [anawîm]* will inherit the earth," and the later Greek translation known as the Septuagint[6] reads, "The *meek* will inherit the earth." The echo in Matthew 5 of this distinction between the Hebrew original and Greek translation of Psalm 37:11 may cause us to think that a similar separation of the economic and the ethical applies to Matthew 5:3 (poor) and 5:5 (meek). However, the promise remains on the historical plane—to possess the kingdom of heaven is to be on earth, to inherit the earth. The importance of this promise does not permit a withdrawal too far from the original connotations and historical context of references to the "poor" and the "meek" in the Hebrew and Greek versions of Psalm 37:11.

3. Those who suffer, those who hunger and thirst for justice, are those who are afflicted for some cause or who lack something as decisive as justice. This is the case whether such expressions are interpreted *in our passage* in their basic sense or, as the context of Matthew's gospel as a whole suggests, as the ethical program demanded by Jesus, which brings as a consequence rejection or persecution.

4. The merciful or peacemakers are those who tend to the necessities or conflicts of others. In our present world, full of "violence-makers," the figure of "peacemakers" acquires great prominence, even more than at the time when Jesus spoke. In all of the above Beatitudes, the social, historical, and human components are notably present.

5. The only beatitude that is more "interior" is the one concerning the pure in heart (Matthew 5:8). This beatitude appears to be framed in

opposition to the "exteriority" of the so-called pharisaic ethic and is em-
bodied in situations anticipated by the law of Moses (see Matthew 6:4, 5–6,
16–18; 15:11, 18–19). The demand of Jesus has to do with practices that
are *social* and therefore manifest a *revealed ethos and way of life*.

Jesus' discourse is preceded by an important indication of the type of
ministry practiced by Jesus (Matthew 4:23–25). Jesus is presented as
teacher, proclaimer, and *healer* (4:23)—not as Messiah! The figure of
Jesus as *teacher* reappears just when the discourse begins (5:2). Luke
6:20–26 situates the language of Jesus more within the prophetic style (especially in the curses of Luke 6:24–26, which accompany the Beatitudes).
In general, then, Luke's Jesus is a new Elijah; Matthew's a new Moses.

Reflection

We need utopian hopes. Utopia—historically unrealizable by definition—
is what sustains hope, for it constantly pushes forward.

The language of future, which is expressed in utopia, is typically confused with a metahistorical—something beyond history—content. This is
how the Beatitudes often have been interpreted: everything would come
"after." Of course, the Beatitudes envision a time "after"—since the present is characterized by poverty, tears, marginalization, and violence. That
time is not, however, after-this-world, but after-the-now and *in this world*.

Properly eschatological themes—resurrection, new world, glory,
heaven—ought, of course, to express a radical change in the mode of existence, but a radical change *as soon as possible*. A lack of understanding
of the structures of religious language has led to an indefinite postpone-
ment of the eschatological hope, which comes to be understood only as
metahistorical. But this is not correct. What Paul describes as the anticipa-
tion of transformation into Christlikeness (Ephesians 2:6; Colossians 2:12;
3:1–14) has its analogy in the transformation of history *as an act of God*.

These Beatitudes could have formed part of the eschatological discourse
of Jesus (Matthew 24), since they presuppose *the experience* of suffering,
of exclusion, of violence, of the corruption of the heart, of injustice, and so
on, and since they have to do with an "after." However, the Beatitudes are
placed at the beginning of all the discourses of Jesus because they describe
experiences typical of those who receive *the text*. But they are also the experiences of our present world in an accentuated form. They are at the beginning of the discourses of Jesus as if to explain that hope for the
transformation of the present suffering can shape the reception of every
other word that will come from him. The ethic proposed by Jesus in the rest

of the discourse on the mountain (Matthew 5—7) and in the whole gospel is directed to people committed to life. As part of life, we are in need and we suffer, but the programmatic promises spoken in these Beatitudes imbue such negative human experiences with a foundation of hope. Far from suggesting a passive submission to reality, the proclamation of Jesus invites change *now*—the "after" is at the same time an "as soon as possible."

A coherent rereading of the Beatitudes demands the exploration of their reservoir of meaning in two complementary directions. First, we ought to open the Beatitudes themselves like a fan. Just as Luke was content to include four, and Matthew expanded these to eight,[7] so should we re-create the list to include many more, or perhaps fewer, according to the concrete situations of our reality. We could imagine that Jesus also said: "blessed are the honest and faithful, because they will be praised," or "blessed are those who have a communal spirit, because they will have life," and so on. The message Matthew ascribes to Jesus was not necessarily said by him in these words, but they re-express the central core or kerygma of the teacher. The creative freedom of the authors of the gospels must be a model for imitation, not so much to change the canon of scripture, but to reclaim it fruitfully and to verbalize its reservoir of meaning.

The second way to contextualize the reservoir of meaning of our gospel text consists of finding contemporary equivalents of the Beatitudes. Every text is written from a given situation and returns to it in the form of the intended reading audience. The author of Matthew 5:1–12 knows *what* he wants to say, *to whom,* and *how* to say it—a closure of sense, not directed to us but to a specific audience. In order for this text to be directed to us, we must appropriate and open it in order to discover aspects that relate to our reality. Instead of "coming out" exegetically from the text, we must "enter" eisegetically[8] into it with our questions in order then to come out of it with answers that are relevant to these questions.

Therefore the "situation" of my world expounded in part one (Context) has allowed me to "enter" in part two (Text) into the text of Jesus' proclamation according to Matthew 5:1–12, and to find there a message relevant for the present in part three (Reflection). Thus a fruitful hermeneutical circle is established from life to the text then later from the text again to life, enriched by the rereading of the message of the Beatitudes of Jesus.

In this way, read today and in my context, the message of Matthew 5:1–12 speaks to me of Jesus' option for the excluded and marginalized who suffer for their ideas because of the corruption of the people and the social systems in power; of his praise for those who build peace in an age of violence and irrational conflicts, for those who opt for honesty in their positions, for those who transform (and not only assist) the needs of the poor, the unemployed, the exiled, and those excommunicated by conflicts or ideas.

If it be read intertextually, Matthew 5:1–12 evokes the parable in Matthew 25:31–46, in which Jesus speaks again:

> When the Son of Man comes in his glory, and all the angels with him, then he will sit on the throne of his glory. 32 All the nations will be gathered before him, and he will separate people one from another as a shepherd separates the sheep from the goats, 33 and he will put the sheep at his right hand and the goats at the left. 34 Then the king will say to those at his right hand, "Come, you that are blessed by my Father, inherit the kingdom prepared for you from the foundation of the world; 35 for I was hungry and you gave me food, I was thirsty and you gave me something to drink, I was a stranger and you welcomed me, 36 I was naked and you gave me clothing, I was sick and you took care of me, I was in prison and you visited me." 37 Then the righteous will answer him, "Lord, when was it that we saw you hungry and gave you food, or thirsty and gave you something to drink? 38 And when was it that we saw you a stranger and welcomed you, or naked and gave you clothing? 39 And when was it that we saw you sick or in prison and visited you?" 40 And the king will answer them, "Truly I tell you, just as you did it to one of the least of these who are members of my family, you did it to me." 41 Then he will say to those at his left hand, "You that are accursed, depart from me into the eternal fire prepared for the devil and his angels; 42 for I was hungry and you gave me no food, I was thirsty and you gave me nothing to drink, 43 I was a stranger and you did not welcome me, naked and you did not give me clothing, sick and in prison and you did not visit me." 44 Then they also will answer, "Lord, when was it that we saw you hungry or thirsty or a stranger or naked or sick or in prison, and did not take care of you?" 45 Then he will answer them, "Truly I tell you, just as you did not do it to one of the least of these, you did not do it to me." 46 And these will go away into eternal punishment, but the righteous into eternal life.

The earlier example of Jesus' teaching—the Beatitudes—speaks to me of a promise in the form of a reversal of situations. The later instance of his teaching—the parable of the sheep and goats—speaks of a judgment on the actions made in this life in favor of the needy and of those excluded from society. There exists here a connection between blessing and judgment.

This connection establishes that the "blessed" of Jesus' initial program (i.e., the Beatitudes) are blessed because their needs and sufferings are attended to in the here and now of history by their brothers and sisters (i.e., the parable). These brothers and sisters will in turn be "blessed" by the Father at the final, eschatological moment because they have blessed their brothers and sisters in the present moment (Matthew 25:34). Does this not signify a program for life?

Notes

1. Translation by Edgardo Colón-Emeric.

2. The so-called Ten Commandments in Exodus 20:1–17 (and Deuteronomy 5:6–21) [editors].

3. For example, the so-called Covenant Code in Exodus 21:1–23:19 [editors].

4. The style itself reflects the wisdom style of speech rather than the style of legal language.

5. See the War Scroll (1QM 14.7) [editors].

6. Hebrew Psalm 37:11 is the same as Septuagint Psalm 36:11 [editors].

7. I regard Matthew 5:11 to be an extension of Matthew 5:10 and thus part of the eighth Beatitude, rather than an independent ninth Beatitude, because both verses have the same subject.

8. The Greek preposition *ex* can be translated *out of,* and the Greek preposition *eis* can be translated *into.* Hence, reading out of a text (exegesis) can be contrasted with reading into a text (eisegesis). Though the latter term is often used disparagingly, of reading one's own ideas randomly into the biblical text, Croatto argues that reading into a text is necessary to discover the fullness of its reservoir of meaning, that meaning which is not limited to the original author and his or her audience [editors].

Matthew 5:1–12
An African Perspective

Hannah W. Kinoti

Context

During the Muslim Idd holiday in 1991, Mrs. Mutahi, who lived in the poorer part of Nairobi with her family, had some friends over for a lunch party. When her guests left, she got busy clearing dishes and throwing the rubbish in the common rubbish bin outside. Later in the evening, she went to throw away some more rubbish and was surprised to find a group of boys hanging on the rubbish bin and picking clean the chicken bones she had thrown away earlier. She invited the boys into the house and gave them the leftovers from the lunch. The boys had no homes to return to, so that night they slept on the floor of the small house. On the following several evenings the boys kept returning in greater numbers until the house proved too small for them. Her daughter who did some tailoring in the city centre offered to take the boys some bread for lunch at a public park in the city. That worked well, but the boys still turned up at the house in the evenings. The lunches were also sometimes rudely interrupted by civic authorities who dispersed the "parking boys," whom they considered a menace.

Eventually Mrs. Mutahi proposed to her "family" of street urchins, which by now included girls, that they should all move to the foot of the Ngong hills, on the outskirts of Nairobi, where she and her husband owned a small plot of land. There they could all construct a much bigger house than the present quarters. Some of the children deserted her because they preferred the dazzle of the city centre, but some twenty children moved with her.

I visited Ngong Hills Children's Home with a group of women from my church, and the stories this woman told moved us to tears. One was about how she "hijacked" an eight-year-old girl from a commune of street boys. The girl needed immediate medical attention due to damage caused by sexual assaults in the commune. In one busy hospital, she only got rebukes for "neglecting your daughter and coming to us too late to do impossible repairs." In another hospital, treatment was forthcoming, but the hospital bill was prohibitive. Overwhelmed and deeply moved by the needs of her new family, this woman of faith resorted to prayer for specifics, and God intervened in numerous instances. The children were wonderful and impressed us by their good manners and spiritual awakening.

Another story concerns the late Bishop Festo Kivengere of Uganda. His small book, entitled *I Love Idi Amin,* is, according to its subtitle, "the story of triumph under fire in the midst of suffering and persecution in Uganda."[1] Kivengere wrote it in exile, having run away upon learning that, after the death of Archbishop Luwun in a "car accident," Amin was after his life also. His claim to love Amin attracted much attention, and Kivengere explains in his biography that, when he contemplated the story of the crucifixion, the Lord Jesus clearly told him he owed Amin forgiveness. In his own words, "My hardness and bitterness towards those who were persecuting us could only bring spiritual loss . . . So I had to ask forgiveness from the Lord, for grace to love president Amin more . . . This was fresh air for my tired soul. I knew I had seen the Lord and had been released: love filled my heart."[2]

Text

In a scene reminiscent of the giving of the law on Mount Sinai (Matthew 5:1–2; Exodus 19—24), Jesus gives a new ethic to his disciples. It is a reversal of the world's standards then and now and cuts across aspects of the sacred law of Moses and some of our cherished traditional moralities. Elsewhere, Jesus instructs his disciples that some of the ways of the world "shall not be so among you" (Mark 10:42–43; Luke 22:25–26). The blessed state belongs to those who are poor in spirit, those who mourn, the meek, those who hunger after righteousness, the merciful, the peacemakers, and those who are persecuted for his sake.

The poor in spirit realize their lack of resources and merit and therefore unreservedly depend on God's help and salvation. Being in touch with God in a vital way, they cannot but do God's will "on earth as it is in heaven." They are humble and simple in contrast to the ostentation of the present age. Further, the spiritually poor mourn for their sin (Psalm 51:3) and plead God's mercy (Luke 18:13). They obtain comfort presently from the great Comforter (Isaiah 61:1) and are assured of it completely in their final state of glory (Revelation 7:17). Those who mourn also sorrow for the sins of others and would willingly receive retribution on behalf of others (Exodus 32:32). At the same time, they deeply sympathize with the sufferings of the oppressed and the marginalized. They deeply share their neighbor's pain. Thus they are the conscience of their times out of a heart of love. At the last judgment, the poor in spirit will be surprised by who they are (Matthew 25:31–46).

The meek are humble-minded, gentle, courteous, considerate, patient, and sensitive in their dealings with other people. They are prompted by goodwill towards their fellow human beings and reverent obedience to God. Instead of self-assertiveness, they have the quiet confidence that everything is theirs because they belong to Christ to whom the earth belongs (Psalm 37:11; 1 Corinthians 3:22).

The hunger and thirst here (Matthew 5:6) refer to both moral and social righteousness; the inner righteousness, not the external conformity associated by Matthew with the Pharisees (Matthew 23); and a stand for justice, liberty, integrity, and human rights. Old Testament prophets had much to say about righteousness (e.g., Amos 5:24; 8:4–6; Micah 6:8, 10–11; Jeremiah 23:10–11).

The merciful (Matthew 5:7) regard the unfortunate with sympathetic loving-kindness, as the parable of the Good Samaritan demonstrates (Luke 10:37; Matthew 17:15). Mercy demands action to alleviate all types of suffering—physical, spiritual, and that which arises from structural injustices. In another sense, the merciful deal with others as they know God has dealt with them (Matthew 6:14–15). In their dealings with other people, purity of heart (6:8) or sincerity is the norm (Psalm 24). Christ's followers are challenged to examine this motive. It calls for singleness of motive against duplicity. Only the pure-hearted will see God.

Peacemakers are they who "seek peace and pursue it" (Psalm 34:14). They are not mere peace lovers who will accept things in order not to cause trouble. Rather, they face issues and deal with them actively, often with considerable struggle and trouble in the process. Reconciliation between God and human beings and between fellow human beings is at the heart of peacemaking. Peacemakers will be called children of God because they are engaged in God's work of reconciliation and spreading peace in its broadest sense of personal and social well-being.

Faithful adherence to Jesus' standards was bound to bring persecution (Matthew 5:10–11). Though persecution is not to be sought after, when it comes the persecuted one is to rejoice. Christ's follower needs to remember that the disciple is not above the master.

Reflection

Jesus is addressing his disciples past and present, not the crowds. The disciples are different. He has called them to follow him. He is their model and standard. He teaches them the reversal of conventional wisdom and behavior.

Reading the Beatitudes today against the backdrop of our situation in contemporary life, we cannot help agreeing that they are "jets of light . . . love kindles against the darkness of age."[3] If they cross the ethic of the time then, they are certainly a very sharp contrast to the spirit of contemporary African society. African society is now living out many contradictions of both traditional African morality and the demands of the gospel of Jesus Christ.

Africa has no shortage of the materially poor, but the proud in spirit might well outnumber them. We seem to have caught the wrong message from the Bible, and the parable of the Pharisee and the publican at prayer (Luke 18:9–14) applies in our society today. In striving to catch up with other peoples, few will admit their inadequacies and shortcomings. Many live above their means materially, being caught by the spirit of ostentation and advertising. Spiritual pride, so characteristic of the many forms of Christianity that fragment the society, is exposed only by the accelerated moral decay so evident everywhere. The Christian giant in Africa turns out to be another Goliath!

Our society is afflicted by many problems, and there is a lot of pain and grief due to civil strife and corruption. The killings, the carnage on our roads, and the loss of property by many to the few who are aggressively mighty are but a few examples. We long for the end of the many injustices in the society. We long even more for the kind of mourning that the Lord describes as "blessed." That kind of mourning would be certain to be part of the solution to our current pains, sufferings, and griefs.

The blessed kind of mourning is firstly that which is prompted by the appreciation of how grievious sin is to God. Blessed are those who are genuinely remorseful for their sins and so cry to God for mercy in the spirit of the publican who could hardly lift his head in God's presence and who was filled with self-recrimination (Luke 18:13). Festo Kivengere, according to his own testimony, found real release for fellowship with God when the cross of Christ made him realize there was no basic difference between him and Idi Amin.

Secondly, the blessed kind of mourning is exemplified by those who genuinely share the misery and the pain of their neighbors. They enter into the agony of others and do something about it. There are many who toss a coin to a street urchin to get rid of the menace for a while, but to enter spontaneously, as did Mrs. Mutahi, into the world of the homeless, the grief-stricken, the sick, and all those afflicted requires a compassion only God can give when we have acknowledged our poverty before God.

Thirdly, the blessed kind of mourning is demonstrated by those who are deeply troubled by the sins and wrongdoings of others, those who count themselves party to the common guilt. They not only petition God on behalf of others but are prepared to play the prophetic role to prick the conscience of their society. Recently Kenya, and the world, lost a frontline cameraman, Mohammed Amin, a Kenyan-born, Asian photojournalist who met his death together with twenty-eight other passengers when a hijacked Ethiopian Airlines plane crash-landed on the shore of Comoro Island. In 1984, Mo, as Amin was popularly known, used his camera to tell the world that in war-torn Ethiopia thousands of innocent civilians were starving, and he stayed his camera long enough to prick the conscience of the affluent. In the forward to Mo's biography, Bob Geldof testifies to the deep effect Mo's images had on him:

I was confronted by something so horrendous I was wrenched from the complacency of another rather dispiriting day . . . unable to turn away from the misery of another world inhabited by people only recognizable as humans by their magnificent dignity.[4]

Geldof says that generally the scenes of horror on TV are shrunk and made bearable in the context of the living room to the extent of making one immune, if not anesthetized. Mo refused to soothe.

But the pitiless, unrelenting gaze of this camera was different. Somehow this was not objective journalism but confrontation . . . Mo Amin had succeeded above all else in showing you his own disgust and shame and anger and making it yours also. . . .

In a brief, shocking but glorious moment Amin had transcended the role of journalist-cameraman and perhaps unwittingly become the visual interpreter of man's stinking conscience. . . . I thank God that Mo Amin sickened and shamed me.[5]

Mohammed Amin had spent months pleading with the Ethiopian authorities to allow him to visit the areas most devastated by the Ethiopian famine. They were reluctant because they feared his camera would focus on guerrilla activity, as Ethiopia was plagued by years of rebel wars. Eventually the world saw what he saw on October 19, 1984. In the words of his biographer, Brian Tetley, who also perished in the same air disaster,

> People lie dying . . . (and Mo among them) like something out of the Bible. Gently, caringly a television cameraman moves among the dying and the dead . . . What passes between him and the victims . . . is so elemental and so profound, that four days from today it will change the world.[6]

What do Mrs. Mutahi, who housed street urchins, Festo Kivengere, who forgave Idi Amin, and Mo Amin, who searched for portraits of misery, have in common with each other and with Jesus' words in the Beatitudes? All four—Jesus, Mrs. Mutahi, Festo Kivengere, and Mo Amin—challenge us to an ethic that translates faith in Jesus Christ into action. The "blessed," the "poor in spirit" of Jesus' vision, are those who mourn, who are merciful, who make peace, who hunger after justice, and who may be persecuted. These words encompass as well the person of Jesus, whose life was spent acting on behalf of the miserable until he died a deplorable death on the cross. Mrs. Mutahi did not stop herself with a vague sense of compassion or guilt but instead took concrete steps to bring to street urchins health and home. Festo Kivengere did not linger on the sidelines of Ugandan politics, content with the so-called spiritual realm, separate from the political, but instead brought spiritual power to the center of a vicious political arena by forgiving Idi Amin. The photojournalist, Mo Amin, abandoned the more typical and profitable beaten path in order to compel the world to encounter the dehumanized faces of starving and perishing civilians in war-torn Ethiopia. Each of these persons was, in the truest sense, a peace*maker,* a bringer of blessings, a blessed one.

Notes

1. *I Love Idi Amin: the Story of Triumph Under Fire in the Midst of Suffering and Persecution in Uganda* (London: Marshall, Morgan and Scott, 1977).

2. *I Love Idi Amin,* 55, 57–62. See also A. Coomes, *Festo Kivengere: A Biography* (Eastbourne: Monarch, 1990) 375.

3. *Interpreter's Bible,* 12 vols. (Nashville: Abingdon, 1951) 7.279.

4. B. Tetley, *Mo: The Story of Mohammed Amin, Front-line Cameraman* (London: Moonstone, 1988) 9.

5. *Mo: The Story of Mohammed Amin,* 9.

6. *Mo: The Story of Mohammed Amin,* 11.

Matthew 5:1–12

An Asian Perspective[1]

Helen R. Graham

Context

While serious peacemaking efforts have been underway in the Philippines since the ouster of President Ferdinand Marcos in the popular uprising of February 1986, a situation of "peacelessness"[2] continues to prevail in the Philippine countryside. More than two decades of war between government forces and members of the two major revolutionary forces—the New People's Army [NPA] and the Moro National Liberation Front [MNLF]—have created an estimated 1.3 million internal refugees. In spite of ongoing peace talks, militarization of the countryside continues unabated, and the major socioeconomic injustices that have fueled the conflict remain with no immediate or long-term solution in sight.

It is into this situation of peacelessness that peace advocates have emerged, making various efforts at third-party intervention in the ongoing peace process. One notable effort is the attempt to establish "peace zones" in different parts of the country. One of the first peace zones was established, in the face of severe tension, in a small village in the southern part of the island of Negros called Cantomanyog. The plan started by forming a "Peace Caravan" to encircle the island, stopping at major cities along the way and ending at the little mountain village of Cantomanyog, where a peace zone was to be set up. The caravan set off for its five-day tour around the island. As it was approaching Cantomanyog, Bishop Fortich and several priests began to prepare for a eucharistic celebration to be held upon the caravan's arrival.

Their plans were frustrated, however, by an artificially gathered crowd that blocked the way the caravan was to pass, two kilometers before

Cantomanyog. A small group, strategically placed within the crowd and led by a masked man, began shouting against the setting up of a peace zone.[3] A military helicopter gunship also arrived and disgorged soldiers in fatigues and armed with M16 assault rifles, who were deployed behind the crowd. The caravan was met by the sight of a small table prepared for liturgy on the other side of an obviously hostile crowd and a row of fully armed military who were blocking their way. In spite of the tension, the eucharistic liturgy was begun, and the priests present among the group gathered on the other side of the barricade, also vested for the liturgy. As the liturgy advanced, some of those at the barricade began to trickle over to where the liturgy was being celebrated. By the time of the liturgy's kiss of peace, the people from Cantomanyog who had been blocked by the barricade had braved their way through and had slipped into the crowd at the liturgy. Amidst many tears, and with the remaining people at the barricade and the heavily armed soldiers with guns pointed, the setting up of the first peace zone in Negros was announced over a loudspeaker by a young woman from Cantomanyog, who was holding a small child in her arms.[4]

Text

Although the Hebrew word *shalom* (meaning *total well-being, peace, prosperity,* and the like) appears more than 350 times in the First (or Old) Testament, and its Greek equivalent some thirty or thirty-one times in the Second (or New) Testament, the noun *peacemaker* is unique to Matthew 5:9, appearing in a beatitude that many commentators ascribe to Matthew's own hand.[5] This seventh beatitude declares that those who work to create peace (literally, who "do" or "make peace") are especially favored by God and will be reckoned as God's children because they resemble God.

A hint of the meaning in Matthew's context may be gathered from the rabbinic expression *'asah shalom* (*to make peace*), which refers to the making of peace between two individuals, of bringing an end to strife. Peacemaking was of foundational importance for rabbinic Judaism, akin to the place occupied by the requirement of love in the Second Testament.[6]

Shortly after the destruction of the Second Temple in 70 C.E., Rabbi Johanan ben Zakkai promised that the salvation formerly obtained through the peace offering could now be obtained through the peacemaker.[7] Rabbi Johanan's insight that peacemaking replaced the peace offering after the destruction of both temple and altar of sacrifice makes the ethical task of peacemaking virtually the equivalent of worship, an idea not unrelated to the earlier prophetic critique of cultic worship in favor of justice.[8]

The rabbis also believed that strife and discord were delaying the Messiah's coming, and that the peacemaker's intervention would be instrumental in hastening the coming of the Messiah and thus ushering in the age of salvation. It was as if the very continuation of the world hinged on the bringing of peace.[9]

The Matthean text blesses peacemakers from within the community's context of strife and discord between Jews who accepted Jesus as Messiah and Jews who did not. The Matthean community is probably best understood as having recently withdrawn from or been expelled from the Jewish assembly, while still maintaining strong ties with its parent Jewish community, with which it was in conflict.[10] It is possible that in the Matthean community the beatitude of "peacemaking," along with the Beatitudes in general, constituted a strategy of survival for a Jewish-Christian minority struggling to follow an alternative vision of Jewish society, based upon an alternative interpretation of the Torah, in the era following the destruction of the Jerusalem Temple.

Reflection

The rabbinic idea that the continuation of the world depends on the bringing of peace, and the Matthean notion of peacemaking as a strategy of survival, opens up possibilities for appropriating anew the Matthean beatitude in our own times. The escalation of conflict in many areas of the world today threatens to reach omnicidal proportions.[11] We are witness to what might be termed "a new epidemic of violence"[12] on a global scale that endangers the very continuation of our world as we know it.

Today's peacemakers are akin to God the Creator, called to profound creativity, called to create peace. Although quite different from that reflected in the Matthean text, the Basic Christian Community (BCC) of Kabankalan, Negros Occidental, has experienced decades of conflict and strife resulting from armed confrontation between military and rebel forces. The BCC members chose to read the Matthean beatitude as a warrant for establishing a peace zone in an attempt to end the violence and free their energies for more creative endeavors. A zone of peace, however, creates only an environment within which efforts toward the creation of an alternative society, a society of genuine peace based on justice, can be pursued. The peacemaker's involvement within that environment in literally "making peace" based on justice, however, often results in personal tragedy.

Prior to the peace zone, efforts on the part of Kabankalan BCC leader Alex Garsales to assist victims of land-grabbing, to follow up their cases against a rich landowner of the area, were met with numerous threats against his life. Undaunted, he continued his work. Because of his untiring efforts to bring about a peace based on justice, the other BCC members chose him to play the role of Jesus in the Good Friday enactment of the passion. Upon accepting the role, he said, "I Alex Garsales promise to be faithful, to offer myself to defend the poor and the oppressed so that peace may prevail in this place . . ." His bullet-riddled body was found in the tall grass on Easter Monday.[13]

While humankind struggles to respond creatively to global crises of enormous proportions that threaten the very survival of the planet, men and women on the local level, following in the footsteps of the one "who is our peace" (Ephesians 2:14), are actually shedding their blood on the altar of sacrifice in the struggle to bring about a peace based on justice. Rabbi Johanan ben Zakkai's teaching that in some way the activity of the peacemaker would replace the sacrificial peace offering in the Jerusalem Temple most probably did not envision that such activity could lead to the actual offering of one's life as a peace offering. The personal cost of making peace may, indeed, be very high.

After Alex's death the BCC members feared for their lives but continued as BCC members. The men began sleeping under the trees outside their houses at night because they believed that they were safer than in their homes, from which they could easily be dragged out and killed. Children served as lookouts whenever the BCC members met, but the continued presence of six battalions of military, plus an additional company of special forces in the area,[14] increases the likelihood of the peacemaker's offering the ultimate sacrifice of actually becoming a peace offering. Blessed [indeed] are the peacemakers, for they will be called children of God (Matthew 5:9).

Notes

1. The author wishes to thank Professor Renate Rose of Union Theological Seminary, Cavite, for her suggestions.

2. A word coined by J. Galtung, *The True Worlds: A Transnational Perspective* (New York: The Free Press, 1980) 94.

3. It was later discovered that the crowd had been brought in from the surrounding villages and that the masked man and the small group of shouters had been trained by a military captain.

4. For the full account, see N. O'Brien, *Island of Tears, Island of Hope: Living the Gospel in a Revolutionary Situation* (Maryknoll, NY: Orbis, 1993) 209–16.

5. The words *to make peace*, however, occur in two places: Proverbs 10:10 [Septuagint] and Colossians 1:20. See also Ephesians 2:15 and James 3:18.

6. W. Foerster, *eirene, Theological Dictionary of the New Testament*. Edited by G. Kittel et al. (Grand Rapids: Eerdmans, 1964) 2.409.

7. See E. Schweizer, *The Good News According to Matthew* (Atlanta: John Knox, 1975) 94.

8. See Amos 5:21–25; Hosea 6:6; Isaiah 1:10–17; Jeremiah 7:1–15; and Psalm 50:7–15.

9. See *Pirke Aboth* 1, 18, cited by Foerster, *eirene*, 2.409–10.

10. See A. J. Saldarini, "The Gospel of Matthew and Jewish-Christian Conflict," in *Social History of the Matthean Community: Cross Disciplinary Approaches*. Edited by D. L. Balch (Minneapolis: Augsburg Fortress, 1991) 41 and *passim*.

11. The word *omnicide* was coined by J. Galtung in his book *There Are Alternatives: Four Roads to Peace and Security* (Nottingham: Spokesman, 1984) 15.

12. R. Kothari, "The Yawning Vacuum: A World Without Alternatives," *Alternatives* 18/2 (1993) 128.

13. I acknowledge Sister Aquila Sy, PVBM, of Kabankalan, Negros Occidental, as the source of the details of this poignant story.

14. Information contained in a personal letter to the author from Kabankalan, dated November 22, 1994.

John 1:1–18

In the beginning was the Word, and the Word was with God, and the Word was God. 2 He was in the beginning with God. 3 All things came into being through him, and without him not one thing came into being. What has come into being 4 in him was life, and the life was the light of all people. 5 The light shines in the darkness, and the darkness did not overcome it. 6 There was a man sent from God, whose name was John. 7 He came as a witness to testify to the light, so that all might believe through him. 8 He himself was not the light, but he came to testify to the light. 9 The true light, which enlightens everyone, was coming into the world. 10 He was in the world, and the world came into being through him; yet the world did not know him. 11 He came to what was his own, and his own people did not accept him. 12 But to all who received him, who believed in his name, he gave power to become children of God, 13 who were born, not of blood or of the will of the flesh or of the will of man, but of God. 14 And the Word became flesh and lived among us, and we have seen his glory, the glory as of a father's only son, full of grace and truth. 15 (John testified to him and cried out, "This was he of whom I said, 'He who comes after me ranks ahead of me because he was before me.'") 16 From his fullness we have all received, grace upon grace. 17 The law indeed was given through Moses; grace and truth came through Jesus Christ. 18 No one has ever seen God. It is God the only Son, who is close to the Father's heart, who has made him known.

John 1:1–18
A Latin American Perspective[1]

José Cárdenas Pallares

Context

The Nahua people of Mexico are farmers whose crops include corn, beans, chili peppers, tomatoes, and squash. This apparently humble vocation and accompanying lifestyle notwithstanding, the Nahuas remain the Indian population of central Mexico to whom the great Aztec nation once belonged, prior to the European conquest. The Aztec language is, in fact, known as Nahua.

God is, according to the Nahua people, "the one who is lived for," "the one who is united to all and to whom all are united," and "the one who thinks or invents himself." God is "night and wind," that is to say, invisible and impalpable.[2] God is *Ometeotl*, God twice; God is *Ometecutli-Omecihuatl*, "God and Goddess of duality," or the reason for being of all reality. This understanding of God was shared by the whole of Mexican society.

In pre-Hispanic Mexico, Ometeotl was not some remote and unknown being, the patrimony of a few intellectuals completely divorced from the popular culture . . . rather he was a God invoked by all in such ordinary circumstances as a pregnancy, known from time immemorial and who if he was not worshipped and regarded more, it was only out of respect, since it was too presumptuous for humans to dare become familiar with him, which is contrasted with the honor given to him *through* lower gods, in spite of recognizing that these were not really gods before him, rather human fictions of an imaginative-poetic type cast to fit our smallness.[3]

This god is approached only with "flower and song," that is to say, with poetry, understood in its fullest, deepest sense, as "the hidden and guarded expression, which on the wings of symbolism and metaphor lead a person to babble and to draw from himself that which in some mysterious and sudden way, he has to be able to perceive."[4]

But what now of contemporary Mexico rather than pre-Hispanic Mexico? Presently in my country, which is 70 percent mestizo and 20 percent Indian, the word *Indian* is associated with *stupid, slow,* and *ugly.* One observation suffices to illustrate this harsh reality: in the virtual television monopoly, not one actor, program director, or commercial announcer has Indian traits.

Today the descendants of "the People of the Sun" are a country of people with chronic low self-esteem, high unemployment, and low wages. Today we are taught in many ways that we are trash, in order for us more easily to be treated worse than animals. In such a context, is it not an unaffordable luxury to apply oneself to the study of a text as exquisite as the Johannine[5] Prologue?

Text

The Gospel of John is written for a community that is despised (John 15:18–25), harassed (John 9:22–34), impugned for its faith (John 6:42–52, 7:52, 9:25), and considered to be cursed rabble that ignores Israelite law (John 7:48). Nevertheless, this community is being asked to remain firm and to deepen its faith; it is being told in various ways that it is worthwhile to run all these risks because nothing and nobody can give them what Jesus Christ gives them: light (John 8:12); life (John 11:25); the irresistible and completely free love of God (John 17:23–26); the unique experience and sense of God (John 17:2); complete intimacy with God (John 14:23); and participation in the very divine life (John 17:3).

This community, despised yet enormously blessed, can possess all of this only through Jesus Christ, because only he is the true light (John 1:9), only he is "the one who is present" in the depth (*eis ton kolpon*) of the Father (John 1:18), only Jesus has close and unbreakable intimacy with the Father. Through Jesus Christ, this despised community has access from now on to eternal life (John 5:24). They are those whom he makes children of God in the fullest sense of the word (John 1:12).

Thanks to this completely new reality, they are no longer dwelling in darkness (John 9:39–41); now they are free from the sin of the world (John 1:29), free from the "mother of all slaveries" (John 8:32). They are no longer subject to the conjunction of destruction and deceitfulness (John 8:44), or to hopelessness before death (John 11:33), or to hatred toward all that life brings (John 11:47–53; 12:21–24). These despised believers are, in fact, no longer under any condemning judgment (John 3:18–5:29;12:48) because they are in communion with the bread of eternal life (John 6:31–58) and because they have accepted without any reservation the revelation of God as pure and overflowing love (John 3:16–17).

This totally new life that the Johannine community has experienced is encapsulated by the author of the Gospel in the phrase from John 1:16 "grace instead of grace" (*charis anti charitos*), in other words, by a reference to the loving response to love received. The small but significant Greek word *instead* (*anti*) is to be understood in the sense of a "response to"; *anti*—as in Matthew 5:38, Luke 1:20, and 1 Peter 1:3–9—as a loving *response to* love received."[6] Grace arises in response to grace, love in response to love.

Out of this quality of life, those in the Johannine community are able to perceive Jesus not merely as human or the instrument of the Spirit of God but as the *doxa*—glory—of the only Son of God. "Only he is the steward of the Father, and therefore in the Glory of the Father."[7]

The author of the fourth Gospel (and his community) does not reduce Jesus to pure flesh, *sarx,* which is good for nothing (John 6:63a), which cannot give eternal life (John 3:36; 6:51, 6:33), or the power to be children of God (John 1:12–13), or free love, that is, the gift of the revelation of God (John 1:16), or transformation of death into life (John 5:24–26). Because this flesh has no life in it (John 5:26) and is not the truth (John 14:6), it cannot give the resurrection (John 11:25), or light (John 8:12–14), or the Word of God (John 1:1), or God, the only son (John 1:18), God himself (John 1:1; 20:28). The flesh cannot give salvation "because no one can give what he does not have . . . nor communicate that which he does not possess, nor convert into what he is not. Salvation can only come from the realm of the Spirit of God, not from the sphere of the flesh, of the earthly, of the human. If Jesus were of human origin, he could not give life, salvation . . . He would only be like Moses and the Baptist, who have not seen God (John 6:32–49), who are not the light (John 1:8). His word would not be the inimitable Word of God, the conclusive self-revelation of God."[8]

On the basis of these observations, it is possible to say that in the Prologue of the fourth Gospel lies the whole Gospel in a nutshell. In the Prologue is expressed the quintessence of the fourth Gospel because "thanks to the experience of having received grace upon grace, the community of witnesses has been able to see in Jesus the divine fullness as 'Doxa' [glory], and likewise, because of this 'seeing' can affirm that the logos [word] was made flesh."[9]

Therefore, Jesus must be believed in completely, with respect to what he explains of God with his entire existence (John 1:18), because his being is equal to the being of God (John 1:1). Because Jesus Christ is "the Word which comes from the very depths of God, of the sovereign freedom and the love of God, because he is God,"[10] he can give to human beings eternal life (John 20:31). For this reason, it is beneficial to continue growing in faith in him, in spite of the insults and reprisals that come upon believers, since only by faith in him is the divine light reached (John 9:1–41).

Reflection

The Logos [Word] became flesh (John 1:14). The Logos is not changed into flesh, nor is the Logos only a carnal costume; here the flesh, that is, the corruptible, the weak (Isaiah 40:6–7[11]) is not what conceals but what *reveals* the immortal and the truth.

The sentence, "the logos became flesh," in John 1:14 "expresses the unmistakable paradox that the logos who dwelt with God, clothed in the full majesty of the divinity and possessing the fullness of the divine life, entered the sphere of the earthly and human, the material and perishable, by becoming flesh."[12] But the form of humanity the Logos took was neither the most luminous nor the noblest, according to human criteria. The Logos became humanity in Jesus, the one from the town of Nazareth, from "where nothing good can come" (John 1:46), that is, in someone "from the margins of the margin," the least from the least colony of the empire. One like him is today called "brownie" or "greaser" by our distant neighbors. In other words, in becoming human, the divine Logos became brother to all; he did not exclude anyone, since he came to those who were the lowest of the human condition.

Believing in Jesus as the Christ and Son of God, giving witness to him in an alienated and fractured society, is to speak with the entire existence of the saving will of God toward all—taken to the extreme in Jesus' taking the form of a slave and washing his disciples' feet (John 13:1–5[13]). Believing in Jesus means to transmit the experience of fidelity and faithful love, the experience of the illumination and life that only God is capable of giving, to dimensions of life that are as concrete, despised, lowly, and ordinary as Jesus' very own.

The reality of Jesus' nearness to the despised of this world, represented so aptly by the despised Johannine community, is all the more remarkable because the origin of Jesus' being is in the "beginning without beginning," in God, who "dwells in unapproachable light, whom no one has ever seen or can see" (1 Timothy 6:16). The divine Logos, the truthful Word, became flesh in Jesus of Nazareth in order to bring light, truth, and love to a community that was harassed, despised, and ostracized. This Word, in Jesus, took the form of a slave, took the towel of the servant, and washed the feet of those whom he illumined.

If the eternal Word of God has done this, we who have accepted his revelation have no alternative but to draw closer and to unite ourselves with all our strength to as many people as possible, for the task of the Christian is not to fill books that confuse and confute but to give witness to God, who is light, who is life, who is truth, who is pure, who is gracious love, who is the pure word of salvation offered to *all* peoples. Equally important, *if a community as small, weak, and deplored as the Johannine community has led the church to the grateful contemplation of the ultimate reality of Jesus, of his divine origin, of his character as divine Word, should we not now learn from communities that lack backing and resources?* Should we not seek to be illuminated by communities who today, like the Johannine community two millennia ago, are regarded as rabble and marginal to the allegedly powerful and successful communities of faith?

The Prologue to John's Gospel has compelling meaning in nations characterized by hypocritical and rancid racism, by corruption and by economic injustice. Its words ought not to be considered the focus of socially irresponsible reflection but rather a strong stimulus in the struggle for a world where light and life reign.

Notes

1. Translation by Edgardo Colón-Emeric.

2. C. Siller, *Flor y Canto del Tepeyac* (Servir, 1981) 31n. 3.

3. J. L. Guerrerim, *Flor y Canto del Nacimiento de México* (Librerí Parroquial, 1990) 240.

4. M. León-Portilla, *La Filosofia Nàhuatl estudiada en sus fuentes* (UNAM, 1974) 144.

5. The word "*Johannine*," an adjective based upon the Greek name John, describes elements related to the fourth Gospel, such as the "Johannine community," that is, the community in which the Gospel was written. The Johannine Prologue is the Prologue to the fourth Gospel [editors].

6. J. Mateos, *El Evangelio de Juan* (Christianidad, 1979) 47.

7. X. Lèon Dufour, *Lecture de l'evangile selon Jean* (Sevil, 1988) 1.120.

8. L. Schenke, "Das Johanneische Schisma und die 'Zwölf'," *New Testament Studies* 38 (1992) 116.

9. H. Weder, "Der Mythos vom Logos (Johannes I)," in *Einblicke ins Evangelium: exegetische Beiträge zur neutestamentlichen Hermeneutik: gesammelte Aufsätze aus den Jahren 1980–1991* (Vandenhoeck & Ruprecht, 1992) 415. J. Blank (*Das Evangelium nach Johannes*, 3 vols. [Düsseldorf: Patmos, 1990] 1a.96) writes, "With this phrase the event to which all other events are subordinate is named; the reality in which the divorce 'in the beginning' is united with a being from here, earthly-historical, in a concrete human named Jesus. This Word, 'became' [John 1:14, "became flesh"], has to be taken against all theological speculation—literally. That the eternal 'Word of God' is given in such a way, that it becomes identical with a particular man, this is the peak of the revelation of God in history; the 'paradox of paradoxes,' as the church fathers said. The 'incarnation,' the realization of the Word of God in the flesh is the central secret of the faith and the miracle of antonomasia [the changing of names], and as such cannot be adequately captured in any formula."

10. Blank, *Evangelium,* 1a.102.

11. "A voice says, 'Cry out!' And I said, 'What shall I cry?' All people are grass, their constancy is like the flower of the field. 7 The grass withers, the flower fades, when the breath of the Lord blows upon it; surely the people are grass."

12. R. Schnackenburg, *The Gospel According to St. John* (Burns and Dates, 1968) 1.266.

13. "Now before the festival of the Passover, Jesus knew that his hour had come to depart from this world and go to the Father. Having loved his own who were in the world, he loved them to the end. 2 The devil had already put it into the heart of Judas son of Simon Iscariot to betray him. And during supper 3 Jesus, knowing that the Father had given all things into his hands, and that he had come from God and was going to God, 4 got up from the table, took off his outer robe, and tied a towel around himself. 5 Then he poured water into a basin and began to wash the disciples' feet and to wipe them with the towel that was tied around him."

John 1:1–18

An African Perspective

Hannah W. Kinoti

Context

In both serious and lighthearted conversation, the Gikuyu people of Central Kenya often repeat the phrases "Cege said . . ." or "As Cege prophesied . . ." Cege was a renowned prophet/seer who "saw" and made pronouncements about many matters that have come to be true. Cege's fame among the Gikuyu is not so much because of his being a seer, however, because there were seers before him and there continue to be seers after him. His fame is due to the timing of his life and times in the corporate life of the Gikuyu people. According to the Gikuyu system of reckoning of an individual's age, Cege belonged to the age-set that was given the name Njihia (malefactors), those initiated into adulthood in 1887. This age-set was so named because the newly initiated warriors deviated from prescribed morality and were rude and disrespectful to elders and matrons. In Gikuyu idiom, they "met elders with their broad chests." But literally they were so full of conceit that they did not give way to elders when they met them on the path but hit whomever they met with their broad chests, and it was left to the old man or woman to step aside.

But Cege was different—even unique. His parentage remained a mystery even though he was known as Cege wa Kibiru (son of Kibiru) or Mugo wa Kibiru (seer son of Kibiru). The story goes that a hunter called Kibiru broke away from other hunters to go and check whether his old traps had caught anything. He found a boy sitting at the foot of a tree near one of his traps. Wondering what a small boy could be doing in the forest alone, Kibiru asked the boy his name and his father's name. The boy responded that he was Cege and his father was God. Then he invited the boy to accompany him, and the boy complied.

After the day's hunt, Kibiru took the boy home and performed the ceremony of adoption, known as *guciaruo na mburi* (to cause to be born by means of a goat or sheep). Such a ceremony traditionally facilitates complete and unreserved incorporation of the person thus born into the clan of his or her adoption. Cege, henceforth son of Kibiru, would go to graze livestock with other boys of the extended family but would wander off from the group and spend hours away from them. When he returned, they would ask him where he had been, and he would reply that he had been in God's place. People began to take note of young Cege as a special person sent by God to the community—a *mugo*. *Mugo* is a comprehensive term given to persons endowed with special gifts, such as healing and prophecy. These gifts are believed to be given by God to certain people for the service and well-being of the community. Cege, for instance, is reputed to have warned individuals against certain courses of action; if the individual did not heed the warning, he or she suffered the consequence. People learned to take his warnings seriously.

The main reason Cege is remembered today is that he prophesied about the coming of the "white" strangers and the many changes that would accompany the encounter of Gikuyu's life and the strangers' ways. It so happens that the Gikuyu experience of colonialism, and the so-called civilizing effect of the white colonial power in Kenya, had such deep-rooted ramifications for good and bad that the Gikuyu remember that Cege warned them. Cege or no Cege, the Gikuyu share the general African belief that words are potent, especially words spoken by special categories of people who are in close touch with the supernatural.

Text

The theme of John's Prologue is the Word (Logos), preexistent, creator, incarnate, rejected by some, yet the only one who reveals God and gives those who believe in God the right to become children of God.

John's Gospel was written in Greek in a manner to appeal both to Jews and Gentiles (Greeks). For the Jews, the words "In the beginning was the Word . . ." (John 1:1–2) echo Genesis 1:1, "In the beginning when God created the heavens and the earth . . ."—the first words in the Old Testament, suggesting an equation of the Word (Logos) with God. These words further recall the hymn of Wisdom (Proverbs 8:22–30),[1] which depicts creation in a manner different from Genesis 1, in relation to the figure of Wisdom. For the Greeks, on the other hand, the words "In the beginning was the Word . . ." would mean "at the root of the universe," in accordance with the Greek concept of Principle. No less than two meanings are, therefore, attached to this statement: (1) The Lord's Word by which the universe was made (and which came to the prophets); and (2) the Principle which is the ground and bond of all that exists in the universe.[2]

"In him was life . . . light of men" (John 1:4) alludes to the life-giving power of the Word, which further endows human beings with spiritual sight to recognize God, the giver of life (see Genesis 1:3; Psalm 36:9). The Word is the revealer of God and, though light and darkness are antagonists, darkness has not overcome light (John 1:5). John 1:9 makes this more explicit, and John 1:14 announces in no uncertain terms that the incarnate Word, the divine revelation, is the Son of God. The incarnation is a past event ("became flesh"), but the light still shines in the Christ, who is alive eternally and to whom the community of believers bears witness (1 John 1:1; 2:8). The antagonism between light and darkness is given expression in the rejection of Christ by the Jews, but finally victory belongs to him who declares, "I am the light of the world" (John 8:12) and "I have overcome the world" (John 16:33).

In a parenthesis within this Prologue to John's Gospel (John 1:6–8), John is presented as the one sent to bear witness to the light so that all may believe through him, the witness through whom God proved the divine sonship of Jesus (John 1:32–34). The main thought is resumed after this parenthesis, underscoring that, by its response to the revelation that the light brings, humankind stands under judgment (John 1:9–11). To those who believed Jesus' claims, he gave the right to become children of God. This privilege of family membership is a gift resulting from faith. It is a regeneration or a birth from above (John 1:12–13; 3:3–12).

Reflection

In a bid to encourage Hebrew Christians facing opposition for their new faith in Jesus Christ, the author of the New Testament letter to the Hebrews (1:1) declares:

> In the past, God spoke to our ancestors many times and in many ways through the prophets, but in these last days he has spoken to us through his Son . . .

Today these words of the writer to the Hebrews cannot be repeated often enough. If the words "in the past"—the words of our ancestors—were not very much with us, the account about Cege wa Kibiru would have been irrelevant. There are many challenges facing Christians in Africa, a continent where Christianity is expanding at a very high rate. One of them is the task of discerning which of the words they hear are from God through Jesus Christ, which are from the white missionary—who was and continues to be an agent of Western culture, colonialism, and new world order—and which emanate from contemporary forms of African prophecy, informed by both the gospel and African religion.

Because oral tradition is strong in African society, and many people are largely dependent on oral communication, the spoken word is respected and taken seriously. The spoken word is potent, but its power and efficacy depend upon its perceived source. In the African tradition, God spoke and continues to speak and to make known God's laws through appointed personalities, including seers, prophets, diviners, and parents. Their words are therefore not empty. A number of sayings in African languages allude to the idea that a word, once fallen, cannot be picked up again (retracted), or a word spoken cannot be unspoken. It does its work for good or for evil: to build up or to pull down, to bless or to curse, to heal or to cause illness, to enhance life or to cause death.

According to the Gikuyu tradition, God is angered when people disregard the laws that God used to communicate through prophets, seers, diviners, and parents. Traditionally the words of these spokespersons have gone forth to build up the community in moral consciousness. People who contravened God's laws faced the threat of damnation through the curse of a parent or the other agents who conveyed God's Word.

It is possible, therefore, to discern a continuity between the Word—the Logos—of John's Gospel and the prophetic words of Cege wa Kibiru, the renowned seer of the Gikuyu people. Just as the word of John 1 brings life to those who believe and damnation to those who refuse to believe, so Cege's words were warnings to his contemporaries about evil deeds, so that those who refused to believe him suffered the consequences of their disbelief. Cege was, like other prophets, an agent of God. Even if we acknowledge that Christ is more than a prophetic agent of God, that Christ is actually God among us, there still exists this level of continuity between the true Logos and the true word of Cege, the Gikuyu prophet.

God's laws, then, have not changed just because the African society has been thrust into the modern era. Isaiah confirms to his people that "the word of our God endures forever" (Isaiah 40:8). Part of the reason that the gospel of Jesus Christ has been received readily in Africa is that it confirms so many of the values underlined by traditional religions of the African peoples. Paramount to the African peoples was the importance of life and the need to sustain it. The traditional African prophet often was simultaneously a seer, a diviner, a counselor, a healer, a witch-hunter, and a judge. All these were roles and functions for the purpose of enhancing the life of the community, both communal and individual. John's Prologue declares that in Christ was life. Christ is the giver and sustainer of life. In beholding Christ we behold God, from whom all life proceeds.

The first chapters of Genesis and the Gospel of John, as we observed, speak in unison about the division of light and darkness. In Africa, the witch-hunting process, prior to and after the coming of the Christian message, has been one way of combating the powers of darkness and death — powers that have done much to undermine the vitality of life. Witch-hunters or witch-bursters, as they may be called, expose the darkness of evil activities in African society. The witches are workers of evil, of antisocial attitudes or antilife activities, whose evil is exposed by the prophet or diviner, whose word is light. To fight evil, the community has had to cooperate with the diviner or prophet. Therefore, figures such as Cege have played a pivotal role in the African quest for vitality of life.

The message of Christ, the conqueror of darkness, in whatever form darkness manifests itself, continues to possess enormous potential for Africa. Whether the potency of the world has traditionally been believed to be for light and goodness (as in blessings and prophetic truth) or for darkness and evil (as in curses and witchcraft), the liberating message of the gospel is relevant. Therefore, Christ needs to be preached as the one who is truly able to free people from destructive beliefs — what some have called superstitions. Such a word must not, however, be understood in opposition to all that has been said by Africa's prophetic ancestors. Cege, for example, spoke words of truth and light which, because they lay in continuity with the truth of the Logos, prepared the Gikuyu people for what was about to overtake them. Cege brought light because his words mirrored the light of the Logos. Cege enhanced life because his sight reflected the divine life of the Logos. As the Word Incarnate claims, "I have come that they may have life, and have it to the full" (John 10:10).

Notes

1. "The LORD created me at the beginning of his work, the first of his acts of long ago. 23 Ages ago I was set up, at the first, before the beginning of the earth. 24 When there were no depths I was brought forth, when there were no springs abounding with water. 25 Before the mountains had been shaped, before the hills, I was brought forth — 26 when he had not yet made earth and fields, or the world's first bits of soil. 27 When he established the heavens, I was there, when he drew a circle on the face of the deep, 28 when he made firm the skies above, when he

established the fountains of the deep, 29 when he assigned to the sea its limit, so that the waters might not transgress his command, when he marked out the foundations of the earth, 30 then I was beside him, like a master worker; and I was daily his delight, rejoicing before him always . . ."

2. John 1:3 declares both the universality of the creative energy of the Word, while potentially countering a form of teaching according to which matter is essentially evil and God used intermediaries to create it (see Colossians 1:16–20; Hebrews 1:2; Revelation 4:11).

John 1:1–18

An Asian Perspective

George M. Soares-Prabhu

Context

Religious pluralism is a conspicuous feature of India. All the major world religions flourish here, alongside other religious expressions, such as the cosmic religions of India's aboriginal peoples, exiled religions like Zoroastrianism and Tibetan Lamaism, which, forcibly expelled from their own land, have found shelter in India, and an impressive array of new cults offering instant salvation to the disillusioned addicts of consumerism, which are now mushrooming all over the country. The dominant "religion" in this lively spiritual bazaar is unquestionably Hinduism, which owns the allegiance of 83 percent of India's 900 million people, and which, because it is as much a culture like Hellenism[1] as it is a religion like Judaism,[2] has influenced every facet of Indian life.

Hinduism is an ancient, sprawling, incredibly diverse system of beliefs, rituals, and regulations, whose enduring unity in diversity matches the unity in diversity of India itself. What holds this amazingly complex system together is its tenacious social structure (the caste system) and its distinctive way of experiencing reality, which I call, somewhat loosely, *the Indian mind*.[3] This way of experiencing things is cosmocentric (centered upon the cosmos), and not (like Western thinking) anthropocentric (centered upon the human being); for the cosmos and not just humankind is the horizon of every Indian experience. So where an anthropocentric Christianity speaks of redeemed humanity as God's family (Mark 3:31–35; Matthew 23:8–10), cosmocentric Hinduism, in its root metaphor, describes the world—the cosmos—as the body of God.[4]

This root metaphor expresses well the perspective of the Indian mind.

Because it is aware of the world as the body of God, the Indian mind is particularly sensitive to the symbolic character of reality. All sensible reality is perceived as a manifestation (the body) of the Absolute (*Brahman*). As such, it is pervaded by "the Lord," as the body is pervaded by the soul. But because it is only a manifestation and not the Absolute itself, the world that we see or the self that we are immediately conscious of is not the "really real" but is only a pointer to it. We need, therefore, continually to "recenter" ourselves, so as to get beyond our normal identification of ourselves with surface levels of reality, and find our center in the true self, which is one with the Absolute.[5]

This understanding of reality is neatly encapsulated in the opening verse of a popular Hindu religious text, the *Isayasya Upanishad,* a verse that Mahatma Gandhi once described as "containing the whole essence of Hinduism."[6] It reads

> *All this, whatever moves in this moving world,*
> *is pervaded by the Lord;*
> *By renouncing it, enjoy it. Do not covet the wealth*
> *of anyone at all.*
>
> (Isha Up 1.1).

Because the true reality of the world does not lie in its outward appearances but in the Lord who pervades it, we can truly enjoy the world only if we renounce it, that is, if we refuse to be caught up in clinging attachments that stop us at the surface appearance of things and prevent us from reaching the reality of "the Lord," which pervades them. We can enjoy the world only if we do not cling to it. The text of the *Upanishad* thus provides a powerful *mantra* against the moral illness of consumerism, which plagues the world today. The Prologue to John, read in the light of this expression of the Indian mind, does the same in a complementary way.

Text

An Indian reader of the Prologue to John's Gospel, reading it as it now stands, without attempting to unearth some purported "original hymn" underlying it,[7] will understand it as a narrative that tells the story of the "Word." The Word (*ho logos*), we are told, was "in the beginning" (from all eternity) with God, and "was what God was" (John 1:1–2).[8] It was instrumental in the creation of "all things" (1:3) and continued to be a vital principle communicating spiritual life and light to every human person, in the darkness of a world where the ultimate meaning of life ("light") is always obscure (1:4–5). To achieve its work of illumination, consistently blocked by the obstinately resistant "darkness" of spiritual ignorance (1:10–11), the Word became a human person and lived among humankind, sharing the fullness of God's love and revealing the reality of the unseeable God to all those who put their trust in God (1:14–18).

Read in this way, the Prologue to John climaxes in the dramatic declaration that the "Word became flesh and dwelt amongst us." Something of the startling paradox that this implies is suggested by the hauntingly beautiful oracle of Isaiah, in which the fragile impermanence of the human condition (flesh) is sharply contrasted with the rocklike solidity of the Word of God:

> *All flesh is like grass, and its beauty is like the flower of the field.*
> *The grass withers, the flower fades, when the breath of Yhwh*
>   *blows upon it;*
> *The grass withers, the flower fades; but the word of our God*
>   *will stand forever.*
>
> (Isaiah 40:6–8)

Isaiah thus contrasts enduring Word and fleeting flesh; the Prologue to John brings them together. But the Prologue ridges an opposition much greater than that described in Isaiah. For both "*Word*" and "*flesh*" mean much more in the Prologue than they do in Isaiah's oracle. The "Word" of the Prologue is not just the "Word of God" (God's message of judgment and grace articulated by the prophet); it is the primal divine reality, the knowability of God, that grounds this and all other words. "Flesh" in the Prologue signifies not only the powerlessness and impermanence of human existence, as it does in Isaiah; it also stands (as elsewhere in the Hebrew Bible) for the solidarity that binds people together into the intimacy of marriage (Genesis 2:23), the oneness of a family (Genesis 37:27), the unity of humankind (Isaiah 58:7), indeed into the totality of all life (Genesis 6:17).[9]

The story of the Prologue describes, therefore, the progressive involvement of the utterly transcendent God in the messy contingency of all human and cosmic history. The Word (God, inasmuch as God is knowable) is involved in the creation of the universe ("all things came into being through him"), illumines all human history ("the light was the life of all people"), and finally takes flesh in a particular human person ("was made flesh and lived among us"). This progressive involvement of the Word implies an increasingly narrowing focus of the divine presence in the world, which, however, never loses its universal significance. For the Word becomes not just "a person" (*anthropos*), much less "a male" (*aner*), but it becomes "flesh" (*sarx*), that is, it manifests itself in the human nature that Jesus shares with all humankind. "He took upon himself the nature of all flesh," says Hilary of Poitiers, and having in this way become "the true vine, he holds within himself the racial strain of every branch."[10] Or, in the words of Athanasius, the Word has "graced the human race."[11]

Reflection

The Prologue to John thus both echoes the "prologue" to the *Isayasya Up-anishad* and takes us beyond it. John too implies that the world, all that lives and moves, is pervaded by the Lord. The Word (*ho logos*) pervades the whole of creation and all human history because all things were made through the Word (John 1:3) and every human being enlightened by it (John 1:9). The Word is a mysterious divine being that is never clearly identified by John, but that would have reminded a contemporary Jew of the person-ified Wisdom of post-exilic Judaism,[12] and might suggest to an Indian reader today *vac* (the primal creative "*speech*" or "*word* " of Vedic litera-ture) or the *sabdabrahman* (the supreme word-principle of the Sanskrit grammarians).[13] But when the Prologue goes on to affirm that the Word be-came flesh and lived among us (John 1:14), it reveals a dimension of God's presence in the world which goes beyond what Hinduism has conceived.

Even the *avatara* doctrine of Hinduism, according to which God in moments of religious crises comes down into the world in the form of a living being (animal or human) in order to restore the cosmic order,[14] does not carry the implications that the incarnation of the Word does. In the *avatara,* God is manifested in an individual being (a Rama or a Krishna) who brings salvation by destroying evil order and restoring the good. The coming down of the God does not affect other human beings intrinsically. But when the Word becomes "flesh," the whole human race is graced. For "flesh," we have seen, implies the interconnectedness of all human be-ings in the oneness of humankind (*ha adam*),[15] which has been created not as a collection of isolated individuals but as an organic whole (Genesis 1:26–28).[16] What happens to one affects all (Romans 5:12–14).[17]

There is a double consequence to this. If the Word has become flesh, ac-cess to the Word (to God as knowable) is through the "flesh." This means, on the one hand, that it is only in the concrete human life of Jesus lived out in radical self-giving and obedience (and not through philosophical spec-ulation, Greek or Indian) that we discover who God really is. Our God is not the God of the philosophers, nor even the God of Abraham, Isaac, and Jacob, but the "Father of our Lord Jesus Christ," who becomes visible to us in the concrete features of the Son (John 14:9).[18] God's self-revelation (the Word) is mediated through the human life (flesh) of Jesus.

But the incarnation also means that our response to this revelation of God is mediated through humankind. The "flesh" that the Word takes up is not just the individual body of Jesus, but the humanity of Jesus, which is part of the human face. The whole of humankind is graced by the "enfleshment" of the Word. Humankind thus becomes the locus of our encounter with God. The specifically Christian way to God is, therefore, not the way of introspection into the nature of the self (the *jnana marga,* or the way of insight of Vedantic Hinduism), not the way of blameless ethical conduct or of the meticulous observance of traditional rituals (what in Hinduism is called the *karma marga,* or the way of "*works*"), not even the way of reverent attachment to Jesus as God-made-human (popular Hinduism's *bhakti marga,* or the way of devotion to a deity). The Christian way, as John will repeatedly insist in his Gospel, is the way of love (*agape*). It is by loving, that is, "doing good" to one another (John 13:33–34; 15:12), that we respond appropriately to God's love for us (1 John 4:7–12). For in becoming flesh, the Word has identified itself with each one of us.

Over against the growing selfishness, the insatiable greed, the savage competitiveness, the aggressive violence of a world that has taken mammon as its god, consumerism as its religion, and the cutthroat competition of the "free" market as its ethical norm, the *Isayasya Upanishad* exhibits an attitude of great reverence for the world. The world is pervaded by the Lord. It is a symbol of the Absolute to be contemplated and enjoyed and not to be compulsively pursued and possessed. The *Upanishad* warns us against our destructive abuse of a world that is the body of God. To this the Prologue to John, which also hints at this symbolic dimension of the world, adds something new. It points to the sanctification of the "flesh" (that is, of all humankind) through the incarnation of the Word, and so warns us that in exploiting humankind (the poor, the powerless, the outcast, the rejected), we are doing harm to the "family of God," the "flesh" of the Word.

Notes

1. Hellenism was the dominant cultural ethos, rather than a religion, of the Greco-Roman era, a period in history formative for Judaism and the period in which Christianity arose [editors].

2. R. C. Zaehner, *Hinduism* (London: Oxford University, 1962) 1.

3. What I have called the "Indian mind" is the mentality of the "great tradition" of classical Hinduism. This is not the only cultural tradition in India, which is culturally very diverse, but it is the dominant tradition and has to a greater or lesser

extent influenced all the others. One can, therefore, with some caution, speak of
the "Indian mind" as representing that which is specific to India.

4. This idea is expressed explicitly in the Upanishadic teaching of the "inner
controller," which abides in all things (*Brhadaranyaka Upanishad* III.vii. 3–23);
in the *Bhagavad-Gita*'s description of Krishna encompassing the whole universe
in his body (XI.13); and in the doctrine of the "self" (*atman*) as the "subtle
essence" of the universe (*Chandogya Upanishad* VI.viii.7-xvi.3).

5. M. Amaladoss, "An Indian Reads St. John's Gospel," in *India's Search for
Reality and the Relevance of the Gospel of John*. Edited by C. Duraisingh and
C. Hargreaves (Delhi: ISPCK, 1976) 7–24 [especially 12].

6. M. K. Gandhi, *Hindu Dharma*. Edited by B. Kumarappa (Ahmedabad:
Navjivan, 1950) 41.

7. R. Brown, in *The Gospel According to John (i-xii)* (The Anchor Bible; New
York: Doubleday, 1966) 22, gives a table of various reconstructions of the original hymn by various contemporary scholars. No two of them seem to agree on its
shape or its provenance!

8. This expression from the New English Bible catches the meaning of John
1:1c, with its anarthous (i.e., without the definite article) use of *theos* better, I believe, than the traditional "the Word was God" (which would require the article *ho
theos*) or the freer translation, "the Word was divine" (which would require
theios).

9. See G. Soares-Prabhu, "The Sacred in the Secular: Reflections on a Johannine Sutra, 'The Word was made flesh and dwelt among us' (John 1:14)," *Jeevadhara* XVII/98 (1987) 125–40.

10. Hilary of Poitiers, *On Psalm 51*, n. 16, in W. A. Jurgens, *The Faith of the
Early Fathers, Volume I* (Collegeville: Liturgical Press, 1970) no. 886a.

11. Athanasius, *Discourse against the Arians 2.27* in Jurgens, *The Faith of the
Early Fathers*, no. 762.

12. For a convenient exposition of the parallels between the Prologue and a
wisdom myth referred to in the Hebrew Bible (Prov. 8:22–30), the Old Testament
Apocrypha (Wisdom 7:22–30; 9:1–10; Sirach 24:1–12; Baruch 3:37; 4:1), and the
Pseudepigrapha (1 Enoch 42:2), see E. Haenchen, *John: a commentary on the
Gospel of John* (Hermeneia; Philadelphia: Fortress, 1984) 125–26; and C. H. Tal-
bert, *Reading John: A Literary and Theological Commentary on the Fourth
Gospel and the Johannine Epistles* (New York: Crossroad, 1992) 68–70.

13. On *vac* as "the total living Word, that is, the Word in her entirety, including her material aspects, her cosmic reverberations, her visible form, her sound,
her meaning, her message," see R. Panikkar, *The Vedic Experience: Mantraman-
jari* (London: Darton, Longman & Todd, 1977) 88–112 [especially 89]. For a sophisticated identification of the word with Brahman as the *sabdabrahman* ("the
Brahman who is without beginning or end, whose very essence is the word"—
Bhartrhari, *Yakyapadiya* 1.1), see the theory of the grammarians expounded in H.
Coward, *The Sphota Theory of Language* (Delhi: Banarsida, 1980) 9–13.

14. The classical formulation of the *avatara* doctrine is found in the *Bhagavad-Gita* IV.7–8: "Wherever the law of righteousness (*dharma*) withers away and lawlessness arises, then do I create myself [on earth]. For the protection of the good, for the destruction of evil and for the setting up of righteousness, I come into being age after age." Translated by R. C. Zaehner, *The Bhagavad-Gita* (London: Oxford University, 1969) 184. For a brief account of the *avatara* doctrine in popular Hindu belief, see J. Dowson, *A Classical Dictionary of Hindu Mythology and Religion, Geography, History and Literature* (London: Kegan Paul, 1928) 33–38; for a discussion of the differences between *avatara* and incarnation, see G. Parrinder, *Avatar and Incarnation* (London: 1970), and, with greater theological precision, Francis X. D'Sa, "Christian Incarnation and Hindu Avatara," *Concilium* (1993, part 2) 77–85.

15. *Adam* represents the Hebrew word that can be translated in a variety of ways, including *"Adam," human, humankind, man.*

16. "Then God said, 'Let us make humankind in our image, according to our likeness; and let them have dominion over the fish of the sea, and over the birds of the air, and over the cattle, and over all the wild animals of the earth, and over every creeping thing that creeps upon the earth.' 27 So God created humankind in his image, in the image of God he created them; male and female he created them. 28 God blessed them, and God said to them, 'Be fruitful and multiply, and fill the earth and subdue it; and have dominion over the fish of the sea and over the birds of the air and over every living thing that moves upon the earth.' "

17. "Therefore, just as sin came into the world through one man, and death came through sin, and so death spread to all because all have sinned—13 sin was indeed in the world before the law, but sin is not reckoned when there is no law. 14 Yet death exercised dominion from Adam to Moses, even over those whose sins were not like the transgression of Adam, who is a type of the one who was to come."

18. "Jesus said to him, 'Have I been with you all this time, Philip, and you still do not know me? Whoever has seen me has seen the Father. How can you say, "Show us the Father"?' "

Acts 2:1–42

When the day of Pentecost had come, they were all together in one place. 2 And suddenly from heaven there came a sound like the rush of a violent wind, and it filled the entire house where they were sitting. 3 Divided tongues, as of fire, appeared among them, and a tongue rested on each of them. 4 All of them were filled with the Holy Spirit and began to speak in other languages, as the Spirit gave them ability. 5 Now there were devout Jews from every nation under heaven living in Jerusalem. 6 And at this sound the crowd gathered and was bewildered, because each one heard them speaking in the native language of each. 7 Amazed and astonished, they asked, "Are not all these who are speaking Galileans? 8 And how is it that we hear, each of us, in our own native language? 9 Parthians, Medes, Elamites, and residents of Mesopotamia, Judea and Cappadocia, Pontus and Asia, 10 Phrygia and Pamphylia, Egypt and the parts of Libya belonging to Cyrene, and visitors from Rome, both Jews and proselytes, 11 Cretans and Arabs— in our own languages we hear them speaking about God's deeds of power." 12 All were amazed and perplexed, saying to one another, "What does this mean?" 13 But others sneered and said, "They are filled with new wine." 14 But Peter, standing with the eleven, raised his voice and addressed them, "Men of Judea and all who live in Jerusalem, let this be known to you, and listen to what I say. 15 Indeed, these are not drunk, as you suppose, for it is only nine o'clock in the morning. 16 No, this is what was spoken through the prophet Joel: 17 'In the last days it will be, God declares, that I will pour out my Spirit upon all flesh, and your sons and your daughters shall prophesy, and your young men shall see visions, and your old men shall dream dreams. 18 Even upon my slaves, both men and women, in those days I will pour out my Spirit; and they shall prophesy. 19 And I will show portents in the heaven above and signs on the earth below, blood, and fire, and smoky mist. 20 The sun shall be turned to darkness and the

moon to blood, before the coming of the Lord's great and glorious day.
21 Then everyone who calls on the name of the Lord shall be saved.'
22 "You that are Israelites, listen to what I have to say: Jesus of
Nazareth, a man attested to you by God with deeds of power, wonders,
and signs that God did through him among you, as you yourselves
know—23 this man, handed over to you according to the definite plan
and foreknowledge of God, you crucified and killed by the hands of
those outside the law. 24 But God raised him up, having freed him from
death, because it was impossible for him to be held in its power. 25 For
David says concerning him, 'I saw the Lord always before me, for he
is at my right hand so that I will not be shaken; 26 therefore my heart
was glad, and my tongue rejoiced; moreover my flesh will live in hope.
27 For you will not abandon my soul to Hades, or let your Holy One
experience corruption. 28 You have made known to me the ways of life;
you will make me full of gladness with your presence.' 29 "Fellow Is-
raelites, I may say to you confidently of our ancestor David that he both
died and was buried, and his tomb is with us to this day. 30 Since he
was a prophet, he knew that God had sworn with an oath to him that
he would put one of his descendants on his throne. 31 Foreseeing this,
David spoke of the resurrection of the Messiah, saying, 'He was not
abandoned to Hades, nor did his flesh experience corruption.' 32 This
Jesus God raised up, and of that all of us are witnesses. 33 Being there-
fore exalted at the right hand of God, and having received from the Fa-
ther the promise of the Holy Spirit, he has poured out this that you both
see and hear. 34 For David did not ascend into the heavens, but he him-
self says, 'The Lord said to my Lord, "Sit at my right hand, 35 until I
make your enemies your footstool."' 36 Therefore let the entire house
of Israel know with certainty that God has made him both Lord and
Messiah, this Jesus whom you crucified." 37 Now when they heard this,
they were cut to the heart and said to Peter and to the other apostles,
"Brothers, what should we do?" 38 Peter said to them, "Repent, and
be baptized every one of you in the name of Jesus Christ so that your
sins may be forgiven; and you will receive the gift of the Holy Spirit.
39 For the promise is for you, for your children, and for all who are far
away, everyone whom the Lord our God calls to him." 40 And he tes-
tified with many other arguments and exhorted them, saying, "Save
yourselves from this corrupt generation." 41 So those who welcomed
his message were baptized, and that day about three thousand persons
were added. 42 They devoted themselves to the apostles' teaching and
fellowship, to the breaking of bread and the prayers.

Acts 2:1–42

A Latin American Perspective

José Míguez-Bonino

Context

When José came to take him to "the meeting," Choque wished he had not agreed to go with him. It was only three weeks since he had come from the north to this poor area of the big city. In January, he had crossed from his little town in Bolivia over to Argentina to work at the sugar cane harvest in Salta, then down south to Tucuman and, when the sugar crop was over, he hitchhiked to Buenos Aires to look for work. He had no luck the first two weeks; his stammering speech—half *Quechua,* half Spanish—did not help. Then José, a neighbor who had given him a place in his own room, helped him to find a "*changa*" (a precarious temporary job) at a construction site and invited him to the Pentecostal meetings which he himself was attending. Out of gratitude, Choque finally got up and went.

There were some 200 people crowded in the room they called "*templo*" (sanctuary). They were singing. Then a woman began to tell the story of her conversion—her miserable life before, her listening to the preaching of the Bible, her feeling the call to faith, crying and praying until she felt the Holy Spirit . . . and then everything changed for her. Choque understood very little: he was too far back in the room and was not used to "Buenos Aires" Spanish! The people were accompanying the "testimony" with "Hallelujahs," "Glory to God," "Yes Lord," "Amen," and brief interruptions that he could not make out. But as the woman continued, he began to have a strange feeling, as if everything was changing. His heart was thumping in his chest, he wanted to embrace the people around him, to say something. Suddenly he began to speak—he did not quite know what he was saying, perhaps in Spanish, perhaps in Quechua, sometimes echoing sounds that others were uttering. Suddenly he realized that the "Amen" and the "Hallelujahs" were responding to him . . .

Choque is one of the hundreds of thousands who, in the last twenty or thirty years, are crowding Pentecostal churches all over Latin America. Social scientists, anthropologists, and students of religious movements offer explanations for this phenomenon. They suggest, for example, that in the transition from a traditional, rural, precapitalist society to a modern, urban, capitalist society, Pentecostalism offers a refuge: it helps people to acquire new values and attitudes needed for the new situation; it gives them a sense of self-esteem, a new identity, a set of "symbolic" elements that give meaning to their chaotic existence; and it provides a community and new "norms" to order their lives. Probably all of this is true. What Choque knew, however, was that he was speaking the language of the Spirit, which he and the others could understand and celebrate!

Text

A careful reading of Acts 2 elicits several observations and several questions, on which interpreters differ.[1] First, the observations. Clearly the "they" of Acts 2:1, who heard the sound from heaven and received "the tongues as of fire," were not only the apostles but also the whole number of disciples—the 120 of Acts 1:15.[2] In addition, we are immediately met with two symbols: the first is "the wind" (*pnoe*), which can easily be related to *pneuma,* the spirit which comes "from the sky" (Acts 2:2); and the second is "the fiery tongues" (Acts 2:3), which in the early Jewish book of 1 Enoch (14:8–15;[3] 71:5[4]) "denote the element of divinity but have nothing to do with languages."[5]

Second is the crucial question of the "tongues" (*glossa* in Acts 2:4 and *dialektos* in Acts 2:6, 8. (*Dialektos* is the word used for the vernacular of a given country). Interpreters have wondered whether Luke uses *glossa* to mean those inarticulate ecstatic utterances that have occurred throughout the history of religions, or specific languages indigenous to the various regions mentioned in Acts 2:9–11, for example, Mesopotamia, Judea, Cappadocia, and Libya. In any case, Luke clearly states that the "Galileans" could not by themselves speak these "languages," and that people were able to understand "each in their own language" (Acts 2:7). What is the precedent for these many languages? Two options are most likely. First, in Early Judaism, the feast of "Pentecost" could be associated with the giving of the law on Mount Sinai. Although Luke does not refer to the law as a "type" of Pentecost, it is possible that he knew the Jewish tradition that, when God gave the law on Sinai, God's word was divided into different languages so that all people could hear it.[6] Second, E. Trocmé sees in the episode the reversal of Babel's confusion: at Pentecost the people received a new language (as in rabbinic Jewish interpretations of Exodus 19) in which they could celebrate God,[7] although it must be noted that it is not to "a new language" but "their own languages" (*dialektoi*) that Luke refers.

Another question concerns the list of peoples in Acts 2:9–11. It is possible to interpret this list in various ways, such as nationalities according to the lines of the Zodiac, an arc of nations going from East to West, or representatives from the widest diversity of the earth.[8] In any case, there is little doubt that Luke wants to emphasize the universal reach of God's message.

Reflection

As we see, Luke has left us with unsettled questions. The main point of the passage is for him, however, crystal clear. The events of the life, death, and resurrection of Jesus, the Christ, are now "the center of time." A new history develops as the gospel, on the wings of mission, moves by stages "to the ends of the earth."[9] Pentecost is the starting point of this new history of what the Christ "continued" to do and teach after he had been "taken up."[10] In this "new time," the gospel embraces all places, all times, all nations, all families, and all languages. The "gospel" is for Luke—and for Paul, his hero—the birth of a new universality.

What kind of universality? Luke reports an early debate on this question in Acts 15, which contains the discussion of whether the Gentiles who converted to Christ should be placed "under the burden" of fulfilling all the requirements of the Jewish law. The decision did not quite settle the issue, but the early church accepted in principle an understanding of "the universality of the gospel" as *not* requiring a Gentile (i.e., non-Jewish) Christian to become socially, ritually, and culturally a Jew in order to enter "the new people of God." Different responses to this question have plagued the history of missions up to our day. For instance, Spanish colonizers wanted "to model [the indigenous people] as human beings," which meant using European clothes, sleeping on a bed, and combing their hair! Similarly, English colonizers in Australia took the children to schools in distant places, away from their parents, in order "to raise them up in Christian habits."[11]

Even Choque's experience is not unambiguous. He finds a new language of the Spirit, which is "his own," and still everybody understands.

In this sense, the native Pentecostal movement has made it possible for many poor people to have access to the "universal" gospel of grace, which expresses itself socially, culturally, and symbolically "in their own language." They have become, not simply consumers of a religious product, but, in the power of the Spirit, producers of their own piety. However, the new identity into which some Pentecostals enter leads them to become culturally, socially, and economically incorporated into "the universal market" and thus transformed from a Bolivian Quechua Indian into a "westerner."

The basic problem this essay attempts to address is the relationship between the universal nature of the Christian faith and the particular cultural, ethnic, social, and linguistic identities of different peoples, social classes, races, and genders. Sometimes, it is easy to ignore the reality of these varieties. For instance, classical Greek thought gave universality a philosophical base. There is a universal "reason" that all human beings share in relation to which all "singularities" become accidental and unimportant. Similarly, the liberal tradition defined "human rights" as the freedom, fraternity, and equality of all without distinctions. But neither tradition asked who defines these rights or which model of "human being" is assumed. It would be ungrateful and dangerous to underestimate or scorn this "universalist" heritage; it is a human achievement that we cannot afford to abandon. But we cannot simply accept this "faceless" universality when the faces are many, varied, and when each individual is important. To find a way through this dilemma is of crucial cultural, social, and religious importance.

In relation to this issue, what the "gospel of Pentecost" tells us clearly is that the "universality" of the history of salvation is not the dissolution of specific spaces—ethnic, cultural, linguistic—which are God's own creation and which are constantly being renewed by God's Spirit. Rather, the "universality" of the history of salvation is the negation of spaces closed in themselves and the affirmation of a space open to "the other" as a revelation of the same universal grace.

Notes

1. For an excellent summary and bibliography, see E. Haenchen, *The Acts of the Apostles: A Commentary* (Oxford: Blackwell, 1971; paperback edition, 1985) 166–89.

2. "In those days Peter stood up among the believers (together the crowd numbered about one hundred twenty persons) and said . . ."

3. In his vision, Enoch sees a wall of white marble, "surrounded by tongues of

fire; and it began to frighten me. And I came into the tongues of fire and drew near to a great house which was built of white marble, and the inner wall(s) were like mosaics of white marble . . ." (1 Enoch 14:9–10).

4. Enoch recalls, after being carried off in a vision, that he saw "a structure built of crystals; and between those crystals tongues of living fire."

5. Haenchen, *Acts,* 168n. 2.

6. For a thorough discussion of these Jewish traditions in relation to the Pentecost narrative, see R. P. Menzies, *The Development of Early Christian Pneumatology with special reference to Luke-Acts* (JSNTS 54; Sheffield: JSOT, 1991) 229–44.

7. E. Trocmé, *Le "Livre des Actes" et l'histoire* (Paris: Presses Universitaires de France, 1957) 202–06.

8. It is also possible that later scribes who copied the book of Acts introduced modifications into the list.

9. Acts 1:8 reads, "But you will receive power when the Holy Spirit has come upon you; and you will be my witnesses in Jerusalem, in all Judea and Samaria, and to the ends of the earth."

10. Acts 1:1–4 reads, "In the first book, Theophilus, I wrote about all that Jesus did and taught from the beginning 2 until the day when he was taken up to heaven, after giving instructions through the Holy Spirit to the apostles whom he had chosen. 3 After his suffering he presented himself alive to them by many convincing proofs, appearing to them during forty days and speaking about the kingdom of God. 4 While staying with them, he ordered them not to leave Jerusalem, but to wait there for the promise of the Father. 'This,' he said, 'is what you have heard from me' . . ."

11. These quotations are not literal but rather typical expressions used by early theologians at the time of the conquest, such as Juan de Zumarraga, OFM, and Jose de Acosta, SJ, in the context of debates concerning how to "christianize" the Indians. A reliable account of the debate is found in H. J. Prien, *Die Geschichtes des Christentums in Lateinamerika* (Göttingen, Vandenhoeck, and Ruprecht, 1978) 211–15.

Acts 2:1–42
An African Perspective

Patrice M. Siyemeto

Context

Zambia adopted plural politics in 1991; since then, political leaders in the ruling party have been preaching about democracy. The same leadership declared Zambia a Christian country. Despite these two foundations, Zambian society seems to be standing on a shaky foundation. The actions of the rulers and their utterances only pay lip service to democracy and Christian principles. Dissenting voices are not tolerated. Alleged political enemies are harassed.

The first quarter of 1996 for Zambian society has been characterized by many political and economic woes, as well as general chaos. There have been many demonstrations organized by opposition parties, NGOs (Nongovernmental Organizations), students, and government workers who are voicing their disagreement and protest against government decisions and its manipulation of the press. In the region in which I live, the country has seen editors of an independent newspaper sentenced to jail by the speaker of the National Assembly, civil servants going on countrywide strikes, students demonstrating to press the government for more meal allowances, and members of parliament walking out of parliament as a protest over the government's intentions to reintroduce the Public Order Act, which regulates public meetings. In all of these situations, there are diverse and varied voices, disagreements, a lack of common understanding, and general confusion.

Various interest groups have formed an organization called the Civil Society and are busy organizing themselves in order to add their voices to the already conflicting voices. Added to this list of interest groups is the existence of more than thirty-four political parties. If one looks at the banners put up by the demonstrators, one will not fail to see that different messages are being put across. Those in power continue to justify their decisions and actions by claiming that the opposition lacks knowledge and is ungrateful and power-hungry, interested only in wrestling power away from them. All such attempts to communicate lead to confusion, further alienation, and chaos. As in the Tower of Babel story (Genesis 11:1–9), no one understands the other.

The Zambian community is at a crossroad. There is the way of democracy, in which everyone participates and is valued and heard. There is also the way of dictatorship, manipulation, with the hero worship of leaders. Only God can intervene as at the time of the Tower of Babel and at Pentecost. God is a God of surprises; from time to time in human history, God has intervened and done the unexpected.

Text

In attempting to interpret the Pentecost event in Acts 2, one would do well to heed W. H. Willimon's warning that no single formulation can do justice to the story. More than one interpretation can be offered for what happened at Pentecost.[1] This is especially true of Acts 2, which is a pivotal text because it is the whole story of Acts *in nuce,* even as Luke 4:16–31 functions in the Gospel of Luke. Three aspects of this text are particularly relevant for our purposes. First is the Pentecost event itself (Acts 2:1–13). Second is the Pentecost sermon by Peter (Acts 2:14–40). Third is the summary of the new community brought about by the Pentecost gift (Acts 2:41–47).

Before turning to these three aspects of the narrative, it is important to understand the background of Pentecost and the association Luke made between that background and the gift of the Spirit. Pentecost means '*fiftieth*' because the festival was held fifty days after another festival, Passover. The feast had two meanings:

> Pentecost was a harvest (agricultural) festival, known also as the Feast of Weeks because it took place seven weeks after Passover;

> Pentecost was also observed as the anniversary of the giving of the law at Mount Sinai—a development perhaps of the so-called inter-testamental period.[2]

In Acts 2, Pentecost is associated with the outpouring of the Holy Spirit (Acts 2:17–21). We can see a parallel between the double symbolism of Pentecost—the giving of the Spirit in Jerusalem and the giving of the law at Mount Sinai—and Yahweh's two promises of the New Covenant to ancient Israel:

"I will put my Spirit in you" (Ezekiel 36:27);

"I will put my law in their minds and write it on their hearts" (Jeremiah 31:33).

The event itself. Luke records that "they were all together in one place" (Acts 2:1). Whatever the place was, whether in the upper room, John Mark's home, or one of the temple premises, the Christians were in one place, and they were all together. This implies that they were united, of one purpose, waiting for the promises of God. It also signals their readiness and preparedness.

To describe the Christians' deep experience with God, Luke uses three phenomena: wind, fire, and tongues (Acts 2:2–3). Is Luke like the Old Testament writers who deliberately used natural elements, such as wind, fire, and tongues, to explain the supernatural and the divine? Or are these actually what he saw and heard, that is, God's using these as supernatural signs accompanying the gift of the Spirit? Wind, fire, and voices were associated with Mount Sinai (God's presence and manifestations), according to Exodus 19.[3] Luke makes it clear that these were supernatural signs, for he observes that the noise was not wind itself but sounded like it; the sight was not fire but resembled it; and the speech was in languages that were not ordinary but in some way "other" (Acts 2:1–4).

Luke seems to emphasize the nature of the audience, which actually reflects the political and cultural situation of their time. It was a diverse audience, consisting of both Jews and Gentiles. Luke records that they "came from every country of the world" (Acts 2:5). Of course, at that time he was referring to the Greco-Roman world situated around the Mediterranean basin. Five groups can be identified:

Parthians, Medes, Elamites, and residents of Mesopotamia (v 9a). These came from the Caspian Sea westwards;

People from five areas in what is called Asia Minor or Turkey, namely, Cappadocia, Pontus, Asia, Phrygia, and Pamphylia;

People from North Africa, Egypt, and parts of Libya near Cyrene;

Visitors from Rome across the Mediterranean; Cretans and Arabs;

People from Judea, where Jerusalem was situated.

It is obvious, then, that it was an international and multilingual audience.

The speakers were mainly uncultured Galileans (Acts 2:7). Neverthe-less, they were enabled by God's Spirit to communicate in such a way that they could be understood (2:8, 11). Pentecost restores communication and breaks down barriers that separate and alienate people. Time and space cannot allow us to discuss the nature of speaking with tongues (*glosso-lalia*). The kernel of the matter is that they were able to communicate to others what the Galileans felt was God's will. It was an event that enabled them to share. Each one heard and understood (Acts 2:6, 8, 11).

Peter's sermon. In the midst of the miraculous, wonder, and astonish-ment, Peter gives an explanation (Acts 2:14–40). He attributes all that has happened to God. All is a fulfillment of what God had purposed to do, as foretold by Joel the prophet (2:16–21). Then Peter draws the attention of his audience to the person and claims of Jesus, linking Pentecost to Jesus. Jesus' coming was the inauguration of the Messianic age, and its final proof was the outpouring of the Spirit. Peter therefore sees the life and ministry of Christ (Acts 2:22), his death (2:23), and his resurrection (2:24–32) as all being part of God's package of salvation, which includes the gift of the Spirit (2:33). This gives us the impression that the Holy Spirit is actually God; the faith community has not just received something extra but has ac-tually experienced God. God is active in their midst. God has intervened and brought the people together. We see a God who creates, unites, and brings a screen community into being.

The new community. Luke emphasizes that people respond to God's in-tervention (Acts 2:41–42). A new community is born at Pentecost. It is a community with new values and attitudes. It is a learning community, a sharing community, and a worshiping community. It becomes also a ser-vant community.

This is a story, therefore, of a people who were diverse in their culture, language, and experiences, but who, through the intervention of God, were made into a community in which people understood each other and shared their lives together.

Reflection

Can a country like Zambia, with its many ills—social, economic, and po-litical turmoil, disease, hunger, alienation, and poverty—become a healed community? From Peter's sermon, we learn that the promise of the Spirit applies not only to the people of Peter's time but even to those "who are far off, as many as the Lord our God shall call to himself" (Acts 2:39). Be-yond the chaos, misunderstanding, and hatred manifested in the political arena, for example, there is still hope for peace, stability, and reconciliation. What this country needs is an encounter with the life-giving wind. Like the wind of creation in Genesis 1[4] that swept across dark waters, the wind once again can sweep across our dark country in order to bring life, unity, and genuine democracy.

One of the major issues of difference between the government and a large section of the country concerns the mode of adopting the republican constitution. The government insists that only parliament can adopt the new constitution; the people, on the other hand, are calling for a constituent assembly. Their fears came in the wake of the proposals the government has made to the draft constitution. They are suspicious that the government is trying to hijack the political system to its advantage, because its proposals do not enhance democracy.

As I write, the Civil Society, which I identified earlier in this essay, is in a convention. Participants are drawn from different walks of life—urban and countryside citizens, rich and poor, professionals and intellectuals. All are seeking consensus and are attempting to form a united front, with its own voice on the constitution, to pressure the government into submitting to the will of the people. The community in Acts 2 also gathered in one place and waited on God. And indeed God came into their situation and restored normalcy.

Although the story of Pentecost brings hope, it nevertheless judges and finds the Zambian church wanting. As the 120 disciples experienced God's spirit, their new lives spilled over to the lives on the streets and touched many people around.[5] Certainly today a spirit-filled church community can serve as a catalyst in renewing our society. The Zambian church is therefore challenged to make a difference. The church needs to repeat what it did in 1990–91, when it acted as a bridge between warring parties. The church cannot shrink from its God-given responsibility to be the agent of the Spirit in renewing the creation. Therefore, commitment and openness to the leading and renewal of the Spirit are called for on the part of the church. It is this life once lived to its fullest by the church that will permeate our society.

The centrality of Christ to everything that the community needs and may experience can be noted in Acts 2. From Peter's sermon (Acts 2:14–40), it is evident that God does all and accomplishes all through Christ, just as other New Testament texts show that creation was done through Christ (e.g., Colossians 1:15–20), that the Spirit is given through Christ (Acts 2:33), and that the church is Christ's body (e.g., Romans 12:3–8; 1 Corinthians 12:1–13). Christ is the head and holds it together. No wonder Peter, in explaining the Pentecost event, focuses upon Christ.

Zambia was declared by the president to be a Christian nation, but can we be Christians without putting Christ at the center of our politics, economics, and social life? It is easy for Zambian politicians to pay lip service to the declaration of Zambia as a Christian nation. However, the claims of Christ cannot be ignored. In Jesus Christ, there is power loose in the world. This power is available both to the church and to the world.

The effect of Pentecost on the church was such that it became a community that was characterized by its devotion to the teaching of the apostles, its commitment to prayer, the breaking of bread, and fellowship (Acts 2:42). The early believers lived a shared life. As a community, they made a large impact on the world. Their presence was felt. It is this that challenges the Zambian church today. Although this account in Acts 2 is only descriptive and does not prescribe the model for today's church, still there are certain principles that are applicable even today. Unity, love, acceptance, reconciliation, sharing, and fellowship are universal ideals that ought to be found in every Christian community, for these can indeed make an impact upon society.

Notes

1. W. H. Willimon, *Acts* (Interpretation; Atlanta: John Knox, 1988) 29.

2. Circa 200 B.C.E.—150 C.E. [editors].

3. Exodus 19:16–20 reads, "On the morning of the third day there was thunder and lightning, as well as a thick cloud on the mountain, and a blast of a trumpet so loud that all the people who were in the camp trembled. 17 Moses brought the people out of the camp to meet God. They took their stand at the foot of the mountain. 18 Now Mount Sinai was wrapped in smoke, because the LORD had descended upon it in fire; the smoke went up like the smoke of a kiln, while the whole mountain shook violently. 19 As the blast of the trumpet grew louder and louder, Moses would speak and God would answer him in thunder. 20 When the LORD descended upon Mount Sinai, to the top of the mountain, the LORD summoned Moses to the top of the mountain, and Moses went up."

4. Genesis 1:1–2 reads, "In the beginning when God created the heavens and the earth, 2 the earth was a formless void and darkness covered the face of the deep, while a wind from God swept over the face of the waters."

5. See, for example, the healings and concomitant speeches in Acts 3—4 [editors].

Acts 2:1–42

An Asian Perspective

Helen R. Graham

Context

A major issue throughout Philippine history has been the complex issue of land, for which Filipino farmers have struggled ever since the Spanish arrived in 1521; this struggle intensified during the revolution of 1898. A century later, the struggle for land continues. Even though the government has enacted several "land reform" programs since the Philippine revolution, none has as yet been effective.

In an interview I had in Tagalog with Mang Simon, a sixty-five-year-old farmer from the island of Mindoro, who was part of a group of farmers demonstrating outside the Department of Agrarian Reform, the situation of so many Filipino farmers was made clear. "I was a tenant farmer until Magsaysay became president," he said.

Magsaysay initiated a land reform program and I got title to three hectares of land. The Green Revolution came and little by little the traditional varieties of rice were eased out in favor of high yield varieties for the city people and for export. These new strains of rice required very expensive fertilizers and pesticides and special irrigation. I had to put aside some rice for seedlings and pay the threshers one out of every ten sacks of rice, so very few sacks remained for me to sell. As a result, very little money came in for me to feed my family. I sold my land little by little and began to cut wood to sell and tried to catch fish for my family to eat. I also began to organize the farmers, and we worked hard together to make things bearable for people during martial law under Marcos. In 1986 our farmers' group supported Cory's [Aquino] election, and we thought things would be better then. But, in January 1987, thirteen of our members were shot by the Philippine marines as we tried to call our president's attention to the plight of farmers. Even now, under President Ramos, our situation still has not improved. It is very dark now, but our hope is still in our people.

It was only after the thirteen farmers were mercilessly gunned down that the bureaucratic process sped up, and a Comprehensive Agrarian Reform Program (CARP), watered down by the predominantly land-owning Philippine congress, was signed into law.[1]

Today, while farmers continue their protest, the government persists in handing over prime rice land for conversion into export processing zones, industrial estates, subdivisions, golf courses, and vacation resorts.[2] Simultaneously, indigenous peoples, in both the north and the south of the country, resist the expropriation and conversion of their ancestral lands into commercial agricultural or industrial estates, which bring great profits to those already rich and dislocate indigenous peoples, upsetting as well delicate ecological balances.

It is not surprising, therefore, that significant numbers of Filipinos, who formerly farmed their own land, are now forced to work as laborers for multinational companies producing luxury food crops for export. On the eve of the third millennium, as the government promotes its "Philippines 2000" program,[3] Filipino farmers describe themselves in a poignant manner reminiscent of that of the poet of Job 24:10–11:

> We create and produce the food and other basic needs of our society. Through our ceaseless toil and with the use of our wisdom, we work the land to bring forth a bountiful harvest. Yet too often, we go hungry.[4]

Text

The account of the Pentecost event (Acts 2:1–13) is traditionally interpreted as the occasion of the inauguration of the mission of the church, as the time of the fulfillment of "the promise of the Father" (Acts 1:4; Luke 24:49). While attention is focused on the event of the outpouring of the Holy Spirit on the early Christian community, it is good to remember that in its origins the feast of Pentecost, the second of the three great agricultural festivals of ancient Israel, was a farmers' festival. In Exodus 23:16, it is called a harvest feast; in Exodus 34:22, it is more specifically designated the festival of the wheat harvest.[5] Amidst the vicissitudes of a rain-dependent agriculture, ancient Israelite farmers joyfully celebrated a harvest festival on the sixth and seventh of Sivan (late May or early June), marking the end of the cereal harvests which had commenced fifty days earlier with the beginning of the barley harvest (the Feast of Unleavened Bread [Lev. 23:6]). After the destruction of the Jewish temple in Jerusalem in 70 C.E., when the first fruits could no longer be offered in the temple, the ancient agrarian festival of Pentecost (also called Weeks) became associated with the giving of the covenant on Mount Sinai and became known in some Jewish traditions as "the [joyful] Season of the Giving of our Torah."[6]

Full joy in the harvest belongs to those free to work their own land and to consume what they have produced. The story of Israel during the period of the monarchy (ca. 1000–587 B.C.E.), however, is the story of how Israelite farmers became landless peasants under the rule of kings who were not entirely faithful to God's vision for justice.[7] Kings, in ancient Near Eastern thought, were often expected to mirror divine justice on earth. Under the influence of this ideology, for example, Israel prayed that God would give justice and righteousness to each new king (e.g., Psalm 72:1–4[8]). But the prophets accused Israel's kings of cruel and savage oppression, of selling "the righteous for money and the poor for a pair of sandals" (Amos 2:6b), of placing "exactions on the poor, and [taking] grain tribute from them" (Amos 5:11a).[9] In short, kings all too often failed to "know justice" (Micah 3:1–3).[10]

After the fall of the Northern Kingdom to Assyria in 721 B.C.E., but long before the fall of the Southern Kingdom and its capital, Jerusalem, to Babylon in 587 B.C.E., the prophet Isaiah looked forward with hope to the coming of a king who would truly embody Yahweh's justice—one upon whom the Spirit of Yahweh God would rest: "the spirit of wisdom and understanding, the spirit of counsel and might, the spirit of knowledge and the fear of the Lord" (Isaiah 11:2). Such a one would not make decisions on hearsay, but "with justice [would] he judge the impoverished peasants, and with equity . . . decide for the poor of the land" (Isaiah 11:3b–4a).[11] Isaiah's prophecy found fulfillment in Jesus, the "great prophet [who] has risen among us" (Luke 7:16).

The Christian community also believed itself to be an expression of the fulfillment of this prophetic hope. The "Holy Spirit" (Acts 2:4) conferred on the Christian community at Pentecost is the same as that which Isaiah the prophet anticipated and which rested upon Jesus at the baptism (Luke 3:22), empowering him for the prophetic mission of bringing good news to the poor, release to captives, restoration of sight to the blind, liberation to victims of crushing oppression, and the proclamation of the year of the Lord's favor (Luke 4:18–19; Isaiah 61:1–2[12]).[13] In the discourse that follows the account of the Pentecost event (Acts 2:14–40), Peter declared that, in fact, the exalted Jesus, "having received from the Father the promise of the Holy Spirit" (Acts 2:33), has poured forth this same Spirit upon the community, thus bringing about the event witnessed by those who listened to his discourse (2:29–36).

Reflection

The outpouring of the Holy Spirit on the occasion of the Jewish feast of Pentecost is reminiscent of the event of the descent of the Spirit upon Jesus at his baptism—an event acknowledged in the synagogue at Nazareth, where Jesus applies the prophetic passage from Isaiah to himself (Luke 4:18–19; see Isaiah 61:1–2a; see also Isaiah 11:3b-4): "The Spirit of the Lord is upon me, because he has anointed me to bring good news to the poor. He has sent me to proclaim release to the captives and recovery of sight to the blind, to let the oppressed go free, to proclaim the year of the Lord's favor." That the outpouring of the Holy Spirit upon the early Christian community links the community to Jesus' prophetic vocation and signals a prophetic vocation for the church is confirmed in Peter's discourse which follows, and interprets, the Pentecost event (Acts 2:33).

By reading the Pentecost event (Acts 2:1–13) within the context of the long history of the feast's development—beginning as a joyful festival of farmers celebrating the grain harvest, and then becoming one of the three major festivals of Israel which, after the destruction of the Temple in 70 C.E., eventually became associated with the giving of the Torah to Moses on Mount Sinai—many dimensions of its meaning are disclosed. The religious dimension of the feast inevitably overshadowed its originally concrete association with the tangible joy of the farmer at the time of the grain harvest. It was the farmer's *real* joy that became a metaphor for the gift of religious joy believed to be among the gifts bestowed by the Holy Spirit at Pentecost.[14]

In the context of an industrializing agrarian society, such as the Philippines, where agriculture still accounts for a large portion of the gross domestic product (GDP), the true joy of the feast can be most meaningfully celebrated only if the real joy of the farmers who till, harvest, and enjoy the fruits of their own land can once again be recovered, as in the biblical vision of Micah 4:4: ". . . but they shall all sit under their own vines and under their own fig trees, and no one shall make them afraid; for the mouth of the Lord of hosts has spoken." The story of the Filipino farmer, however, parallels that of the farmer of biblical Israel who, under the rule of kings who did "not know justice" (Micah 3:1), became a landless peasant. Inspired by the Pentecostal spirit, Filipino farmers, many of whom are active in Basic Christian Communities (BCCs), continue the struggle for land and thus bear witness to Mang Simon's words, that "our hope is still in our people."

By virtue of the gift of the Holy Spirit at Pentecost, the followers of Jesus are empowered to carry forth Jesus' liberating mission in the world. For the farmers, and those in solidarity with them, this often involves real endurance in the struggle, as is exemplified by the case of those farmers who exerted heroic effort to obtain title to a small parcel of land on the boundary between Bacolod and Bago on the island of Negros. The land, a small portion of 78 hectares left by a wealthy widow to her children, and leased to a third party, had been left idle in the early 1980s, when the sugar industry was experiencing a severe crisis. Organizing themselves into the Hacienda Bonifacia Farmers and Laborers Association (BOFALAS), the farmers began to plant rice and corn. Toward the end of the 1980s, the landowner accused the farmers of squatting, forcible entry, and various other crimes. By 1992, however, the land was placed under Compulsory Acquisition and was to be distributed to the farmers as part of the agrarian reform program. While the landowner devised schemes to keep the land from them, such as bulldozing their crops and driving them off with the help of armed groups, the farmers stood firm. Even after the Provincial Agrarian Reform Adjudication Board issued an order allowing the farmers to take physical possession of the land, the order was not carried out. Finally, after long hours of dialogue and heated arguments with the government officials, the farmers, armed with a court order, were able to convince the police to escort them to the land. They were jubilant when they finally set foot on their own piece of land, for which they had struggled for so long. The tangible joy of farmers free to work their own land and to enjoy its fruits was once again visible in this small community of farmers. Their joy was somewhat clouded, however, as the former lessee attempted to intercept a truckload of their sugar harvest, an action that led to further heated arguments and prolonged legal battles.[15]

If the farmers of BOFALAS did not immediately see a connection between their struggle for land and the church's feast of Pentecost, it was not because there is no connection. Traditional liturgical practice is too often so spiritualized and sterile, so divorced from the everyday lives of the common tao,[16] that it seems unrelated to the people's lives. A brief review of the historical development of the feast of Pentecost demonstrates its concrete connection to the joyous celebration of farmers at the conclusion of the grain harvest. Such a feast is profoundly relevant to the long history of the Filipino farmers' struggle for land. The farmers must reclaim the agrarian origins of this feast and its connection to their own lives as farmers. Is it not possible that, just as the tangible joy of the farmer became a metaphor for the spiritual joy of Pentecost, so the true meaning of the feast might be seen to lie in the actual concrete joy of farmers' harvesting and enjoying the fruits of their own land? Therefore, as we stand on the threshold of the third Christian millennium, asking that the gift of God's Spirit of wisdom, understanding, counsel, power, knowledge, and the fear of the Lord be poured out upon us (see Isaiah 11:2), we will also be challenged to commit ourselves to participate in the struggle toward a transformed future, a future in which Filipino farmers, and indeed all the world's farmers, might once again, in accordance with the vision of Amos,[17] truly rejoice in the joy of the harvest.

Notes

1. The present Minister of Agrarian Reform is committed to making CARP work.

2. See, for example, the documentation prepared by the Center for Alternative Systems Foundation, Inc., and the Cordillera News Agency regarding the Philippine government's comprehensive conversion and development plan for the former U.S. military Camp John Hay, Baguio City, entitled *Beware of Dragons Bearing Gifts* (Center for Alternative Systems Foundation, Inc., and Cordillera News Agency: Baguio City, 1994).

3. The government of President Fidel V. Ramos aims to bring the Philippines into the status of a Newly Industrialized Country (NIC) through its five-year (1993–1998) Medium-Term Philippine Development Program popularly known as "Philippines 2000."

4. Taken from a policy statement of the Peasant Organization of the Philippines, as reproduced in *Sowing the Seed: Proceeds of the International Solidarity Conference for the Filipino Peasantry (ISCFP)* (Kilusang Magbubukid ng Philipinas, 1988). The Job passage reads: "They go about naked, without clothing; though hungry, they carry the sheaves . . . they tread the wine presses, but suffer thirst" (Job 24:10–11).

5. See Deuteronomy 16:9–17 and 2 Chronicles 8:13. For ritual directives for the celebration of the feast, see Leviticus 23:15–21.

6. J. H. Hertz, *The Authorized Daily Prayer Book* (rev. ed.; New York: Bloch Publishing Co., 1965; originally published 1948) 790. See also E. Lohse, *"pentekoste," Theological Dictionary of the New Testament.* Edited by G. Kittel *et al.* (Grand Rapids: Eerdmans, 1968) 6.48–49.

7. See Exodus 20:17, Deuteronomy 5:21, 1 Kings 21, and the prophetic oracles of Amos and Micah, all of which reflect the situation resulting from the changing land-tenure patterns and the resultant impoverishment of the peasantry.

8. "Give the king your justice, O God, and your righteousness to a king's son. 2 May he judge your people with righteousness, and your poor with justice. 3 May the mountains yield prosperity for the people, and the hills, in righteousness. 4 May he defend the cause of the poor of the people, give deliverance to the needy, and crush the oppressor."

9. These translations of Amos are essentially those of J. A. Dearman, *Property Rights in the Eight-Century Prophets* (Atlanta: Scholars, 1988) 19, 28.

10. "And I said: Listen, you heads of Jacob and rulers of the house of Israel! Should you not know justice?—2 you who hate the good and love the evil, who tear the skin off my people, and the flesh off their bones; 3 who eat the flesh of my people, flay their skin off them, break their bones in pieces, and chop them up like meat in a kettle, like flesh in a caldron."

11. Author's translation.

12. "The spirit of the Lord God is upon me, because the Lord has anointed me; he has sent me to bring good news to the oppressed, to bind up the brokenhearted, to proclaim liberty to the captives, and release to the prisoners; 2 to proclaim the year of the Lord's favor, and the day of vengeance of our God; to comfort all who mourn."

13. It should be noted that the announcement of the year of favor, or the jubilee year (Luke 4:19), also has its background in the problem of land and land loss (see Leviticus 25:8–17, 25–28).

14. Isaiah 9:3 (9:2 in Hebrew text) reads, "You have multiplied the nation, you have increased its joy; they rejoice before you as with joy at the harvest, as people exult when dividing plunder."

15. For a fuller account, see "Negros: Under the Heel of Oppression," in *Sparks* [The Official Newsletter of the Rural Missionaries of the Philippines] 6.3 (October-December 1994) 3–5.

16. *Tao* is a Tagalog word for *people*.

17. Amos 9:13–15: "The time is surely coming, says the Lord, when the one who plows shall overtake the one who reaps, and the treader of grapes the one who sows the seed; the mountains shall drip sweet wine, and all the hills shall flow with it. 14 I will restore the fortunes of my people Israel, and they shall rebuild the ruined cities and inhabit them; they shall plant vineyards and drink their wine, and they shall make gardens and eat their fruit. 15 I will plant them upon their land, and they shall never again be plucked up out of the land that I have given them, says the Lord your God."

1 Corinthians 15:1–58

Now I would remind you, brothers and sisters, of the good news that I proclaimed to you, which you in turn received, in which also you stand, 2 through which also you are being saved, if you hold firmly to the message that I proclaimed to you—unless you have come to believe in vain. 3 For I handed on to you as of first importance what I in turn had received: that Christ died for our sins in accordance with the scriptures, 4 and that he was buried, and that he was raised on the third day in accordance with the scriptures, 5 and that he appeared to Cephas, then to the twelve. 6 Then he appeared to more than five hundred brothers and sisters at one time, most of whom are still alive, though some have died. 7 Then he appeared to James, then to all the apostles. 8 Last of all, as to one untimely born, he appeared also to me. 9 For I am the least of the apostles, unfit to be called an apostle, because I persecuted the church of God. 10 But by the grace of God I am what I am, and his grace toward me has not been in vain. On the contrary, I worked harder than any of them—though it was not I, but the grace of God that is with me. 11 Whether then it was I or they, so we proclaim and so you have come to believe. 12 Now if Christ is proclaimed as raised from the dead, how can some of you say there is no resurrection of the dead? 13 If there is no resurrection of the dead, then Christ has not been raised; 14 and if Christ has not been raised, then our proclamation has been in vain and your faith has been in vain. 15 We are even found to be misrepresenting God, because we testified of God that he raised Christ—whom he did not raise if it is true that the dead are not raised. 16 For if the dead are not raised, then Christ has not been raised. 17 If Christ has not been raised, your faith is futile and you are still in your sins. 18 Then those also who have died in Christ have perished. 19 If for this life only we have hoped in Christ, we are of all people most to be pitied. 20 But in fact Christ has been raised from the dead, the first fruits of

those who have died. 21 For since death came through a human be-
ing, the resurrection of the dead has also come through a human be-
ing; 22 for as all die in Adam, so all will be made alive in Christ. 23
But each in his own order: Christ the first fruits, then at his coming
those who belong to Christ. 24 Then comes the end, when he hands
over the kingdom to God the Father, after he has destroyed every
ruler and every authority and power. 25 For he must reign until he
has put all his enemies under his feet. 26 The last enemy to be de-
stroyed is death. 27 For "God has put all things in subjection under
his feet." But when it says, "All things are put in subjection," it is
plain that this does not include the one who put all things in subjec-
tion under him. 28 When all things are subjected to him, then the Son
himself will also be subjected to the one who put all things in subjec-
tion under him, so that God may be all in all. 29 Otherwise, what will
those people do who receive baptism on behalf of the dead? If the
dead are not raised at all, why are people baptized on their behalf?
30 And why are we putting ourselves in danger every hour? 31 I die
every day! That is as certain, brothers and sisters, as my boasting of
you—a boast that I make in Christ Jesus our Lord. 32 If with merely
human hopes I fought with wild animals at Ephesus, what would I
have gained by it? If the dead are not raised, "Let us eat and drink,
for tomorrow we die." 33 Do not be deceived: "Bad company ruins
good morals." 34 Come to a sober and right mind, and sin no more;
for some people have no knowledge of God. I say this to your shame.
35 But someone will ask, "How are the dead raised? With what kind
of body do they come?" 36 Fool! What you sow does not come to life
unless it dies. 37 And as for what you sow, you do not sow the body
that is to be, but a bare seed, perhaps of wheat or of some other grain.
38 But God gives it a body as he has chosen, and to each kind of seed
its own body. 39 Not all flesh is alike, but there is one flesh for human
beings, another for animals, another for birds, and another for fish.
40 There are both heavenly bodies and earthly bodies, but the glory
of the heavenly is one thing, and that of the earthly is another. 41
There is one glory of the sun, and another glory of the moon, and an-
other glory of the stars; indeed, star differs from star in glory. 42 So
it is with the resurrection of the dead. What is sown is perishable,
what is raised is imperishable. 43 It is sown in dishonor, it is raised
in glory. It is sown in weakness, it is raised in power. 44 It is sown a
physical body, it is raised a spiritual body. If there is a physical body,
there is also a spiritual body. 45 Thus it is written, "The first man,

Adam, became a living being"; the last Adam became a life-giving spirit. 46 But it is not the spiritual that is first, but the physical, and then the spiritual. 47 The first man was from the earth, a man of dust; the second man is from heaven. 48 As was the man of dust, so are those who are of the dust; and as is the man of heaven, so are those who are of heaven. 49 Just as we have borne the image of the man of dust, we will also bear the image of the man of heaven. 50 What I am saying, brothers and sisters, is this: flesh and blood cannot inherit the kingdom of God, nor does the perishable inherit the imperishable. 51 Listen, I will tell you a mystery! We will not all die, but we will all be changed, 52 in a moment, in the twinkling of an eye, at the last trumpet. For the trumpet will sound, and the dead will be raised imperishable, and we will be changed. 53 For this perishable body must put on imperishability, and this mortal body must put on immortality. 54 When this perishable body puts on imperishability, and this mortal body puts on immortality, then the saying that is written will be fulfilled: "Death has been swallowed up in victory." 55 "Where, O death, is your victory? Where, O death, is your sting?" 56 The sting of death is sin, and the power of sin is the law. 57 But thanks be to God, who gives us the victory through our Lord Jesus Christ. 58 Therefore, my beloved, be steadfast, immovable, always excelling in the work of the Lord, because you know that in the Lord your labor is not in vain.

1 Corinthians 15:1–58
A Latin American Perspective[1]

Elsa Tamez

Context

There are many battered and raped women in Latin America and the Caribbean. Organizations that are dedicated to the defense of women against violence provide an infinite number of testimonies. Women are beaten, raped, and sexually abused by their husbands, friends, lovers, teachers, bosses, police, priests, pastors, or soldiers. Even small girls do not escape this violence. In times of war, when women who are organized or members of a guerrilla movement are imprisoned, their bodies are constantly humiliated, bathed in blood and semen.

The blows, the rape, and the incest often generate in women a hate for their own bodies and a profound deterioration of their self-esteem, as well as an absolute lack of confidence in others and in life itself. Institutions that stand with and try to support these women psychologically find that it is very difficult to help them to love themselves and their bodies or to recover confidence in themselves or in others. Very few women recover completely. Most feel guilty and are never able to overcome the humiliating experience of such abuse.

The women who are most able to overcome this experience of spiritual and bodily humiliation are those who have been immersed in popular liberation struggles—in neighborhood organizations, in the struggle for land, in guerrilla movements, or in public demonstrations against the high cost of living. These women have an objective and struggle for it despite knowing the risks. They resist repression and abuse because they have faith in the possibility of achieving their ideal.

From a Christian point of view, we might say that they organize because they believe that resurrection follows crucifixion. They believe that, even though their bodies are beaten, abused, and bloodied by torture, nevertheless life conquers death, and they will rise again in the bodies of many others. Thus, the crucifixion of their bodies is viewed as a consequence of their action for justice. An important task of solidarity is for these women, who believe in the resurrection, to pass on their faith in the resurrection to other women who have been raped and abused. However, since many women are not oriented toward a liberating horizon, it is difficult for them to believe in the resurrection of the body.

Text

1 Corinthians 15 offers elements for a feminist rereading of liberation that starts from the abused body and moves toward the resurrection of bodies. Paul, as an apostle of Jesus Christ, gives witness to his life of faith by taking on in his body the impact of the gospel message. Because he preaches the gospel's good news of liberation to all, Jews and non-Jews alike, he suffers many kinds of abuses in his body and risks his life more than once (2 Corinthians 6:5[2]). Each day, he says, he is in danger of death (1 Corinthians 15:31). The apostle takes on in his own body the marks of the death of Jesus of Nazareth, the crucified One.

In 2 Corinthians 4:10, Paul says this explicitly: "We always carry in our bodies the death of Jesus." Before he talks about the resurrection of Christ in 1 Corinthians, Paul leads his readers to look at the crucified body of Jesus. For this reason, he says to the Corinthians that he wants to hear nothing among them except Jesus Christ crucified (1 Corinthians 2:2). But in 1 Corinthians 15, Paul is scandalized because some of the Corinthians do not believe in the resurrection of the dead. And he urges them to see that faith in the crucified One has no meaning if Jesus has not been raised from the dead (15:14).

Not only has Christ himself been raised, but also, because of him, the dead are raised. Jesus Christ is the first among many bodies to be raised (1 Corinthians 15:21–22). Hope does not lie solely in Christ's resurrection but in the reality that the dead arise because Christ arose. Conversely, if there is no new humanity, faith in the resurrection is a lie because Christ has not been raised (15:13).

Moreover, faith in the resurrection gives Paul the strength not to lose courage in the struggle to carry on so that life might be manifested. The apostle affirms that, if he did not believe in the resurrection of the dead, there would be no reason for his struggle against his enemies (1 Corinthians 15:32). Paul, who takes on the death of Jesus in his battered body, also takes on the life of Christ in his body in the midst of struggle (2 Corinthians 4:10–12[3]). The struggle, understood in more general terms, is for the creation of a new humanity with new resurrected bodies. What makes it possible to continue in that struggle is the faith that this new humanity has already been made known by the resurrection of the Second Adam (human), Jesus (1 Corinthians 15:22).

Reflection

Many women involved in popular liberation struggles, who have been imprisoned for defending just causes on behalf of the community, have taken on in their bodies the marks of the crucified Jesus. These are the same as the marks shown on the weak body of the apostle Paul. The intention of these women in their struggle has been that life might be made known in their bodies and in the body of their community. They struggle for things that are necessary for the body: food, housing, clothing, education, work, a time to celebrate. The response has often been physical blows, torture, rape. However, their sacrificed bodies become resurrected sanctuary. When they are assassinated, they believe that they will be resurrected in the body of their companions, who continue the struggle.

On the other hand, many women and girls who are not organized and who walk through life naively have been beaten and raped for nothing— only for having a woman's body. Sin has been enraged against them, and it has been publicly manifested through violence with the permission of the law in a patriarchal culture and the silence of many men and women. The same thing happened with the body of Jesus; it was sacrificed for sin and was exhibited publicly on the cross with the permission of the law and the approval of the multitudes. The women in the gospel accounts—Mary Magdalene, Joanna, Mary, the mother of James, and Salome—believed that Jesus had risen (Mark 16:1–8; Matthew 28:1–10; Luke 24:1–12), and they saw him. Similarly, many contemporary women active in liberation organizations also believe it. But many women and girls of today still cannot see signs of resurrected bodies. They do not view as credible the faith that women's bodies can also rise, that they are beautiful, a gift from God.

It is essential in our context to share the faith in the resurrection of the body. Only when there is faith in the resurrection of the body in continuity with our human history will it be possible to have confidence in one's self and in others. When this faith is grasped, then one's own body and others' bodies can be valued. The possibility of a dignified life for all can be believed, and there is strength to struggle in this life. The revived body is claimed as a gift of God, offered in the resurrection of the Messiah, the human God, the first raised of many men and women.

Notes

1. Translation by Gloria Kinsler.

2. Paul lists among them, ". . . beatings, imprisonments, riots, labors, sleepless nights, hunger . . ."

3. ". . . always carrying in the body the death of Jesus, so that the life of Jesus may also be made visible in our bodies. 11 For while we live, we are always being given up to death for Jesus' sake, so that the life of Jesus may be made visible in our mortal flesh. 12 So death is at work in us, but life in you."

1 Corinthians 15:1–58
An African Perspective[1]

François Kabasele Lumbala

Context

The notion of the person in Africa is characterized by a certain ontological pluralism; several vital principles are united to the body. Human life is born of this union. The definitive end or cessation of life-giving action of these vital principles provokes death. What should be underlined in this African anthropology is the unity of the human being; body and spirit are inseparable. For example, to announce that John is dead, one would say, "John has taken the ground's position," or even, "John is lying on the ground." The entire person can be freed, influenced in his or her being, through a fragment of nail, a piece of skin, a hair, a word. The body is intimately linked to the being of a person.

On earth, we are voyagers, passengers on destination to an invisible world, the beyond. There is, in other words, a continuation of life. The life of virtuous people exists alongside the ancestors—a village with fertile approaches, where one continues to be what one was on earth in this life. The life of wicked and hateful people is glum, spent in continuing to bother humans with their spiteful wanderings. Whatever it may be, however, life after death is never considered a place of delight to the point that one could desire it. Humans are only happy as beings on earth, even if a person knows he or she is "condemned to die," for life always has the last word. Even in death, the infant who is born announces the parents' death, but at the same time carries the victory of life over death.

Life ultimately finds its meaning only in this communion with the beyond, in this solidarity between the living creatures of the earth and the living dead—between the human and ancestral communities—a solidarity that love and good reinforce, but which hate and evil betray. That is why for us, life on earth, like life beyond, is always a struggle in which *everyone* is involved, the living dead and living creatures. Only the communion between the two can be the arm to victory.

Text

The Corinthians knew that Jesus had survived, and they did not doubt that Christ was "resurrected" by a special privilege from God. But they doubted the general resurrection of the dead, that is, the hope that all people, or the righteous, would rise in a single resurrection. The Corinthians came to doubt this general resurrection because they disbelieved that the body, this *prison of the soul,* could once again take up its attributes in material form. For Paul, to doubt this possibility for all people was also to doubt it for Christ, the one who lived as the human prototype and who carried the human species toward God's design. Paul argued that one cannot believe in the resurrected Christ if one does not believe that what happened to Christ will happen to the believer, for it is the same force of God that is at work in both Jesus Christ in the past and in the believer in the present. Just as God condemned humanity in Adam, so God justifies humanity by raising Jesus from the dead. Therefore, Paul reasons, through Jesus, God will resurrect humanity. Christ's resurrection is not a singular, self-contained event. It is all at once a fundamental event that reveals God's design for humankind.

How will this happen? 1 Corinthians 15:35–44 answers the question concerning the body in which humanity will be resurrected. They will be resurrected, argued Paul, with another body. Just as the dead seed makes way for the plant with a new body, so in the resurrected body is still the same being, but it is completely transformed from corruptible to incorruptible, from miserable to glorious, from weak to powerful, from physical to spiritual. If Christ is the first to be resurrected, that means that resurrection is not merely a mechanical phenomenon but the realization of a divine project, the accomplishment of one of God's designs, which was initiated with the resurrection of Jesus. This divine design intimately includes our participation, compelling us to live in the present situation for God and not for oneself; the divine design is for all of us to sow good.

Reflection

That there is survival after death is, for our African peoples, part of what is accepted as evident; survival after death is not "news." "Good news" will make itself heard in the form of the survival described by Paul in the message of the resurrection. It is for this reason that the teaching in 1 Corinthians 15:35–44 constitutes the central point of this text for many of our people.

The resurrected body is totally transformed. To illustrate this for our context, where Paul uses the image of the seed, we see the image of the caterpillar, a food in high supply that appears only at certain times of the year in tropical Africa. The caterpillar, which could not be picked up by people in February, withdraws on a tree leaf. There it closes itself up in a cocoon made of small stalks of wood held together by a kind of glue. The cocoon is really a coffin that is hermetically closed. On the inside of the cocoon, a painstaking process of profound and radical change takes place. A few months later, the cocoon breaks open and out comes a new being, the butterfly. Whereas the caterpillar crawled on grass and leaves, the butterfly flies; whereas the caterpillar fed on grass, the butterfly drinks flower nectar; whereas the caterpillar was food for people, the butterfly is no longer a food for them. There is a total transformation of body and of life. This image speaks more to us with regard to resurrection than does Paul's image of the seed.

There is, however, a difference in this transformation by God, who is the master and the artisan. This is one of the great novelties of resurrection for our people: it is God who resurrects, for God's love is stronger than death. God raises a person to a more plentiful life, to a life that fully communes with the divinity, to a life that is no longer the simple continuity of powerful terrestrial life.

Humanity's role in this resurrection is not to be neglected, even if God is the artisan. It is at this point where we rejoin Africans, for whom the love and communion between living creatures and the living dead is the principle weapon against death. In our African traditions, everyone is completely responsible for what happens to them after death; their fate depends upon whether there was a ferment of union and understanding between persons. In this case, the ancestral figure becomes the paradigm of resurrection, for not just any sort of dead person was considered an ancestor; only those who had lived in the exemplary nature of love and generosity and who never slowed life down could become ancestors. So it is for us that the witches, the evil-doers, will not resuscitate but will sur-vive.[2] They have already condemned themselves. Thus for us resurrection takes place in the present, that is, it begins now in the way we act, in the nature of our relationships; otherwise, it will never be. Of course, there was a "before" and an "after" in the Christian event, in the resurrection of Jesus, but for the majority of Africans, the distinction between the two planes does not contradict their coexistence within each other.

According to African belief, those who did not have offspring were excluded from the camp of the ancestors. They were cursed as they were buried so that they could "never come back." Sometimes they were even buried with a stick of bamboo implanted in their kidneys. But with the Christian message, the borders of the ancestors' camp, those who are resurrected, are determined, not by such an arbitrary physical integrity, but by love. This is to say that resurrection in the Christian message expands the horizons of African beliefs in the afterlife even while it is included among those beliefs.

Notes

1. Translation by Nancy Grey.
2. The original French is *sur-vivraient,* which constitutes a play on words. The English translation cannot capture this feature.

1 Corinthians 15:1–58
An Asian Perspective

Daniel C. Arichea

Context

Filipinos in general believe in the existence of an immortal soul that separates from the body at death. As long as this soul has not found its way out of this earth, it is able to affect and influence people—either in a positive or negative way—especially relatives and others who have had dealings with the deceased. The common rituals related to the dead are aimed primarily at helping the soul find its way out of this earth. In some cases, a fire is lit at the entrance of the place where the body lies; this fire is to provide light for the soul's journey. In other cases, food is placed at strategic places outside the place where the body lies; this is meant to be picked up by the soul in order to provide food for its journey. In most cases, the watch for the dead lasts for three nights; it is believed that on the third night the soul makes its final attempt to influence the living before it finally departs for another world. There are many stories regarding the visible appearance and audible activities of the soul during the third night. When I was young, I remember my late mother, a devout Christian, telling the story of how, on the third night of our helper's death, my mother heard her cleaning the house and washing the dishes. In some instances, the watch for the dead lasts for nine days, representing the *novena* in the Roman Catholic ritual.[1] In still other cases, the watch lasts for forty days; this practice is thought to have been influenced by the account in the first chapter of Acts, where it is reported that the resurrected Jesus stayed on with his disciples for forty days. Whether the watch is for three days or nine or forty, the focus is the same, namely, to facilitate the departure of the soul from earth.

It is believed that when the soul leaves this earth, it journeys into the presence of God, where it faces judgment for its actions while it dwelt within the body of a person. It is therefore important for a person to make sure that his or her soul passes the judgment and does not go to hell, from where it cannot escape. An important part of preparing the soul to face judgment is participation in religious rituals and exercises.

In the Philippines, there are dangers that result from this overemphasis upon the soul. One danger is minimizing the importance of the body. Filipinos go to church and engage in spiritual exercises to take care of the needs of the soul; what they do with their bodies afterwards has very little relation, if any, to the religious rituals they have gone through. Thus belief in the immortality of the soul leads to a rigid division between the spiritual and the material aspects of life. If the soul stands for the spiritual side of life, and the body for the physical and material, then the dichotomy between soul and body leads to a dichotomy between the church and the world. This dichotomy affects all of Filipino life and society. The religious part of one's life is for the immortal soul, and that has little to no influence on how one acts in society. In fact, many of those who engage in immoral acts are religious in the sense that they go to church and participate in various religious rituals and exercises. Thus it can truly be said of many Filipinos that for them it is the cross on Sunday and the double-cross on weekdays.

A second danger that results from overemphasizing the soul is a lack of concern for social ills. If the goal of life is the salvation of the immortal soul, then why should there be any preoccupation with the things of this world? It does not matter whether people are poor in the physical sense as long as they are rich in the spiritual sense. It does not matter whether there is poverty and injustice, for, after all, what is of prime importance is making sure that the soul finds its immortal rest.

Text

The resurrection of the dead was difficult for the Corinthian believers to accept. A great number of them were saying that there was no such thing as the resurrection of the dead. In their understanding, faith and hope in Christ are relevant only for life on earth and not for life after death; to this conviction Paul responds emphatically, "If for this life only we have hoped in Christ, we are of all people most to be pitied" (1 Corinthians 15:19).

In order to address their lack of understanding, Paul begins, not with doctrine, but with Christ. Faith in Christ includes, in fact demands, faith in the resurrection of the dead. Conversely, a denial of the resurrection of the dead is tantamount to a denial of Christ. Paul's logic proceeds in this fashion: if the Corinthians believe in Christ, they must accept the tradition about him, which has been handed down to Paul and which Paul himself has handed down to others. This tradition includes the fact of Christ's death, burial, and resurrection. The evidence for Christ's resurrection from the dead is found in the risen Christ's appearance to many followers, including Paul himself. Paul takes enormous pains to emphasize this point as he begins to address this Corinthian problem (15:3–8):

> For I handed on to you as of first importance what I in turn had received: that Christ died for our sins in accordance with the scriptures, 4 and that he was buried, and that he was raised on the third day in accordance with the scriptures, 5 and that he appeared to Cephas, then to the twelve. 6 Then he appeared to more than five hundred brothers and sisters at one time, most of whom are still alive, though some have died. 7 Then he appeared to James, then to all the apostles. 8 Last of all, as to one untimely born, he appeared also to me.

The main part of the tradition is the resurrection of Christ, upon which Paul elaborates further in 1 Corinthians 15:14–19. Here Paul discusses the consequences if Christ has not been raised from death. One consequence is that Christian faith would be useless, since there is nothing to *believe*. Another consequence is that, since there is nothing in which to believe, then Christian proclamation would also be useless because there is nothing about which to *preach*. Christian proclamation would, in fact, be misrepresenting God, because central to the Christian proclamation is the affirmation that God has raised Jesus from death. A third consequence is that the faith of the Corinthian Christians would also be ineffective, and they would still be what they were before they heard the gospel; that is, they would still be living in their sins—there would be nothing to *save* them. Furthermore, there would be nothing in store for the Corinthian believers who have died already—there would be nothing for which to *hope*. Without the resurrection of Jesus, as it was recounted in the tradition (15:3–8), there would be for Christians no faith, no proclamation, no salvation, and no hope!

Paul also asserts that the suffering of believers would be meaningless apart from a future resurrection (vv. 31–32). He uses his own difficult experiences to illustrate what he means: "I die every day! That is as certain, brothers and sisters, as my boasting of you—a boast that I make in Christ Jesus our Lord. If with merely human hopes I fought with wild animals at Ephesus, what would I have gained by it? If the dead are not raised, 'Let us eat and drink, for tomorrow we die.'" However, it is very likely that Paul also has the sufferings of the Corinthian believers in mind. Suffering, Paul seems to say, is inevitable if we take our faith seriously. Why should we endure all that trouble if all of life is what happens here on earth, if everything ends at death, with no hope for a life after this life? If that were so, then we should not take life seriously but simply attempt to enjoy every moment of it while it lasts.

It is therefore not possible for believers in Christ to deny his being raised from death. In so many words, Paul tells this to the believers in Corinth: "You cannot believe in the resurrection of Christ without believing in the resurrection of the dead. Conversely, you cannot deny the resurrection of the dead without also denying the resurrection of Christ."

Reflection

As we have already noted, the situation of the Corinthian believers is similar in many ways to that of the Filipino context. Many of the Corinthian believers did not believe in the resurrection of the dead, and they explicitly and unabashedly said so. While many Filipinos do not explicitly assert unbelief in the resurrection of the dead, their unbelief is exhibited in their ritual practices and in their way of life. In addition, many of the Corinthian believers did not understand the relationship between the resurrection of the dead and the resurrection of Jesus Christ; they failed to see that a denial of the former would be tantamount to a denial of the latter. Similarly, while Filipinos in general would not deny the resurrection of Jesus Christ, it does not seem to be central to their faith. If it were, then why is the most celebrated religious day in the Philippines not Easter or Christmas but Good Friday? On Good Friday, the services of both Roman Catholic and Protestant churches are completely full; it is the day for everyone to go to church although it occurs in the thick of summer, with intolerable heat and humidity. Death is, in fact, celebrated additionally at least twice a year as a national holiday: All Saints Day and All Souls Day (November 1 and 2). On these days, burial plots are cleaned and tombstones are washed and repainted. What is the attraction of death—of Good Friday? It is the day to remember the death of Jesus, and it is his death, not his resurrection, that is central in the Filipino's understanding of Christ.

Because of the similarities in the Corinthian and Filipino contexts, Paul's approach to dealing with the issue of the resurrection of the dead can become a model for the Filipino church. In terms of approach, Paul took seriously the Corinthian context in order to communicate effectively with them. In this respect, he began, as we have seen, with the reality of his own suffering and theirs. His words about the resurrection have authenticity because his identification with their suffering was evident. Paul's reference to the Corinthians' suffering and the connection between suffering and resurrection is especially relevant to the Filipino context. There is still so much suffering among Filipinos. While it is true that there is an economic boom in the Philippines, the vast majority of Filipinos continue to remain impoverished. The gap between rich and poor is not being bridged; in fact, it can be said that the rich are getting richer and the poor poorer. Millions of children are subjected to various kinds of exploitation and abuse. In this context, a reaffirmation of a future resurrection gives hope to those who suffer and at the same time prods the Christian community—through the way it values the material as well as the spiritual dimensions of life—to work for a proper balance between spiritual and material concerns.

In addition to underscoring the relationship between suffering and resurrection, Paul even took questionable elements of the Corinthians' context and beliefs seriously. For instance, he did not excoriate the Corinthians for their baptism on behalf of the dead (1 Corinthians 15:28–29). Whatever that practice meant, Paul took care to relate it to the resurrection and the future reign of Christ: "When all things are subjected to him, then the Son himself will also be subjected to the one who put all things in subjection under him, so that God may be all in all. Otherwise, what will those people do who receive baptism on behalf of the dead? If the dead are not raised at all, why are people baptized on their behalf?" In the same way, there is a need to incorporate the Filipino context in order to address effectively their predicament with regard to the resurrection of the dead. For example, one approach would be to incorporate explicit references to the resurrection in existing liturgies for the dead. The Philippine church ought, for instance, to continue to worship in ways that incorporate liturgies such as the one prescribed for funerals and memorial services in the Book of Worship of the United Methodist Church. The first two lines of the "Service of Death and Resurrection" read, "Dying, Christ destroyed our death; rising, Christ restored our life." The greeting in this liturgy emphasizes the centrality of the resurrection: "May God grant us grace, that in pain we may find comfort—in sorrow hope, in death resurrection."

Finally and most importantly, there is a need to recover a holistic Christology in the Philippine church. For the apostle Paul, the solution to the Corinthians' lack of faith in the resurrection of the dead was a reaffirmation of faith in Jesus Christ, who lived and died, was buried and raised from death, and who was believed to be alive and present in the Corinthian community. Similarly, the best way—in fact, the only way—to convince

Filipinos of the resurrection of the dead is to point to Jesus Christ and to invite Filipinos to affirm their faith in him as their living Lord and Savior. That can be done only if Jesus Christ is alive today and present within Philippine society. And Jesus can be a living Lord only if, in fact, he is also the Lord who has been raised from death. Faith in Jesus as the risen Lord leads to an affirmation of the resurrection of the dead because he is the first born from the dead; that is, he is the guarantee that those who are in union with him will share in his resurrection. The paramount question, then, is this: Do Filipinos believe in the risen and living Christ or not? Are they willing to take the risk of putting their trust in someone who lived and died and was *raised from death in the body*? If they are, then they must also accept the possibility of their own resurrection.

Notes

1. The *novena* is a term applied to a period of nine days spent in private or public devotion, the intent of which is to receive some special grace. Although this practice dates only to the seventeenth century, it is based ultimately upon the nine-day wait for the Holy Spirit mentioned in Acts 1:13–14 [editors].

Revelation 21:1–22:5

Then I saw a new heaven and a new earth; for the first heaven and the first earth had passed away, and the sea was no more. 2 And I saw the holy city, the new Jerusalem, coming down out of heaven from God, prepared as a bride adorned for her husband. 3 And I heard a loud voice from the throne saying, "See, the home of God is among mortals. He will dwell with them as their God; they will be his peoples, and God himself will be with them; 4 he will wipe every tear from their eyes. Death will be no more; mourning and crying and pain will be no more, for the first things have passed away." 5 And the one who was seated on the throne said, "See, I am making all things new." Also he said, "Write this, for these words are trustworthy and true." 6 Then he said to me, "It is done! I am the Alpha and the Omega, the beginning and the end. To the thirsty I will give water as a gift from the spring of the water of life. 7 Those who conquer will inherit these things, and I will be their God and they will be my children. 8 But as for the cowardly, the faithless, the polluted, the murderers, the fornicators, the sorcerers, the idolaters, and all liars, their place will be in the lake that burns with fire and sulfur, which is the second death." 9 Then one of the seven angels who had the seven bowls full of the seven last plagues came and said to me, "Come, I will show you the bride, the wife of the Lamb." 10 And in the spirit he carried me away to a great, high mountain and showed me the holy city Jerusalem coming down out of heaven from God. 11 It has the glory of God and a radiance like a very rare jewel, like jasper, clear as crystal. 12 It has a great, high wall with twelve gates, and at the gates twelve angels, and on the gates are inscribed the names of the twelve tribes of the Israelites; 13 on the east three gates, on the north three gates, on the south three gates, and on the west three gates. 14 And the wall of the city has twelve foundations, and on them are the twelve names of the twelve apostles of the Lamb. 15 The angel who talked to me had a measuring rod of gold to measure the city and its gates and walls. 16 The city lies foursquare, its length the same as its width; and he measured the city with his rod, fifteen hundred miles; its length and width and height are equal. 17 He also measured its wall, one hundred forty-four cubits by human measurement, which the angel was using. 18 The wall is built of jasper, while the city is pure gold, clear as glass. 19 The foundations of the wall of the city are adorned with every jewel; the first was jasper, the second sapphire, the third agate, the fourth emerald, 20 the fifth onyx, the sixth carnelian, the seventh chrysolite, the eighth beryl, the ninth topaz, the tenth chrysoprase, the eleventh jacinth, the twelfth amethyst. 21 And the twelve gates are twelve pearls, each of the gates is a single pearl, and the street of the city is pure gold, transparent as glass. 22 I saw no temple in the city, for its temple is the Lord God the Almighty and the Lamb. 23 And the city has no need of sun or moon to shine on it, for the glory of God is its light, and its lamp is the Lamb. 24 The nations will walk by its light, and the kings of the earth will bring their glory into it. 25 Its gates will never be shut by day—and there will be no night there. 26 People will bring into it the glory and the honor of the nations. 27 But nothing unclean will enter it, nor anyone who practices abomination or falsehood, but only those who are written in the Lamb's book of life. 22:1 Then the angel showed me the river of the water of life, bright as crystal, flowing from the throne of God and of the Lamb 2 through the middle of the street of the city. On either side of the river is the tree of life with its twelve kinds of fruit, producing its fruit each month; and the leaves of the tree are for the healing of the nations. 3 Nothing accursed will be found there any more. But the throne of God and of the Lamb will be in it, and his servants will worship him; 4 they will see his face, and his name will be on their foreheads. 5 And there will be no more night; they need no light of lamp or sun, for the Lord God will be their light, and they will reign forever and ever.

Revelation 21:1–22:5

A Latin American Perspective

Jorge Pixley

Context

The most important inspiration for the organization of popular movements in Latin America during the last three decades has been the revolutionary project of the Cuban people. Thousands of sick people from the region have received free surgery and other medical care in excellent Cuban medical facilities. Thousands of young people have benefited from scholarships to study technical and military specializations in Cuba, thereafter returning as agronomists, physicians, or architects.

The health care delivery system in Cuba, the educational system with its multiple university specialties, the attention provided for the elderly, and the many facilities provided to rural communities are the dreams of poor people who have had occasion to enter into some form of contact with Cuba.

The Cuban Revolution has been guided from the beginning by a nationalist affirmation. That affirmation has been understood as an active struggle against imperialist domination, which had reached a very high level of penetration in the pre-revolutionary Cuba. Early in the revolutionary experience, in 1961, the leadership declared that the struggle had to be carried out with a socialist political, economic, and cultural program. As the 1960s continued, the Soviet Union and its allies became the sole trading partners as a result of the U.S. blockade and political difficulties with China, an otherwise viable alternative.

For the purpose of this essay, it is essential to realize that the Cuban government held to the utopian vision of a free nation organized in such a way as to erase social differences. This powerful utopian vision fueled the possibility of building a society that reached, before the collapse of the Soviet Union, a living standard above that of most Latin American nations, with unrivaled health and educational systems. Cuba was able to resist an embargo by the United States, which exhibited the characteristics of a blockade for thirty years, thanks to Cuba's privileged relation with Eastern Europe. However, due to subsequent calamitous changes in Eastern Europe, Cuba is now forced into economic crisis by the continuation of this blockade. That crisis has also produced a crisis in the utopian vision itself.

Text

Revelation 20—22 contains the utopian vision of John and other Asian Christians in the years circa 90–100 C.E. This utopian vision is remarkable for several characteristics that reveal how these men (yes, men!) saw their social predicament.

(1) This is an *urban* world, both the present one that is passing away (Revelation 21:1; 17:1–17) and the new one that is to come: "the holy city, the new Jerusalem" (Revelation 21:2). This vision contrasts with the utopia of Paradise (Isaiah 11:1–9; Luke 23:43) and with the rural dream of living "each under his own vine and fig tree" (Micah 4:4).

(2) This is an *exclusive* city, from which the impure and the outside aggressors are excluded (women too, apparently, according to Revelation 14:4). The "cowardly, faithless, and polluted" in 21:8 should be read in reference to those condemned in the letters of Revelation 2—3 for a lack of fidelity under persecution and for sexual license. The "murderers, fornicators, sorcerers, and idolaters" refer rather to the rulers and merchants of "the great Babylon" (e.g., Revelation 17:5), who have received the sign of the beast. The sign allows them to trade in this world, which is condemned to destruction (Revelation 13:16–17). "The liars" is a designation that refers to "those who say that they are Jews and are not" (Revelation 2:9; 3:9) and to Jezebel, "who calls herself a prophet and is teaching and beguiling my servants to practice fornication and to eat food sacrificed to idols" (Revelation 2:20). The prominence of judgment in this book reveals a community that feels surrounded by hostile outside elements and mined by treasonous elements within the churches.

(3) The new city comes from heaven down to earth (Revelation 21:10). This signifies a totally *alien basis* for the hope of a utopian city. There is no workable project for humans either to carry out the necessary judgment or to establish the new heavens and new earth. These are perceived to come from God.

(4) The city itself is presented predominantly by geometric shapes and consists of minerals and precious stones. Aside from the tree of life (Revelation 22:2) and the life-bearing water (Revelation 22:1–5), there is little that suggests the presence of living beings or the satisfaction of bodily needs. This vision arises from a community that feels surrounded by depravity to such a degree that the *purity of stone and metal* is preferable to warm beings who are potential agents of pollution. The exclusion of women contributes to this lack of bodily life in the new Jerusalem.

(5) This is a vision of *power*. Although it is exercised by the Lamb, this power is capable of destroying the Great Babylon and of throwing Satan and his followers into the lake of fire (Revelation 20:14–15). The redeemed who live in the new Jerusalem, deprived of most of the joys of living, derive their own pleasure from power — "reigning forever" (Revelation 22:5).

In sum, this is a vision of the perfect society as dreamed by the prophet of a group that felt besieged from outside by the powers of the Roman Empire and betrayed from within by false brothers (and sisters, e.g., Jezebel). The reason for this vision is not difficult to grasp. Asian Christians[1] found themselves in dramatically new circumstances during the late first century. Their vision of the perfect society had to be adapted. Under these circumstances, the vision of John, an Asian Christian in exile, replaced the earlier utopian vision of the Synoptic Gospels, the focal point of which was a banquet with Abraham (Matthew 8:11), at which all the redeemed would drink new wine with Jesus (Mark 14:25).

Reflection

Utopias are by definition models that exist nowhere and that cannot be literally realized. They are not historical projects that can guide historical and political action, but they are necessary to motivate and to inspire social action. The Cuban Revolution would not have been possible without two crucial elements in its utopia: first, a society free from imperialist impositions and thus able to develop according to its own internal economic and social requirements; and second, a socialist economy where the production is collectively owned and distributed in an egalitarian fashion. These utopian elements arose out of specific problems faced by Cuba in the pre-revolutionary years, that is, domination of the Cuban economy and society by the United States and a grossly unequal distribution of the national product. The consequent utopian vision generated specific historical projects. On the one hand, it established a national army designed for defense against the United States and a structure of military alliances with the Soviet Union. On the other hand, its internal organization of the economy reduced the free market to a minimum, centralized profit accumulation in the State, and gave priority to health care and education in the national budget. The Cuban utopia shared with John's utopia in Revelation a harshness imposed by the overriding demand of being prepared to defend the nation against a powerful empire only a short distance away. The emphasis on social equality in the Cuban utopian vision lent it a human warmth that John's vision lacks, especially since this equality was understood above all as equal access to health care and education.

The alteration produced by the new configuration of world forces, which accompanied the drastic reordering of Eastern Europe, begun in 1989, demanded a revision of the Cuban national project. This revision is already well under way, with the depenalizing of possession of foreign currency and the introduction of some margins of tolerance for a free market in agricultural produce. Although the promotion of tourism, which goes back to the period prior to 1961, and permission for family visits from Cubans in exile have introduced an element of social unrest among ordinary Cubans, this disruption resulting from contact with the outside world is deemed necessary for Cuban economic survival.

The introduction of such major changes requires a transformation of the national utopia, the dream of the Cuban revolution. The need for this change, which is "theological" or "mythical," has a direct bearing on the survival of the revolution and the level of satisfaction of the Cuban population. It also affects the impact of the Cuban revolution on the rest of Latin America. Like John, who became the prophet of a newly besieged Christian community in Asia, a prophet, one or many, must arise to give a new order to Cuban dreams. The free market, which was perceived as a depraved but attractive Jezebel, is now tolerated. Foreign influence and foreign currencies, previously denounced as insidious, are now regarded as necessary in the struggle for the survival of the revolution. A modified utopia is evidently called for, a new dream that can be shared by the large majority of Cubans—as was the former dream which has now been rendered obsolete.

What John did for Asian Christians with the visions of Revelation, we must do for Latin American Christians besieged by an aggressive global economy. I share the view of those Cubans who feel that the new utopia must be socialist and anti-imperialist in order to maintain its Cuban roots and to achieve social consensus, but this utopia must also be modified to take into account the new global reality of a monopolar world and the inner-Cuban need for a mixed economy. This utopia will share with John's vision of Babylon (Rome) an anti-imperialism that in Cuba goes back to

José Martí in the nineteenth century, but it will also incorporate a human warmth, which Asian persecution excluded from John's city and which the defensive needs of the Cold War hardened in Cuba. Its anti-imperialism will, we hope, now be softened.

All of these observations underline the intimate relationship that exists between reality and dreams. It is possible to suggest that only a softening of the United States' blockade will make possible a softening of the prophetic vision. John teaches us something of the dynamics of prophetic vision—but also some of its pitfalls. Is it too much to hope that we in Latin America have learned some lessons?

Notes

1. Christians in Asia Minor, e.g., Turkey, rather than Asia in the sense of nations such as China [editors].

Revelation 21:1–22:5
An African Perspective

Timothy G. Kiogora

Context

Marriage is regarded as the pillar of African societies. In every known African society, all men and women are expected to marry and to raise a family, to become elders or wise persons who are respected in society, and to prepare to pass on to another life even as they enter the final phase of life, which is grandparenthood. Although many things are in a state of flux in Africa today, it is safe to say that the ethos within which marriage is practiced in sub-Saharan Africa still exists. This ethos is characterized by a strong sense of community and continuity.

Among the Meru of Kenya, a small community of Africans who belong to a larger African group generally referred to as the Bantu peoples of Central, East, and South Africa, marriage is a pivotal event in life. I grew up among these people. I remember when my time to marry came. As a member of this community, I was expected to look for a bride. This is risky business. You do not marry just for your sake (that is, to have a companion) but for the sake of all your family, community, and nation (that is, all the extended family). I knew I had to inquire carefully about a girl I had seen, and, with enough background information, I began courting her. But that was not all. You do not elope with somebody's daughter. You have to make your intentions known to your future wife's family and give them time to run a check on you and your family. Then you must demonstrate that you are worthy of marrying your bride by making a symbolic "payment" for her: it costs something to live with somebody and to raise a family, and it will cost you something to undo a marriage relationship. By marrying, you have become a generous person to the community, and this requires that you become a person of means. The "payment," or dowry, is not symbolic in the sense that someone can buy another; the focus rather is on the future and a commitment to the life of the community and relationships therein.

When the bride is finally released to the bridegroom among the Meru, she is adorned accordingly, both morally and materially. She is the epitome of the future itself. She is an ideal because through her the future will be continued and relations among different people cemented and extended. It is hoped that she will have children, for not to have children places enormous stress on the community and the marriage itself. Her name will be changed to "mother of—" when and if she has a child or children. The husband is also named "father of" so and so. When I was growing up in Meru, I did not know the names of many older women except by their titles of prestige, which were simply "Ngina-wa—" or "mother of—." Thus a bride moves from the particularities of history (her past name) to the futuristic space characterized by the new (the children). Spouses in many African communities are, to this extent, expected to play vicarious roles in a serious normative sense: they are to embody the future through their struggle to bear and raise children, and with disciplined patience they are to wait upon their children's children and, all being well, depart from this life having been "renewed" by their grandchildren. That is to say, they have already "lived in the future." Among the Meru, children are named after the immediate family members, beginning with all the grandparents. In this way, the beginning becomes a part of the end, and vice versa.

Text

Two traditions come together in John's vision of the new heaven and the new earth: the bride and the new Jerusalem. John describes "the holy city, the new Jerusalem, coming out of heaven from God, prepared as a bride adorned for her husband" (Revelation 21:2). As if this identification of the new Jerusalem as a bride were inadequate, John describes again his vision: "Then one of the seven angels who had the seven bowls full of the seven last plagues came and said to me, 'Come, I will show you the bride, the wife of the Lamb.' And in the spirit he carried me away to a great, high mountain and showed me the holy city Jerusalem coming down out of heaven from God" (Revelation 21:9–10).

The entire book—its many visions, its words of warning and encouragement, its pain and agony—finds its climax and is eclipsed by this vision of "a new heaven and a new earth" (Revelation 21:1), a city that has no need of sun or moon, "for the glory of God is its light, and its lamp is the

Lamb" (21:23). The bridal image evokes the occasion of a festive marriage, a day on which there is no place for the mourning, weeping, pain,
and death that have permeated the prior visions of this book (21:4). Therefore, at long last, the book of Revelation, with its doom and devastation,
becomes a book of hope.

To understand the force of this vision of the new Jerusalem, it is necessary to assess briefly the role Jerusalem played in the history of Israel. After the people of Israel left Egypt, they evoked God's presence in the
tabernacle in the wilderness in the days of Moses and Aaron (Exodus 25–
30; Numbers 2:1–31). This tabernacle was a mobile sanctuary that suited
the nomadic existence of their tribal pattern. The universal God was believed to dwell with the people, and the nomadic people worshiped God as
a tribal God, that is, as the God who dwelt peculiarly with them. In Canaan,
the promised land, the Israelites built a permanent sanctuary to house the
tabernacle at Shiloh; Shiloh was a center of worship under the leadership
of Samuel (Joshua 21–1 Samuel 4).

Later, after David made Jerusalem the capital city of Israel, Solomon,
David's son, built the temple in Jerusalem. The temple marked the fixing
of God's presence at one earthly place (1 Kings 8). This temple came to be
considered the place of God's choosing, with the result that many Israelites
believed that God's presence in the temple made Jerusalem invulnerable to
attack. The temple came to comprise the center of a powerful tribal religion, so to speak. God was, it was said, bound up with some specific space
called the "holy of holies" within the temple. During the eighth century
B.C.E., Isaiah tried to rid the people of such a misplaced conviction that
God would invariably protect Jerusalem, when he sang, "Ah, Ariel, Ariel,
the city where David encamped! Add year to year; let the festivals run their
round. 2 Yet I will distress Ariel, and there shall be moaning and lamenta-
tion, and Jerusalem shall be to me like an Ariel. 3 And like David I will en-
camp against you; I will besiege you with towers and raise siegeworks
against you" (Isaiah 29:1–4). Jeremiah, prior to the fall of Jerusalem to
Babylon in 587 B.C.E., tried to associate God's presence with justice rather
than with the misguided belief that God dwelt in the temple of a poisoned
people: "Thus says the Lord of hosts, the God of Israel: Amend your ways
and your doings, and let me dwell with you in this place. 4 Do not trust in
these deceptive words: 'This is the temple of the Lord, the temple of the
Lord, the temple of the Lord.' 5 For if you truly amend your ways and your
doings, if you truly act justly one with another, 6 if you do not oppress the
alien, the orphan, and the widow, or shed innocent blood in this place, and
if you do not go after other gods to your own hurt, 7 then I will dwell with

you in this place, in the land that I gave of old to your ancestors forever and ever" (Jeremiah 7:3–7). Ezekiel received a vision in which God's glory departed from the temple, not because of the Babylonian siege during the decade prior to 587 B.C.E. but because of Jerusalem's sinfulness (Ezekiel 8–11).

When Jesus appeared in Jerusalem, he stood within this prophetic tradition in his effort to convince Israel during the first century C.E. that Jerusalem represented God's presence in a different way. It was, to put it in our experiential language, a presence born of the recognition of the absence of righteousness, the absence of comfort to the dispossessed, and more especially the absence of "the true spirit," which Jesus himself was to embody. Like Isaiah, Jesus wept over Jerusalem, indicating the pain he felt over "what could have been" had his contemporaries listened to him (Matthew 23:37–39). Even after Jesus had been killed and had risen from the dead, his disciples continued to experience his departure as an absence: indeed this was the most critical absence in Jerusalem because it crippled them, compelling them to retreat to a room to wait upon a new time. That new time was marked by the coming of the Holy Spirit (Acts 2), which transformed Jesus' absence into a dynamic presence. The proclamation of the gospel would now begin in Jerusalem and extend to the ends of the earth, just as Jesus commanded: "But you will receive power when the Holy Spirit has come upon you; and you will be my witnesses in Jerusalem, in all Judea and Samaria, and to the ends of the earth" (Acts 1:8). Thus, Jerusalem came to symbolize the future for the church, a people that was not fixed to any geographical space. The church became the hope of one nation—the whole world as this nation, free of that which is parochial, tribal, and ethnic.

The relevance of the visible church must henceforth be understood in the context of the new reality "from heaven." The special privilege of being a church is to live as the adorned bride lives for the future. The holy presence of God, in Revelation 21, is a gift to all people from God, and the new Jerusalem (the church) is a symbol of that presence (21:22–27).

Reflection

John is a reliable witness. It is from his experience as an exile on the island of Patmos (Revelation 1:9) that his knowledge of events makes him a messenger to the seven churches (Revelation 2–3), indeed to all churches in all times. He sifts through the trash of human history to make this point. Two millennia later, we are not at a new historical juncture, after all the years of lapsed memories, pretensions to power, and the seduction of materialistic visions and fixed religious images. John's vision still issues a call to all people to seize the new moment if they are to experience God's blessings (21:7). The new Jerusalem does not refer to the restoration of an earthly city in Palestine called Jerusalem. The new Jerusalem is a new earthly reality characterized by the presence of virtuous life among all people. What, however, has a Jewish city, historical or renewed, to do with Africa?

Like the people of ancient Israel, African peoples had localized, tribal experiences of God. Among the Meru and Kikuyu of Kenya, for example, God was a fixed reality high on Mount Kenya, the highest mountain in their area. For this reason, God was associated with a specific place, although such tribes acknowledged God's capacity to "hear" and "see" everything, implying God's omnipresence. Nomadic African communities, like the Masai of East Africa, associated God with their yearnings in a mobile existence.

When the Christian gospel was preached in Africa, Africans saw the possibility of expanding what they knew about what they did not know. Here the "strangers" who brought the gospel were "mysteries" from God, so to speak. Where the Christian gospel was embraced, it was accepted uncritically. However, many of the churches that resulted were built for specific ethnic communities. For example, in East Africa, many denominations are still structured along ethnic lines: Methodists are by and large from the Meru tribe; Presbyterians are mostly from the Kikuyu; the Luo would be in the main Anglican, or descendants of the original Church of England. It is safe, then, to say that the more things changed, the more they remained the same. African tribalism was transformed into Christian tribalism. The "new life in Christ" became just another African "mystery" among many. The church did not become an open-ended, potentially universal community.

In this kind of situation, John's vision of the new Jerusalem, the bride adorned and descending, in Revelation 21 is simultaneously good news and bad news for much of Africa. It is good news because the new sense of community found in this text introduces Africa to a fresh look at who God's people truly are; it is bad news because it is judgment upon our inability or unwillingness to deal with glaring ethnic tendencies in our church practices in Africa. The symbol with which we are so familiar—"a bride adorned for her husband"—a symbol so central to life in Africa, a symbol that is the conclusion to a period of selecting, courting, testing, and being tested, a symbol rich with hopes for a new generation, suggests that the bride's dress and makeup come from heaven this time! Thus, the vision of

Revelation 21 serves to convict us of tribalism and to offer a vision for the renewal of the church's fundamental self-understanding, as we enter a new millennium in Africa.

This vision offers hope. We observed that the visions of the book of Revelation are eclipsed by this vision of "a new heaven and a new earth" (Revelation 21:1), in which death and tears are no more. We who live in Africa know why hope is necessary because we are only too familiar with the struggle between God and the Satanic forces in the forms of ethnic conflicts, hostile droughts, colonization and its aftermath, incurable diseases, and tribal rulers. The purpose of life is for us to align ourselves with "life forces" as opposed to evil forces of death. Thus, one cannot escape from being involved one way or the other with either the forces of life or the forces of death. Many Africans believe that one cannot be neutral. Life is a struggle every day. In the struggle between God and Satan, there is much wear and tear, and one has to hang on to life often by the skin of the teeth, as it were. Nevertheless, we in Africa smile and play in situations of critical "absence"—absence of justice, absence of compassion, absence of the true spirit. We must recognize that this is God's world, not ours, and that hope in this world comes from God rather than from the harsh reality of our surroundings. Hope comes from the vision of a bride descending from heaven in preparation for the grand marriage ceremony about to take place, from the conviction that death and tears will disappear, rather than from the Satanic warfare with evil, which otherwise marks the book of Revelation and our lives in Africa. In Africa today, then, in spite of what happens around the lives of many people, hope is always present.

The dimensions of "the bride, the wife of the Lamb" (21:9) are carefully laid out: the gates, the foundation stones, the names on the gates, and even the number of layers of foundation stones and gems on them. Why this precision? Apparently, the purpose of the bride is not to serve the pleasure of her husband but to create a carefully guarded community: "a city" 1,500 miles from every angle—*very* spacious (21:16); a community or city with fortified walls (21:17). It is a pure city (21:18). The bride is a visible sign that points to this pure, glorious, anticipated community. I confess that I still do not know the name for *church* in my own mother tongue, Meru. *Church* is construed as some kind of gathering, often of like-minded people, who live a limited and limiting existence. In contrast, my ability to express the unbounded, hopeful, and universal language of John's vision of the beautiful bride, of the new Jerusalem, in the Meru tongue is a wonderful experience. In Meru, as in many other parts of Africa, the old images meet the new, and nothing can ever be the same.

Revelation 21:1–22:5
An Asian Perspective

Choan-Seng Song

Context

We human beings live in a global village today, we are told. We are to think globally, envision globally, plan globally, strategize globally, from politics to science and technology, to communications, and, of course, to economy and trade. When it comes to the global economy, where does it begin? Does it begin with New York, London, or Tokyo, those financial and trade centers of the world? No, it does not begin there. It begins with the story of people such as Yati, a twenty-three-year-old woman who works for Reebok in Tangerang, Indonesia.

> Yati earns 165,000 rupiah—not quite $80—for a month of sewing bits of leather and lace for shoes that bear the name of Reebok. She works 40-hour weeks plus 90 hours of overtime.
>
> It costs less to live in the sweltering villages of rural Indonesia than almost anywhere else in the world. And Reebok goes to great lengths to portray itself as a conscientious promoter of human rights in the Third World.
>
> But when Yati leaves the clean, well-lighted factory, she has only enough money to rent a 10-by-12 foot shack with dirty walls alive with gecko lizards. There is no furniture, so Yati and two roommates sleep in fetal curls on a mud-and-tile floor.
>
> Through a translator Yati asks, "How much Reebok cost, U.S.?" The answer is on the bottom line of her monthly pay stub. Having suspected as much, Yati shuts her eyes and nods.
>
> . . . in her shanty, bathed by the yellow-brown light of a single

naked bulb, Yati shares her dream of leaving the factory to become a secretary. But after four years of making Reeboks, she has neither the savings nor the time to pursue it, and the dream is growing dim.

Asked to imagine her future, her bright face turns to a scowl, and she waves a hand in the air. "I can't," Yati says. "This is all there is for me."[1]

Yati cherishes a simple dream—leaving the factory to become a secretary. But that dream is beyond her reach. Although she has worked forty normal hours and ninety overtime hours a week for four years, she has neither the savings nor the time to pursue her dream. This ought to compel those politicians, economists, and company presidents who talk in global terms to think more than twice. It also reminds Christians not to paint a vision of a new heaven and a new earth too easily and too glibly.

Yati's is not an isolated story. Stories such as Yati's abound in many developing nations in Asia and in other Third World countries. They were very much at the center of the Mission Conference held in Cipanes, near Jakarta, Indonesia, in September 1989, organized by the Christian Conference of Asia. Awakened to the realities such stories portray, more than 200 Christians—lay and ordained women and men from churches in Asia—found themselves denouncing "the massive dehumanization [in Asia] manifested in the forms of hunger, malnutrition, oppression of women and children, disabled persons, cultural minorities and indigenous peoples, landless peasants, industrial workers, fisher folks, stateless citizens, and victims of political oppression." They were anguished by "the domination of global and national powers" that continue to exploit "the human and material resources of Asia," the exploitation that "keeps the majority of Asian peoples in perpetual enslavement" and brings about an environmental crisis. And they had to deal with the painful awareness that "religions, including Christianity, have been collaborators with these principalities and powers . . . even to the extent of giving religious justification to the powers-that-be."[2]

Text

Confronted with "the massive dehumanization" in the world today, what are Christians to make of Revelation, especially chapter 21, with its talk of "a new heaven and a new earth?" For most Christians in Asia, who are sheltered in the church and removed from violence done to helpless women, men, and children in society, the Book of Revelation offers a cozy reason for faith: they are among those chosen to enjoy "the kingdom of God" to come in glory and splendor. Never mind words of warning issued to some

of the seven churches mentioned in the opening chapters (Revelation 2—
3). Those words are not meant for our church! Never mind either that tense
silence that envelopes heaven when the seventh seal is opened: "When the
Lamb opened the seventh seal, there was silence in heaven for about half
an hour" (Revelation 8:1). What terrifying scenes of destruction unfold as
the angels successively blow their trumpets, each time more terrifying than
the previous time (Revelation 8:2–9:21)! And there is Armageddon in Revelation 16, where violence of a cosmic magnitude erupts to destroy the enemies of God: "The sixth angel poured his bowl on the great river
Euphrates, and its water was dried up in order to prepare the way for the
kings from the east. 13 And I saw three foul spirits like frogs coming from
the mouth of the dragon, from the mouth of the beast, and from the mouth
of the false prophet. 14 These are demonic spirits, performing signs, who
go abroad to the kings of the whole world, to assemble them for battle on
the great day of God the Almighty. 15 ('See, I am coming like a thief!
Blessed is the one who stays awake and is clothed, not going about naked
and exposed to shame.') 16 And they assembled them at the place that in
Hebrew is called Harmagedon." Christians are, of course, not those enemies of God! Just the contrary. They are God's, chosen "to reign with
Christ a thousand years," to live out a millennium of bliss (20:4).

The Book of Revelation can thus be read and misread, interpreted and
misinterpreted, applied and misapplied by many Christians and churches.
Most parts of it—twenty chapters out of twenty-two, in fact—read like cosmic warfare between God and Satan, the sole purpose of which is to vin-
dicate Christians and to avenge their enemies and persecutors. John, who
is the author of those strange and vivid visions of horrors, devastations, and
death, also envisioned a decisive defeat of the Roman principalities and
powers that had inflicted so much pain, suffering, and death on Christians.
He himself, "according to a firm tradition in the early church . . . was banished by order of the Roman emperor"[3] to a small island called Patmos "because of the word of God and the testimony of Jesus" (Revelation 1:9).

What John has accomplished in those extraordinary visions and images
is to profess a faith told as stories of warfare between God and God's enemy, between good and evil, between light and darkness—a familiar literary device that produced much fine religious literature in the ancient world,
the East and West, North and South.[4] It is the faith of men and women who,
even though harassed, hunted down, burnt with fire, or thrown to the
beasts, remained faithful to their God in the midst of afflictions. "Be faithful until death," the church in Smyrna is encouraged, and then it is given a
promise, "I will give you the crown of life" (Revelation 2:10).

This promise concerns faith in the God of life and future. True, there is destruction and death all around. This is a fact of life. This is what happens in history. Even nature is not free from it all. Oppressed and persecuted, John and his fellow Christians projected human afflictions and natural catastrophes as God's judgment on the world that inflicts pain and death on them. But the future of life does not belong to Christians alone. It belongs as well to the entire creation of God. Just as the entire created world is subject to death, so is that creation the recipient of life. John, in the Spirit on the Lord's day (Revelation 1:10), was also made aware of this.

It may be that the visions of horrendous destruction have made John realize that what God wants to bring about is not just the vindication of Christians and the salvation of their souls but the restoration and renewal of the entirety of God's creation—a new heaven and a new earth. The turmoil in the universe and tribulations in the human community in his visions are, after all, not the judgment God meted out only to a human world hostile to Christians. They are in fact the birth pangs of the creation to be newly born. "The whole creation," to quote what Paul wrote in his letter to the Christians in Rome, "has been groaning in labor pains until now" (Romans 8:22).

Reflection

What John, on the island of Patmos, has shown us, then, is that "the whole creation is groaning in labor pains" for "a new heaven and a new earth" (Revelation 21:1). It has taken him a long time to get to this point, as long as twenty chapters out of twenty-two. But from the old creation to a new creation is a long, long time. It is a time that cannot be measured by human time. It is God's time. And as God's time, it is neither under our control nor at our disposal. In this between-times, there are endless nights of doubt, fear, and anguish. And John has described for us experiences of those dark nights in terrifying images and symbols.

No less than John, the participants of the Mission Conference at Cipanes in Indonesia, in 1989, were also confronted with this between-times of doubt, fear, and anguish. They came to the conference to "consider our vision of a new earth."[5] But while these words were still on their lips, and the ink in which these words were written was not yet dry, they had to hear the story of Yati's unfulfilled dream of leaving her shanty and becoming a secretary. They had to know that they had been talking about a new heaven and a new earth while people like Yati were saying, "I can't imagine my future. This is all there is for me." They realized that stories such as Yati's lead to a larger picture of what is happening in many countries in Asia. It became clear to them that they had to reckon with an alarming fact: "Our lands are being devastated for the profit of others not dependent on them. Thus, for example, the denuding of the forests on the western and eastern Chats of India is causing drought; excessive logging in Sri Lanka, Thailand, and the Philippines is severely disrupting the whole ecosystem, turning fertile lands to wastelands."[6]

This is the human and ecological crisis that the people of Asia are facing, the crisis created by the drive for economic growth and the prosperity of rich nations. Is there, then, no hope for people in Asia such as Yati? Is there no future for the massive continent of Asia, which is relentlessly exploited for economic gains? Faced with such questions, the participants of the Mission Conference articulated their Christian vision. "Our vision," they said, "is the new earth based on the reign of God . . . of justice and freedom."[7]

But the distance between Asia's exploited people and God's reign of justice and freedom, between the old heaven and the old earth and a new heaven and a new earth, is enormous. We cannot cover that distance with one giant leap. Nor can we reduce it by taking a shortcut. It takes all the tribulations, both personal and communal, for John the seer finally to envision that new heaven and earth. And he knows that the churches have to be tested and tried before they can be given glimpses of a new heaven and a new earth. It must be the same for Christians in Asia. Theirs is a vision of a new heaven on earth, that part of the mother earth called Asia. But they cannot just wish that vision into becoming a reality. Nor can they hail it from nowhere. They have to become actively engaged in efforts to redress the causes of the crisis. They have to commit themselves "to try our best, with our belief in Christ as the life of the world."[8]

This brings us back to the vision of a new heaven and a new earth, in which John hears "a loud voice from the throne saying" (Revelation 21:3), among other things, that God "will wipe every tear from their eyes. Death will be no more" (21:4). But there is death, and signs of death are everywhere. How many of John's fellow Christians had to die because of their faith in Jesus! How many tears those left behind had to shed for their loved ones taken away from them violently! Again, between suffering and freedom from suffering, there is a huge chasm. Between tears and laughter, there is a large gulf. And between death and life, there is an insurmountable abyss.

You and I cannot cross that gulf by waving a magic wand. We cannot bridge that chasm by just thinking positive thoughts and keeping out negative ones. And it is not in our power to overcome that abyss by taking refuge in meditation and contemplation. John knows it. It is God, he tells us, who will wipe every tear from our eyes. And God does it by dwelling with us as our God (Revelation 21:3). Immanuel! God with us! The theology of the Book of Revelation is not a theology ready-made in heaven and transplanted on earth. The faith it seeks to inspire is not packaged in paradise only to be opened and distributed to Christians worshiping in church.

What John is engaged in is the theology of Immanuel, a theology that God shares our human sufferings, that God is involved in the tribulations of the universe. That theology of Immanuel, translated into Asia, insists that for God to be God, God must be the God to be heard in Yati's story, to be perceived in the groaning of a natural world devastated by human greed. And for us human beings to be human beings, we must be able to resonate with that God in Yati's story and in the groaning of lands, forests, and rivers polluted by our industries and economic activities. This Immanuel—this God with creation and creation with God—is a new heaven and a new earth.

What the author of the Book of Revelation has shown us, then, is *not* a vision of a new heaven and a new earth *but* a vision of *a new heaven on earth,* in the very same world that the Roman Empire ruled with brutal force. And what the participants at the Mission Conference in Indonesia perceived as "a new heaven on earth in Asia" is what many women and men are striving for: "industrial workers' fight for their rights and the landless peasants' demand for land reform, ethnic people's clamor for self-determination and identity, women's demand for equality and larger share in the decision making processes of churches and community, people's call for justice, democracy and peace."[9] The efforts to remedy all these problems are not by themselves a new heaven on earth in Asia. They are its signs. They are in fact more than signs. Without them, there will be no new heaven on earth in Asia. The mission of the Christian community is to identify such signs and to be part of such signs.

John also shares with his readers an astonishing sign: he "saw no temple in the city" (Revelation 21:22). A new heaven and a new earth have no temple! Temple is the heart of a religious community. It commands the devotion and loyalty of its believers. But how much blood has been shed and how many lives have been lost because of it? What an irony! Heaven and earth are new precisely because the temple is gone, that cause of conflict is removed. In that new realm of life, no blood is going to be shed and no life will perish on account of what one believes. No, it is much more than that. There, religion itself ceases to exist. It is simply no longer needed. It is not religion but God who commands the devotion and loyalty of all nations and peoples.

A city without a temple is a powerful image for Christians in Asia, who share not only living space with people of other religions but also their sufferings and longings, their despairs and hopes. The story of Yati's plight transcends religious boundaries. The effort to redress that plight is not inspired by a sectarian spirit but by the awareness of a common destiny in God. A vision such as this should inspire all of us, including Yati, to envision our future and should empower us to face the world of injustice, helplessness and pain: "this is *not* all there is for us."

The road towards a new heaven on earth in Asia is a long and hard one. Likewise, the new heaven and new earth that our author, banished to the island of Patmos, saw in the Spirit on the Lord's day continues to frustrate as well as to inspire those men and women who rise to its call. But the journey has already begun, and there is no turning away from it. This, after all, is the journey of none other than Jesus our Lord, who prayed that God's will be done on earth as in heaven.

Notes

1. The story is taken from the article "The Hidden Cost of Free Trade," *San Francisco Chronicle*, Sunday, July 24, 1994, section A, page 8, and section A, page 10.

2. The quotations are from the report of "Section I: Discerning Christ's Work among People," in *People of Asia, People of God, a Report of the Asia Mission Conference 1989* (Hong Kong: The Christian Conference of Asia, 1990) 122.

3. P. E. Hughes, *The Book of the Revelation: a Commentary* (Grand Rapids: Eerdmans, 1990) 24.

4. Such literature is usually designated "apocalyptic literature." Examples from the Greco-Roman era, during which period the biblical Book of Revelation (in Greek, *apocalypsis* or *apocalypse*) was composed, include the Book of Daniel, 4 Ezra, 2 (the Syriac Apocalypse of) Baruch, and several documents from among the Dead Sea Scrolls, such as the War scroll (1QM) and the third and fourth columns of the Community Rule (1QS 3–4) [editors].

5. *People of Asia, People of God,* 130.

6. *People of Asia, People of God,* 130.

7. *People of Asia, People of God,* 133, 124.

8. *People of Asia, People of God,* 130.

9. *People of Asia, People of God,* 124.

Select Annotated Bibliography

For an introduction to global biblical interpretation in general, a starting point is R. S. Sugirtharajah (ed.), *Voices from the Margin: Interpreting the Bible in the Third World* (Maryknoll: Orbis, 1991), which is a collection of previously published articles by men and women from many Two Thirds World contexts. The volume is divided into five parts: (1) "Use of the Bible: Methods, Principles and Issues"; (2) "Re-use of the Bible: Examples of Hermeneutical Explorations," consisting of miscellaneous illustrative studies, e.g., an Indian interpretation of John 2:1–11; (3) "The Exodus: One Theme, Many Perspectives," in which the exodus is interpreted from the perspectives of the Korean *minjung,* Palestinians, Native Americans, etc.; (4) "One Reality, Many Texts: Examples of Multi-faith Hermeneutics," which consists of articles written in light of other Asian religious traditions; and (5) "People as Exegetes," a significant section of biblical interpretations by non-scholars in Malawi, Nicaragua, Indonesia, South Africa, and China. J. S. Pobee (ed.), *New Eyes for Reading: Biblical and Theological Reflections by Women from the Third World* (Geneva: WCC, 1986) contains brief reflections by Two Thirds World women on biblical texts in which, for the most part, women are featured. The style is conversational rather than analytical. Although the foci of J. R. Levison and P. Pope-Levison, *Jesus in Global Contexts* (Louisville: Westminster/John Knox, 1992), are portraits of Jesus in Latin American liberation theology, Asia, Africa, and North American feminist and black theologies, this book introduces the issues faced by each context and the resulting portraits of Jesus, as well as sources and methods used in each context, including the Bible. The conclusion contains a summary of hermeneutical methods and biblical starting points, and a thorough bibliography is included.

The earliest influential books to stake a claim for Latin American biblical hermeneutics from a liberation perspective were L. Boff, *Jesus Christ Liberator: A Critical Christology for Our Time* (Maryknoll, NY: Orbis, 1978) and J. Sobrino, *Christology at the Crossroads* (Maryknoll, NY: Orbis, 1978). E. Tamez's *Bible of the Oppressed* (Maryknoll, NY: Orbis, 1982) is an introduction to contemporary Latin American readings of the Bible that presupposes no technical knowledge. A sense of liberation theology's approach to the Bible can be gleaned from J. Míguez-Bonino (ed.), *Faces of Jesus: Latin American Christologies* (Maryknoll: Orbis, 1984), particularly in the section on "Christ and Politics." J. L. Segundo, *The Historical Jesus of the Synoptics* (Maryknoll: Orbis, 1985) should be read only after an initial foundation in historical-critical methods is laid. Following a theoretical discussion of his hermeneutics, Segundo implements the methods of historical-criticism to defend the thesis that the political dimension permeated the life of Jesus. J. S. Croatto's *Biblical Hermeneutics: Toward a Theory of Reading as the Production of Meaning* (Maryknoll, NY: Orbis, 1987) presupposes an acquaintance with literary theory.

Two of the earliest books to compare African conceptions with biblical ones were K. Dickson and P. Ellingworth (eds.), *Biblical Revelation and African Beliefs* (London: Lutterworth, 1969) and J. S. Mbiti, *New Testament Eschatology in an African Background: a study of the encounter between New Testament Theology and African Traditional Religion* (Oxford: Oxford University, 1971). The central features of African biblical interpretation can be culled from Christological analyses. J. S. Pobee (ed.), *Exploring Afro-Christology* (Frankfurt, New York: Peter Lang, 1992) contains articles by black theologians in sub-Sahara Africa, North America, and the Caribbean. R. Schreiter (ed.), *Faces of Jesus in Africa* (Maryknoll: Orbis, 1991) contains survey articles of various aspects of African Christology, as well as specific Christologies: Jesus as master of initiation (rites of passage), chief, ancestor and elder brother, and liberator. From a South African perspective, I. J. Mosala interprets Micah and Luke in *Biblical Hermeneutics and Black Theology in South Africa* (Grand Rapids: Eerdmans, 1989). A recent volume of the journal, *Semeia,* volume 73 (1996) contains several relevant articles: G. West, "Reading the Bible Differently: Giving Shape to the Discourses of the Dominated"; I. J. Mosala, "Race, Class, and Gender as Hermeneutical Factors in the African Independent Churches' Appropriation of the Bible"; M. W. Dube, "Readings of Semoya: Botswana Women's Interpretations of Matt 15:21–28"; J. S. Pobee, "Bible Study in Africa: A Passover of Language"; and J. S. Ukpong, "The Parable of the Shrewd Manager (Luke 16:1–13): An Essay in Inculturation Biblical Hermeneutic."

Two valuable early works that represent two aspects of the Indian context—mystic experience versus the public life of nation-building—are R. Panikkar, *The Unknown Christ of Hinduism* (London: Darton, Longman and Todd, 1964) and M. M. Thomas, *The Acknowledged Christ of the Indian Renaissance* (London: SCM, 1969), respectively. More general discussions of Asian biblical interpretation include: G. M. Soares-Prabhu, "The Historical Critical Method: Reflections on its Relevance for the Study of the Gospels in India Today," in *Theologizing in India,* edited by M. Amaladoss, G. Gispert-Sauch, and T. K. John (Bangalore: Theological Publications in India, 1981) 314–67; idem., "Two Mission Commands: An Interpretation of Matthew 28:16–20 in the Light of a Buddhist Text," *Biblical Interpretation* 2 (1994) 264–82; S. J. Samartha, *The Search for New Hermeneutics in Asian Christian Theology* (Madras: CLS, 1987) probes general issues related to biblical interpretation in Asia; and R. S. Sugirtharajah, "The Bible and its Asian Readers," *Biblical Interpretation* 1 (1993) 54–66, which contains a survey, critical analyses, and bibliography. K. P. Lan offers an interpretation of the Bible in the context of religious pluralism and women's experience in Asia, in *Discovering the Bible in the Non-Biblical World* (Maryknoll, NY: Orbis, 1995).

Index of Subjects

African
 afterlife, conceptions of, 189–91
 ancestors, 191–92
 anthropology, 189–90
 healers, 43, 45–46, 148–49
 oral tradition, 148
 marriage, 23, 207–8
 myths, 17–24
 naming ceremony, 23
 prophecy, 145–49
 proverbs, 5, 22, 43, 81–82, 84, 85,
 105
 songs, 5, 21, 66, 105–6
 traditional religion, 148–49
 tribalism, 211–12
African Synod, 44
Amin, Mohammed, 129–30
Athanasius, 154

Basic Christian Communities, 133,
 177
Bible
 and contemporary hermeneutics,
 2–3
 and hermeneutical circle, 121–22
biblical characters, events, gods, insti-
 tutions, nations
 Aaron, 209
 Abel, 29
 Abraham, 20, 23, 109, 203
 Absalom, 20
 Adam, 19, 31, 157 nn.15, 17; 187,
 190
 Armageddon, 215
 Assyria, 14–15, 71, 103
 Baal, 39

Babylon, 1, 14–15, 71, 96–97, 103,
 110, 202, 204, 209–10
Beatitudes, mountain of, 118
Cain, 29
Canaan, 209
Covenant, See covenant
Creation, 18–19, 52–53, 133, 146,
 154, 171, 216
Cyrus, 96–97, 99 n.1, 106 n.2
David, 20, 209
Eden, 19, 31
Elijah, 120
Egypt, 38–40, 45, 58, 70, 71, 103
Eve, 19, 31
Ezekiel, 210
Holy Spirit, See Holy Spirit
Isaac, 20
Isaiah, 175, 209, 210
Jeremiah, 209
Jerusalem (Zion), 109–10, 168–69,
 175, 202–5, 208–12
Jesus, See Jesus
Jezebel, 202, 204
Joanna, 187
Job, 112
John the Baptist, 141
Joseph, 20
Jubilee, year of, 179 n.13
Kings, Israelite, 39, 70, 175
Lamech, 29
Logos, 142–143
Mary Magdalene, 187
Mary, mother of James, 187
Messiah, 120, 133
Moses, 105, 106 n.3, 118, 120, 141,
 209

biblical characters, events, gods, insti-
    tutions, nations (*continued*)
  Nazareth, 142, 176
  Nebuchadnezzar, 110
  Nimrod, 14
  Noah, 19
  Patmos, 210, 215, 219
  Persia, 71, 96–97
  Peter, 168, 170, 171, 176
  Pharisees, 119–20, 128
  Prophets, Israelite, 175
  Roman Empire, 203
  Salome, 187
  Samuel, 39, 209
  Sarah, 23, 109
  Satan, 203, 212, 215
  Servant of Yahweh (suffering),
    96–99, 102–6, 109–13
  Shiloh, 209
  Sinai, 45, 53, 118, 126, 162–63,
    168–69, 175
  Solomon, 38, 39, 209
  Smyrna, 215
  Tabernacle, 209
  Temple, 38, 39, 134, 175, 209,
    218–19
  Tree of life, 203
  Wisdom, 83, 146, 149–50 n.1, 154,
    156 n.12
Buddhism, 112
burakumin, 87–88, 90–92

capitalist market, 37, 39–40, 77,
    201–2, 203–5
caste system, 49–54, 151–52
church
  in Africa, 45–47, 65–66, 104–6,
    171–72, 211, 212
  in Asia, 50, 71–72, 133–34, 177,
    193–94, 196–98, 214, 216–19
  in Latin America, 13–14, 95–96,
    142–43, 161–62, 163–64, 203–5
colonialization, 28, 139, 145–46,
    147–49, 163, 173
conquistadors, 1, 13
countries and regions
  Argentina, 4, 5, 14, 16 n.1, 161–62

Australia, 163
Bolivia, 161
Caribbean, 185–86
China, 27–28
Costa Rica, 5
Cuba, 201–2, 203–5
Eastern Europe, 202, 204
Ecuador, 13
El Salvador, 95–96
Ethiopia, 129–30
Ghana, 5, 23–24
Guinea, 16 n.1
India, 2, 5, 49–54, 91–92, 151–52,
    154–57, 217
Indonesia, 5, 213–14, 216–17
Japan, 27–28, 30, 69–70, 72, 87–88,
    92
Kenya, 5, 6, 63, 64, 125–26,
    129–30, 145–50, 207–8,
    211–12
Korea, 69–72, 107–13
Mexico, 5, 76, 139–40
Nicaragua, 5, 6, 37, 40, 75, 77,
    95–96, 98–99
Philippines, 4, 5, 6, 131–35,
    173–74, 176–79, 193–94,
    196–98, 217
Portugal, 16 n.1
Soviet Union, 37, 40, 201–2
Spain, 1, 13, 16 n.1
Sri Lanka, 217
Taiwan, 5, 27–28, 30
Tanzania, 65
Thailand, 217
Uganda, 65
United Kingdom, 16
United States, 16, 37, 201–2,
    203–5
Zaire, 5
Zambia, 5, 6, 167–68, 170–72
covenant
  in Africa, 43–44, 45–47
  and Ancient Near Eastern peoples,
    48 n.5, 52
  code, 51
  and Israelites, 23, 45
  of Jesus Christ, 47

at Sinai, 53, *See also* Index of
    Scripture References, Exodus 20

dalits (ex-untouchables), 6, 49–50,
    51–54

education, 75, 98, 201–2
epicureanism, 83
eschatology, *See* hope
exile, 96–99 n. 1, 103, 109–10,
    209–10
exodus, 38–40, 45, 209

fetishes, 17, 43

Geldof, Robert, 129–30
God
    African view of, 17–18, 21–25, 81,
        146, 148, 211
    as anointer, 70–71
    Aztec view of, 139–40
    compassion of, 110, 218
    and covenant, *See* covenant
    as creator, 83, 133, 216
    and diversity, 15–16
    and incarnation, 152–55
    in Hinduism, 151–52
    as host, 59, 65
    and humanity, 21–24, 30–32, 112,
        218
    as liberator, 15–16, 58–59, 78,
        112
    as protector of the poor, 40, 91
    reign of, 217
    and resurrection, 191
    and Satan, 212, 215
    and sky, 22
    as shepherd, 58–60, 64, 66–67,
        70–71
    as Yahweh, 23, 38–39

hellenism, 76, 151, 155 n.1
hermeneutics, 2–3, 121–22
Hilary of Poitiers, 154
hinduism, 2, 49–53, 151–52, 154–57,
    171
Holy Spirit (Spirit of God), 6, 71, 141,

162, 164, 168–70, 174–79, 210,
    216, 219
hope, 77–78, 84–85, 103, 104,
    111–13, 120, 175–78, 186, 195,
    201–5, 212, 216–18

immortality
    in African belief, 23, 189–92
    in Filipino belief, 193–94, 196–98
incarnation, 140–44, 146–50, 152–57
indigenous peoples and languages
    Akan, 17, 21–22, 23
    Ashanti, 18, 21
    Aztec, 139–40
    Bambara, 82
    Bantu, 5, 7, 43, 44, 46, 47, 81–82,
        84–85, 101–2, 104–6, 207–8
    Basuto, 21
    Dinka, 17
    Ewe, 21, 23
    Gikuyu, 5, 145–46, 147–49, 211
    Incas, 1, 13
    Kikuyu, *See* Gikuyu
    Luba, 43
    Lunda, 21
    Massai, 21, 211
    Meru, 207–8, 211–12
    Mestizo, 140
    Nahua, 5, 139–40
    Ngombe, 21
    Nuer, 17, 18, 22
    Quechua, 13, 161–64
International Monetary Fund (IMF),
    37, 40, 78 n.2
Islam, 125

Jesus
    at baptism, 176
    and creation, 152–55, 171
    as crucified one, 186
    as head of church, 171
    and Holy Spirit, 171, *See* Holy
        Spirit
    as human flesh, 141, 153, *See* incar-
        nation
    and Jerusalem, 210
    as lamb, 208–9, 215

Jesus *(continued)*
  as liberator of oppressed, 2, 121–22,
    177
  as light, 140–41, 142–43, 147, 149,
    152–54
  as logos (word), 142–44, 146–47,
    152–57
  and mystical experience, 2
  as resurrected one, 186, 194–98
  and Sermon on the Mount, 118–23
  as shepherd, 57–58, 66
  as slave, 142
  and Suffering Servant, 104, 110
  in synagogue at Nazareth, 176
Judaism, 3, 83, 132–33, 162–63

land reform, 173–79

martyrdom, 95–99, 101–2, 103,
    133–34, 215, 217
Messiah, 120, 133
minjung, 71–72, 107–9, 111–13 n.1

nations, *See* countries and regions

oppressed, words for
  burakumin, 87–88, 90–92
  dalits, 6, 49–54
  minjung, 71–72, 107–9, 111–13 n.1

pentecostalism, 161–62, 163–64
poetry and song
  in Africa, 5, 21, 66, 105–6
  in Latin America, 140
political leaders, *See* world figures

religious leaders, *See* world figures
resurrection
  collective Israelite, 97–98
  of Jesus, 98–99, 186–87, 190,
    194–98

and solidarity of women, 185–86,
    187–88
and suffering, 187–88, 196–97
See also immortality

sabbath, 38–39, 40, 44–45
songs, *See also* poetry and song

utopias, 77, 120, 201–5

witchcraft, 43, 81, 149
women
  abuse of, 6, 185–86
  in Africa, 44
  and crucifixion, 185–86, 187–88
  and resurrection, 185–86,187–88
world figures
  Alexander the Great, 76
  Amin, Idi, 65–66, 126,
    128–30
  Aquino, Cory, 173–74
  Biko, Steve, 96
  Gandhi, Mahatma, 49, 152
  King, Jr., Martin Luther, 7, 96
  Kivengere, Festo, 126, 128, 130
  Malcolm X, 96
  Marcos, Ferdinand, 131, 173–74
  Park, Chung Hee, 108
  Ramos, Fidel, 174, 178 n.3
  Romero, Oscar, 96
  Sandinistas, 98–99
  Somoza (Anastasio Somoza De-
    bayle), 98
world religions
  Buddhism, 112
  Hinduism, 2, 49–53, 151–52,
    154–57, 171
  Islam, 125
  Judaism, 3, 83, 132–33

Zakkai, Johanan ben, 132

Index of Ancient References

Old Testament

Genesis

1:1	31, 53, 146
1:1–2	172 n.4
1:2	22
1:3	147
1:26–27	52
1:26–28	154, 157 n.16
1	146, 171
1–11	xi, 24 n.8, 33 n.2
2:15	32
2:23	153
3:4–5	31
3:6	19
3:21	19
3:22	20, 22
3:22a	19
3:22b	19
3:24a	19
3:24b	19
4:1–16	29
4:23–24	29
6:1–4	19
6:5–7	19
6:17	153
7:1–24	19
10–11	15
10:8–10	14
11	28
11:1–9	1, 3–4, 11, 13, 17, 19, 27, 168
11:2	14
11:2–3	14
11:4	30
11:4a	19, 20
11:4b	20, 29
11:5	15
11:6	20, 30
11:6–7	15
11:7	15, 20, 30
12	23
12:2	23
12:3	16
21:12	20
37:27	153
48:15	72 n.3
48:16	20
49:24	72 n.3

Exodus

2:23–25	48 n.6
3:1–6	106 n.2
3:13	61 n.4
3:13–14	58
19	163, 169
19:16–20	172 n.3
19–24	38, 126
20	6, 39, 45, 51
20:1	40 n.2, 51
20:1–2	45
20:1–11	51
20:1–17	3–4, 35, 37, 40 n.2, 43, 49–50, 123 n.2
20:2	38
20:3	38
20:6	44
20:10	45
20:12	45
20:12–16	51
20:17	51, 179 n.7
20:22–23:19	51–52
21:1–23:19	123 n.3
21:15	9 n.12
21:15–17	51
21:35	9 n.12
22:21–26	52
23:16	174
25–30	209
31:15	51
32:32	127
34:14	38
34:14–26	50
34:22	174
34:28	40 n.2, 53

Leviticus

17–26	51–52
18:6–18	50
19:9–10	52
20:10	51
23:6	175

Leviticus (*continued*)

23:15–21	178 n.5
25:8–17	179 n.13
25:25–28	179 n.13
25:39–46	53

Numbers

2:1–31	209

Deuteronomy

4:13	53
5:6–21	123 n.2
5:21	179 n.7
10:4	53
12–26	51–52
15:1–3	53
15:1–18	52
16:9–17	178 n.5
17:14–17	52
27:15–26	50

Joshua

21–1 Samuel 4	209

1 Samuel

8:1–15	39
8:4	41 n.6

2 Samuel

18:18	20

1 Kings

5	38
5:13	41 n.5
8	209
12	38
21	179 n.7

2 Kings

24:1–4	110

2 Chronicles

8:13	178 n.5

Ezra

1:2–4	99 n.1
6:3–5	99 n.1

Job

24:10–11	174, 178 n.4

Psalms

2:1–2	70
11	70
11:1	64
11:4–7	72 n.2
23	4, 58–59, 65–66, 70–71
23:1	70–71
23:1b	70
23:1–3	64, 71
23:1–4a	58
23:1–4	58
23:1–6	3, 55, 57, 63, 69
23:2	58–59
23:2–3	70
23:3b	58–59
23:4	58, 65, 70
23:4b–5	58
23:4–6	72
23:5	59, 70–71
23:5a	59
23:5–6	65
23:6	64
23:6b	61 n.5
24	127
27:1–6	64
27:2b	61 n.5
28:9	72 n.3
34:14	127
36:9	147
37:11	119, 123 n.6, 127
50:7–15	135 n.8
51	156 n.10
51:3	126
62:1–8	64
72:1–4	175, 179 n.8
74:1	72 n.3
77:20	72 n.3
78:52–53	72 n.3
79:13	64
80:1	64, 72 n.3
95:7	64, 72 n.3
100:3	72 n.3
121:3–8	72 n.3
137:1–3	109

Proverbs

8:22–30	146, 149 n.1, 156 n.12
10:10	135 n.5

Ecclesiastes

1:2	76, 78 n.4, 88
1:9	88
1:17	83
2:20–23	76, 78–79 n.7
3	7, 84
3:1–8	3–4, 73, 75–76, 81, 87
3:2–4	89
3:7	89
3:8	92
3:14	92
3:15	91
3:16	91
3:17	91
3:17–18	78, 79 n.13
4:1	76, 78 n.6, 89
4:2	89
4:3	89
5:8	76, 79 n.8
5:18	83, 88
8:3–4	76, 79 n.9
8:12–13	78, 79 n.14
8:14	76, 79 n.10

9:7–10   78, 79 n.16
12:8   76
12:14   78, 79 n.15

Isaiah
1:10–17   135 n.8
1–39   106
9:3   179 n.14
11:1–9   202
11:2   175, 178
11:3b–4a   175
11:3b–4   176
29:1–4   209
30:21   64
40:1–11   96
40:6–7   142, 144 n.11
40:6–8   153
40:8   148
40:11   72 n.3
40–55   96–97,
            99 n.1,
            102, 106 n.1,
            110
41:1–5   96
41:8   96
42:1–4   96
42:2–4   96
44:1   96
45:1   106 n.1
45:1–3   96
45:1–7   96–97
45:4   96
49:1–6   96
49:3   109
49:9–10   72 n.3
49:10   64
50:4   96
50:6   96
50:7–8   97
51:1–2   109
52–53   102, 110
52:7–10   103
52:12   110, 112

52:13–53:12   3–4,
            93–95, 101,
            103, 106 n.1,
            107, 110–11
52:13   110–11
52:14   110
52:15   99, 103, 111
53   9 n.14
53:3   96, 110
53:4   102, 110
53:5   99, 110
53:7   110
53:7–9   104
53:8   110, 112
53:8–9   97
53:10   110
53:11   110
53:11–12   104
53:12   97, 110
58:7   153
61:1   126
61:1–2a   176
61:1–2   176,
            179 n.12

Jeremiah
7:1–15   135 n.8
7:3–7   210
23:1–4   72 n.3
23:10–11   127
31:10   72 n.3
31:33   169
49:19–20   72 n.3
50: 17–19   72 n.3

Ezekiel
8–11   210
34:1–10   67–68 n.2
34:1–16   61–62 n.6
34   60, 67,
            67 n.2, 72 n.3
36:27   169
37:1–13   99 n.2

37   97

Hosea
6:6   135 n.8

Amos
2:6b   175
5:11a   175
5:21–25   135 n.8
5:24   127
8:4–6   127
9:13–15   179 n.17

Micah
3:1   177
3:1–3   175, 179 n.10
4:4   176–77, 202
4:6–8   72 n.3
6:8   127
6:10–11   127
7:14   72 n.3
10–11   127

*Apocrypha, Pseude-
pigrapha, and
Dead Sea Scrolls*

Baruch
3:37   156 n. 12
4:1   156 n. 12

**Community Rule
(1QS)**
3–4   219 n. 3

**1 (Apocalypse of)
Enoch**
14:8–15   162
14:9–10   164–65 n. 3
42:2   156 n. 12
71:5   162

Sirach (Ecclesiasticus)
24:1–12   156 n. 12

War Scroll (1QM)
14.7   123 n. 5

Wisdom of Solomon
7:22–30   156 n. 12
9:1–10   156 n. 12

New Testament

Matthew
1–2   xiv
4:23   120
4:23–25   120
5   119
5–7   118, 121
5:1   118
5:1–2   126
5:1–12   4, 115, 117,
      121–22, 125, 131
5:2   120
5:3   119
5:3–7:27   118
5:5   119
5:6   127
5:7   127
5:8   119
5:9   132, 134
5:10–11   127,
                     123 n.7
5:38   141
6:4   120
6:5–6   120
6:8   127
6:14–15   127
6:16–18   120
8:11   203
10   118
13   118
15:11   120
15:18–19   120
15:21–28   222
17:15   127

18   118
23   127
23–25   118
23:8–10   151
23:37–39   210
24   120
25:31–46   122,
                           127
25:34   123
28   118
28:1–10   187
28:16–20   118, 223

Mark
3:31–35   151
10:42–43   126
14:22–25   48 n.8
14:25   203
16:1–8   187

Luke
1:20   141
1:51   16
3:22   175
4:16–31   168
4:18–19   176
4:19   179 n.13
6:20–23   118
6:20–26   120
6:24–26   120
7:16   175
10:37   127
16:1–13   222
18:9–14   128
18:13   126, 128
22:25–26   126
23:43   202
24:1–12   187
24:49   174

John
1   148

1:1c   156 n.8
1:1   141–42
1:1–2   146, 152
1:1–18   4, 137, 139,
                      145, 151
1:3   150 n.2, 152,
                           154
1:4   25 n.16, 147
1:4–5   153
1:5   147
1:6–8   147
1:8   141
1:9   140, 147, 154
1:9–11   147
1:10–11   153
1:12   140
1:12–13   141, 147
1:14   142, 144 n.9,
            147, 154, 156 n.9
1:14–18   153
1:16   141
1:18   140–42
1:29   140
1:32–34   147
1:46   142
2:1–11   221
3:3–12   147
3:16–17   141
3:18–5:29   141
3:36   141
5:24   140
5:24–26   141
5:26   141
6:31–58   141
6:32–49   141
6:33   141
6:42–52   140
6:51   141
6:63a   141
7:48   140
7:52   140
8:12   140, 147

8:12–14	141	2:1–4	169	15:1–58	4, 181–183,
8:32	140	2:1–13	168, 174,		85, 189, 193
8:44	141		176	15:3–8	195
9:1–41	142	2:1–42	4, 159–61,	15:13	186
9:22–34	140		167, 173	15:14	186
9:25	140	2:2	162	15:14–19	195
9:39–41	140	2:2–3	169	15:19	194
10:1–18	58,	2:3	162	15:21–22	186
	60–61 n.2	2:4	162, 175	15:22	187
10:3–5	64	2:5	169	15:28–29	197
10:4	64	2:6	162, 170	15:31	186
10:10	149	2:7	162, 170	15:31–32	195
10:14	64	2:8	162, 170	15:32	186–87
11:25	140–41	2:9–11	162–63	15:35–44	190–91
11:33	141	2:11	170		
11:47–53	141	2:14–40	168,	**2 Corinthians**	
12:21–24	141		170–71, 176	4:10	186
12:48	141	2:16–21	170	4:10–12	187, 188 n.3
13:1–5	142,	2:17–21	168	6:5	186, 188 n.2
	144 n.13	2:22	170		
13:33–34	155	2:23	170	**Ephesians**	
14:6	141	2:24–32	170	2:6	120
14:9	155, 157 n.18	2:29–36	176	2:14	134
14:23	140	2:33	170–71, 176	2:15	135 n.5
15:12	155	2:39	170		
15:18–25	140	2:41–42	170	**Colossians**	
16:33	147	2:41–47	168	1:15–20	171
17:2	140	2:42	172	1:16–20	150 n.2
17:3	140	3–4	172 n.5	1:20	135 n.5
17:23–26	140	15	163	2:12	120
20:28	141			3:1–14	120
20:31	142	**Romans**			
		5:12–14	154,	**1 Timothy**	
Acts			157 n.17	6:16	143
1:1–4	165 n.10	8:22	216		
1:4	174	12:3–8	171	**Hebrews**	
1:8	165 n.9, 210			1:1	147
1:13–14	198 n.1	**1 Corinthians**		1:2	150 n.2
1:15	162, 164 n.2	2:2	186	11:10	x
2	4, 6, 162, 168,	3:22	127		
	171–72, 210	12:1–13	171	**James**	
2:1	162, 169	15	4, 6, 186	3:18	135 n.5

1 Peter

1:3–9	141				

1 John

1:1	147
2:8	147
4:7–12	155

Revelation

1:9	210, 215
1:10	216
2:9	202
2:10	215
2:20	202
2–3	202, 210, 215
3:9	202
4:11	150 n.2
7:17	127

8:1	215
8:2–9:21	215
13:16–17	202
14:4	202
16	215
16:12–16	215
17:1–17	202
17:5	202
20:4	215
20:14–15	203
20–22	202
21	210–12, 214
21:1	202, 208, 212, 216
21:1–4	53
21:1–22:5	4, 7, 199–201, 207, 213

21:2	202, 208
21:3	217–18
21:4	209, 217
21:7	211
21:8	202
21:9	212
21:9–10	208
21:10	202
21:16	212
21:17	212
21:18	212
21:22	218
21:22–27	210
21:23	209
22:1–5	203
22:2	203
22:5	203